WORLD EXECUTIVE'S DIGEST LIBRARY
THE EXECUTIVE OMNIBOOK

THE
EXECUTIVE
OMNIBOOK

Seven authoritative books
on key management topics
compiled and condensed by
the editors of
World Executive's Digest

Hong Kong

CONTENTS

CONTENTS

HOW MANAGERS MAKE THINGS HAPPEN

George S. Odiorne

George S. Odiorne is Professor of Management and former Dean of the School of Business Administration at the University of Massachusetts at Amherst. Previously, he was Dean of the College of Business at the University of Utah, Director of the Bureau of Industrial Relations at the University of Michigan and Professor of Management and Economics at Rutgers and New York Universities.

He has also been associated with General Mills, American Can Company and other major U.S. Corporations. He obtained his M.S. and Ph.D. from New York University.

His books include *MBO II: a System of Managerial Leadership, Management and the Activity Trap, Management Decisions by Objectives and Green Power: Corporation and the Urban Crisis.*

"People, it has been said, can be placed in three classes: the few who make things happen, the many who watch things happen, and the overwhelming majority who have no idea what has happened."

                                                     NICHOLAS MURRAY BUTLER

Management Means Action— Not Reaction

In a metal working plant in the East two department managers were in competition for a plant manager's vacancy. The first was admittedly a good administrator. His knowledge of the affairs of his department was thorough and systematic. He worried over reports and controls which came to his desk daily. He held regular meetings to get ideas. Yet he didn't get the job because his *results* weren't good enough.

It went to another fellow who was frankly poor in many of the administrative skills. The successful candidate received few formal written reports. He held conferences only when it couldn't be avoided. He had no charts on his walls showing him the level of various key indices. Most of his time was spent out in the plant talking with people. He always had time to look at any new gadget which one of the mechanics had put on a machine.

He was chosen over the other solely because he made things happen. His output per hourly wage dollar spent was more than fifteen percent higher than that of his colleague who was such a fine administrator.

Now, what was the difference between the two? The important point here is that there is a difference between *management* and *administration*. This big difference is that the manager makes things happen by whatever means are required, while the administrator follows certain procedures mechanically.

The administrator follows a stereotype pattern whether it applies in his situation or not. The manager sizes up the situation as it exists and decides to do those things which will make things happen whether they fit into the text or not. It's perfectly true that these administrative techniques may be just the ticket in some situations. In such circumstances the manager follows them, *as long as they continue to produce results.* When they cease doing that the manager does something different until he finds the techniques that produce the desired results.

In short, management means making things happen; administration means following certain textbook procedures mechanically whether they produce the results desired or not.

Management is not a passive art. One of the major complaints of the experts in management development is that too many executives are looking for "a gimmick."

The enchantment of the gimmick or formula whether it's psychological tests, work simplification, or a five step plan for selecting workers, is intriguing. The big attraction of such a formula is that it reduces management to something which is passive or mechanical. Simply learn how to use the formula, wait for people to bring the problems to you, apply the formula and the answer becomes obvious.

This would be a wonderful labor-saving device, but unfortunately there isn't one such formula worth mentioning.

Underlying every successful organization is a corps of hard working people in management and staff positions who are actively seeking out flaws and defects which need remedying, and who also fix them up. But there's more to it even than that.

A manager is more than a problem solver. He's a goal setter. Without waiting for others to ask him, he envisions things that should happen, and thinks through some possible paths by which the goal can be reached. At this stage he has few, if any, people who would agree with him that the goal is possible. Because he's active in deed as well as in thought, however, he converts them into action in his plan, and enlists their talents toward reaching the goal which he dreamed up. Before long he has a full scale movement afoot and people become ego-involved in his goal just as if they themselves had thought of it. During the struggle to accomplish it, the battle to overcome competition, costs, and other problems in the way, he's there to help. He keeps them pointed toward the objective, and suggests and sets examples of how it can be reached.

Now he may do this by good administrative methods it's true. Being a good manager *doesn't preclude* being a good administrator. It merely implies that he's not a passive administrator who's more concerned with a "clean desk" or proper decor for his office because he's been told that is how administrators should look. Nor is he overly obsessed with procedures for control and review. The dominant trait of the manager who makes things happen is that he's *goal oriented*. It means further that he's actively and intelligently seeking that goal. He's doing more than presiding over a group of people, he's leading them somewhere. Furthermore, while he's doing that the chances are that he's hatching up even more ambitious objectives beyond that one.

Making growth a company goal. *Company growth* is one present day goal which seems to spur executive action and make things happen. Studies by the Stanford Research Institute of several hundred companies with records of growth show that there are several traits which are common to most of them. For one thing they are oriented to growth industries. Not only are the managements of these companies alert to where opportunities lie, they are not averse to dropping lines which are shrinking in market importance and future opportunity. Growth, and management action to accomplish it, are less likely to be found in the hay and grain business, or horse shoe manufacturing than in electronics, missiles, atomic energy, pharmaceuticals or chemicals. Far too many companies fail to grow, the Stanford studies show, because the managements of these companies have a sentimental attachment to products or processes which were once growing and profitable, but which time has now proven outmoded.

Stanford's studies also showed that those companies which have growth patterns have been led by management of great moral courage in making decisions in favor of growth and sticking with them to make the growth occur.

To summarize this point: action-getting management means more than hustlers in management positions. It means intelligent choice of good goals, among the most prominent being the goal of company growth.

The forces of inertia. More often than competitors or actual opposition from those who have different objectives, the manager who makes things happen finds himself fighting a force called organizational inertia. This inertia takes many forms.

The first is the natural tendency of inertia within the manager himself. The tendency to coast along, or to look back "and see how far I've come" overtakes some managers and they turn into administrators. The truly action-oriented manager seldom spends much time walking around his accomplishments admiring what he's done in the past. He's too often engrossed in getting things moving toward the next higher goal.

Even when he hasn't this inward desire to taper off his efforts, the action getter finds that he has the heavy responsibility for spurring others to overcome their own inertia. This demands that he have several important capacities. He's got to be able to move projects and people off dead center and get them rolling toward his goals. He's got to generate enthusiasm for these goals so that people adopt them as their own, with the result that they generate enthusiasm on their own part for getting there. He must further instill a desire to excel and do the job fully and without mistakes or faltering. To do this demands several traits in the action-getting manager which he must assiduously cultivate at the risk of failure.

1. He's going to have to maintain optimism if he's going to overcome inertia. Most managers who make things happen have ego drives that push them on personally, and unbounded optimism and confidence that others will ultimately see his vision of what's to be accomplished despite repeated defeats and failures.

2. He needs a sound knowledge of people to impel them to produce and create. He needs to know what incentives are required to get action from others, and to have some artistry in using them.

3. He needs a certain callousness in demanding high standards of performance from others who are helping him.

One of the greatest wellsprings of inertia in an organization is its *size*. The big organization develops built-in inertias, simply because it's so big. Kenneth Boulding of Michigan University compares the giant corporation to a dinosaur, and warns that unless the big organizations overcome the inertia and ineptness which overtook the dinosaur, they might suffer the same fate. *Power* alone isn't enough to survive. It requires the ability to move with agility and vigor, and to handle a variety of problems, both big and small, which confront the big organization.

A number of things occur when an organization grows in size. The first effect is that communications between the top and bottom, and between the various members, becomes difficult. This means that the left hand sometimes does things that duplicate or conflict with what the right hand is doing.

Another effect of bigness is that the personal touch between the owners and the employees is lost; or in the case of a publicly owned organization such as a manufacturing corporation, between the management and its staff and employees. Since it's this personal touch which is often at the heart of getting action in an organization the top man finds he is limited greatly when he has a great organization to run, and must accordingly organize to overcome the effects of too much bigness.

Because the organization is big it requires more rule of law (called procedures and policies) in order to govern it. These are perfectly sound things to install, but they are part of that body of knowledge called *administration,* and at the same time they make it possible for managers to function at all, they aren't by any manner of means a guarantee of movement and growth. That happens when the manager in favor of action, makes his personal impact on the organization.

To sum up this point: There's nothing about an administrative procedure which will overcome inertia. It takes an action-getting manager to make things happen.

Profit requires action. Being a successful manager in a commercial and industrial enterprise means a profit-minded one. Conversely, it's the profit-minded manager at any level who stands the best chance of moving upward. This is more than simple avarice, or single-minded love of money for itself. It's largely because profit is a universal standard for measurement that is easily grasped by managers and quite clearly understood by those who judge his performance.

It's entirely possible that someday a more commonly held standard will come along, for example— service; but it must always meet the standard which profit has become— immediate, easy to calculate, universally accepted. Profit, for all the criticisms leveled against it, is the best available instrument and standard of managerial success and organizational performance. With adaptations it applies to any organization, even in Soviet Russia.

It's widely held fiction that profit is something exact and precise which comes without deviation or man-made influence out of the impersonal exactitude known as "the books" of the company. This of course is nearly as fallacious as the pious assumption of its divine nature. All of the ingredients which come out at the end of the year under the over-all label of "profit" are quite flexible and under the control of individual decisions of managers or administrators.

Such things as expenditures for research, training, public relations, personnel management, and so on are all drains on the immediate profit in the current accounting period. You'll note that all of these are the results of the decision of management to spend money out of current income in order to assure the future growth and stability of the company.

Profit, then, is more than an accounting term. It's a positive creation and standard for measuring effectiveness of management action and decision making.

Let's illustrate this. A large company begins by having some kind of trade advantage— either a patent right to exclusive manufacture of a product, or a dominant position in a market due to aggressive salesmanship. Theoretically each company has such a special advantage which keeps it alive in the face of competition.

Yet companies go bankrupt. One study of the 100 largest firms in the United States in 1927 shows that only 50 per cent of them still exist. Oswald Knauth, former treasurer of Macy's store, once said that "almost all trade advantages can be duplicated." Except for certain patent arrangements or exclusive access to raw materials there are few advantages which a company can acquire that will preclude the necessity of managers who continue to discover and build up advantages for their own firm through personal leadership. These include actions which will build up its internal and external position, and the development of people, trade connections and experience which results in profit.

Profit is the result almost wholly of the *actions of managers* who exercise initiative and leadership of a dynamic nature, and of the people who respond to this leadership to carry through toward the goals of the organization.

There is probably no company in business today which couldn't be out of business through lack of profit inside of ten years if its management attempted to conduct its affairs simply through mechanical application of administrative practice, at the expense of the more vital, personal, and human application of individual leadership.

The manager and the world outside of business. This individual leadership which produces action and results isn't limited to the four walls or administrative boundaries of the firm. Profit, survival, and growth of the firm today— and in the future— will demand that managers be able to make things happen in circumstances in which important variables won't be under their jurisdiction. Let's look at a few of them:

• The company which isn't attuned to public opinion is taking undue risks with its future.

• Government actions have a vital part in business policy.

• What's happening abroad is sufficiently close to business decisions today that they must be part of the action-getting manager's calculations.

The new action-getting manager must be one who can make his force and result-getting talents felt on both internal and external matters to the company.

The problems of labor management relations are also more serious than the loss of profits to workers and company when the process of collective bargaining strikes serious snags, such as a major steel strike. In our highly specialized world the list of what Stuart Chase once labelled the "paralytic trades" has increased. These are the occupations which are infinitesimally small in relation to the whole population, but whose control over some vital aspect of our super specialized life is sufficiently great that public convenience and often public health and welfare suffer when they are stopped from exercising their skills through disagreements with their employers which result in strikes.

Clarence Randall, for many years chief executive of Inland Steel, points to the two major areas confronting management in the future.

The first of these is added acceptance of the responsibility of business management for carrying out its share of social responsibility in the community in which it works. In this regard Mr. Randall feels that business management has come a long way.

Beyond this Mr. Randall feels that equally responsible behavior by managers must be forthcoming to discharge its responsibilities and apply equal resourcefulness in the face of world problems.

Good management then means action— and not reaction— to both internal conduct of its affair, but also action for greater social responsibility in the narrow community in which it operates— and in the world beyond.

"It is well for the world that in most of us, by the age of thirty, the character has set like plaster, and will never soften again."

WILLIAM JAMES

The Status Quo—
It's Not Good Enough

Ten rules for identifying business stagnation. The specter of stagnation is always just ahead of us in individual companies, or departments of them. Despite the economic forces which make for vitality and growth there still remains the overbearing necessity for managerial action to make the growth occur. What indicators could we find that the danger point of stagnation is setting upon an organization?

Usually the stagnant organization has ten key characteristics:

1. *Its officials are out of touch with broad trends.* Often the organization at rest is headed by officials who have become inbred within their own company and see little significance in what the economy, or their competitors are doing. Often this state occurs when some slight technical difference in the business from most others, seems to exist. The phrase "our com-

pany is different" is often the first sign of decadence in management, since it indicates a general unwillingness to keep abreast of new ideas.

2. *Unwillingness to experiment.* The management which hesitates overly long in accepting new methods or of relinquishing old ones may be headed for oblivion.

3. *It never looks beyond its own markets.* When they run into hard times with product marketing, their only reaction is to mine deeper in the same vein rather than seek new fields for utilizing their products— or their organization— to recoup losses.

4. *It demands great conformity from its people.* The organization which doesn't allow at least a few mavericks who will question and probe present methods and programs will probably stagnate shortly if it hasn't already done so.

5. *It neither rewards merit nor punishes failure.* The organization which operates with a "civil service" mentality, without paying for performance alone, is on the verge of stagnation.

6. *Managers and staff do little self-development.* One of the bench marks of the stagnant organization is the managerial staff which makes little or no effort of its own accord to learn new methods, study new techniques, discuss ways of improving, or show any evidence of a thirst for better ways of operating.

7. *It is inbred.* One certain evidence of stagnation in an organization is its isolation from new ideas, new people, and fresh viewpoints. Such a company seldom permits its people to attend professional meetings, permits little exchange of information with other companies, and abhors consultants. The overall climate is one of smugness, self-satisfaction, and self-congratulation.

8. *It is overly obsessed with immediate profit.* A company which is unwilling to invest certain of its present income in enlargement and development activity such as personnel,

public relations, management development, scientific research, marketing research, or long range investment in intangibles soon begins to show organizational hardening of the arteries.

9. *It attracts passive and dependent people.* These are people who are frightened of the boss, who seek security rather than opportunity, whose principal trait is obeisance not only to orders but to what they *think* the boss would want. Such a climate soon repels the vital and energetic man of ideas and ambitions and he seeks out a livelier and more fertile climate for his talents.

10. *The stagnant company is a boring place to work.* Ruled by seniority, privilege, and low turnover, it has a dull, colorless, and nearly lifeless passivity about it. There is little fire which comes with innovation, change, and the conflict and confusion which comes with growing pains, but which are signs of life and energy. Often it's a humorless place, in which the officials take themselves seriously, and treat restlessness and desire for change as discordant influences which must be put down.

Often the organization which is afflicted with these symptoms can be identified simply by walking through it. There is little of the hustle and burgeoning activity which seems to surround the organization on the move. In some cases it's apparent by the appearance of its managers, who are dull people, and occasionally by its decor which is outmoded and plain. There's little of the stormy, husky, or brawling nature of the broadshouldered organization.

Why change is necessary. However restful the stagnant organization may appear, the disruptive and sometimes exciting world of change is the route to survival for the well managed company. Some of the major reasons for this imperative need for change in a business organization might look like this:

Costs have reached such a scope in most firms that near herculean efforts are required to keep them from running the firm to the wall, if the firm is careless about them. The secular— and constant— trend of costs upward through rising labor costs, rising material costs, the higher costs of government— the only hope of holding inflationary forces under control is the vigorous and active leadership of management. It's perfectly true that this pressure was suspended in large part for many years in its more serious forms through the simple mechanism of shifting the incidence of costs to the consumer through price increases. This circularity in economic management however, inevitably has its bad consequences in inflation which devalues fixed incomes, and did in fact create substantial consumer resistance to further price rises. Thus the only remaining alternative for managements in the face of such pressures— sometimes identified as the "cost-price squeeze"— is to cut other costs in the face of rising labor costs.

Competition of a new order in the economy requires that the firm which would survive make constant change a way of life for itself in all of its ways of doing business. This is most often gradual change, conducted along orderly lines, but often is disruptive in its scope.

The dynamics of management. The fact of this changing world puts demands upon the skills and practices of management which promise to create a whole new breed of people in charge of our business enterprises. We've alluded to some of the ways in which this new management leadership is different from the "model administrator." The significant differences lie in this desire and ability to bring about change and improvement, and to force innovation into the position of being a primary skill of the manager.

Perhaps the first step in the changing fashion of management will be the decline of those powers which we sometimes ascribe to administrators known as *control* and *veto power.* Study the functioning of the typical administrator in the traditional sense and you'll find that much of his time and effort is designed to accomplish *review* and *control.* Actions by subordinates or other managers are channeled in such a way that they must feed through the filter of the "exception principle." Exceptions, and in some cases routine actions by subordinates, are structured to feed through the mechanism which measures them, stopping them in midflight for the purpose of being assessed by the administrator. Those which have conformed to the predetermined pattern of the administrative directive and procedural instruction are permitted to pass on. Those which vary in the slightest are either altered or rejected to be returned to its originator for retouching. However laudable this may be in terms of preventing some backward slipping in the organization, it is essentially a provost marshal's approach to management and does nothing more than maintain the status quo.

Controls tell what's happened or is happening. They don't make things happen by themselves.

As a major preoccupier of management time, controls have several basic defects which make them unsuitable in an economic environment where change is so sorely needed and improvement becomes the pressing requirement for growth—and survival. More, there's some doubt in many quarters about the necessity of arming the organization for controlling things when the controls themselves are more costly than the potential losses which could occur from errors in procedure.

Diametrically opposed in philosophy to this static form of control and administrative practice which serves to maintain the status quo, is the dynamic concept of *action* being the primary requirement of the manager.

A recent example which I saw in a manufacturing plant occured when a new plant manager took over. As he walked around the plant he struck up conversations with the several foremen in charge of departments. As he went into one department he noted that housekeeping was nearly perfect. The machines were painted, the floor clean, and over the bulletin board was a plant safety award for the best departmental accident record. His assistant informed him that this department was managed by Jim C, who was by far the best foreman in the plant. In production, quality, housekeeping, safety, spoilage, yield, maintenance, and grievances he stood far above the rest. The plant manager sought out this paragon and introduced himself.

"Jim, I understand that you run the best department in the plant."

"Could be."

"What is your accident frequency and severity rate per million employees?"

"Damned if I know."

"Well, what is the hourly average from your machines for the past month and the past six months?"

"Beats the hell outa me."

"And your spoilage rate per thousand pieces for the year to date?" The foreman shrugged indifferently.

"Look Mr. X," he said, "I'm so damn busy running this place well I don't have time to keep score."

Obviously we might want a little more knowledge of the "score" from a manager than Jim C professed. Certainly if Jim is going to move upward he's going to have to learn to use records. The point, however, is that we might also legitimately wish that more of the others, who probably knew their statistics cold, could have Jim's attitude of attention to fundamentals— which was getting things done first, and counting the figures afterward.

No manager ever produced anything by merely watching a figure, and management dynamics emphasizes the doing first, and the administrative totting up second.

Why innovation gets top priority. Change can be of two sorts. It can be simply the change which comes about because the people running the business can't make up their minds on the best way and keep flitting from one method to another without making real progress. The second kind is based on change which is rooted in *innovation*. This innovation is the process of infusing new and better products, methods, and processes into the concern to do the job better, faster, cheaper. Charles Percy, president of Bell and Howell, reports that 65 per cent of his company's sale are in products which weren't even in existence five years ago.

Professor Fred Harbison and his associates at Princeton University have studied innovation and have concluded several things about the companies in which it occurs. For one thing it has a way of changing the personnel make-up of the organization. There usually ends up more high talent, trained professional and technical and managerial manpower when innovation hits an organization. This new concentration of high talent manpower, in turn, because it's been attracted or assembled in a climate of innovation, creates more innovation which attracts more highly trained people.

From this we can conclude that building a strong organization which has the talent to grow and get action for corporate growth is centered around innovation.

Innovation then is a force for improvement through infusing new ideas and products into the organization as a whole, which requires top priority if a company is to grow.

How innovation and control are related. One of the mysterious features about improvements in management methods and organization is the phenomenon which we may call the "back-sliding" characteristics of innovation and improvement over time.

Take the case of the typical sales contest. The sales and marketing managers dream up a wonderful plan to boost sales through a giant promotional campaign. In order to cash in on it they announce a contest for salesmen. The winner will get a free trip to Paris, along with his wife, at company expense.

During the months that follow the pressure and hoopla continue unabated, and the red line on the thermometer chart on the sales manager's wall goes up and up until the top is blown off.

The following month no charts are kept, and a good

thing! Sales have fallen well below the peak of the contest. In fact, it is somewhat below the monthly average before the contest began and even the same month for the last five years.

What happened?

Here the sales manager and his team developed (innovated, you might say) a new idea, and carried it off beautifully, but the slump is worse than anything ever seen.

An investigation shows that the salesman who won can well afford to take time off for the trip to Paris, because if he were out covering his territory he probably wouldn't get an order from any of his regular customer anyhow. Knowing that the contest was a temporary figure to beat, the canny winner had used pressure and persuasion to get them to stock up for awhile ahead during the contest.

Good innovation has built-in snubbers which are designed to prevent any sliding backward after temporary gains.

This implies some controls, and really pinpoints the place where controls enter the picture, preventing losses and backsliding from the newly won positions.

Organizations on the move seldom take time to dig defensive positions in the middle of their bayonet charge. Once they've achieved their first objectives however, and are pausing to reload their guns before jumping off again, it's wise strategy to post sentries and outposts to prevent loss of the things already accomplished. In management these are the establishment of sensitive control reports to reveal promptly signs of sliding back.

Let's look again at our sales contest and see just what happened. First, the objective of the breakthrough was clearly defined. The real purpose management had in mind in running a sales contest wasn't just to give sales a temporary spurt. Its goal was to raise the general level of sales for the company, permanently, it was fondly hoped by the planners.

Secondly, the entire incentive plan was aimed at causing the salesman to speed up rather than do anything different. Yet the contest merely whipped up enthusiasm for *more,* and with the wonderful reward for selling more so dramatically spelled out, the salesmen went out to sell more in the easiest way, thereby winning themselves a free prize.

Building controls into the contest may be done in several ways:

1. Make only new sales as qualifying for the prize. That is, sales to customers who were now buying from competitors exclusively have extra value over sales of more products to old customers.

2. Tie the awards to sales of new products to customers who had never bought them before.

3. Run the contest over a longer period of time such as six months or a year. This wouldn't arouse the fervor of enthusiasm of a one-or two-month campaign it's true, but the raising of general levels of sales would have probably been more permanent.

4. More importantly than any of these, it might have been prefaced by some careful diagnosis of markets and sales patterns, and the incentives tied to breakthroughs into new and untapped markets, with no incentives for repeat sales, or extra "pushing" of goods for advance stock to old customers.

5. It might have been supplemented by additional incentives for "business held for six months." These and several other steps which smart sales managers all know, might be considered as practical techniques for preconditioning innovation by building in controls for maintenance of new levels.

Campaigns which are based on pressure, and pep talks that have as their objective the speed up of effort, are always destined to be followed by a let down.

Genuine innovation, based on careful diagnosis, has built in controls to maintain the new levels of performance and prevent sliding back after installation.

The dynamic basis for business action. Despite the fact that stagnant organizations are characterized by certain traits and even certain physical characteristics, it's not easy for a company to recognize that it's falling behind merely because it's standing still. This knowledge only has pertinence and meaning when it falls into the hands of a management which can make things happen which will alleviate the situation.

Such managers have two major characteristics. The first is that they are action oriented and are willing to put aside their preoccupation with score keeping when they are in the middle of the contest, and concentrate upon getting things moving and keeping them headed in the right direction. This means that they not only stimulate innovation from the top, but gear the whole organization to accept innovation and create new things themselves. Yet innovation and moving forward requires that the action getter have supplementary characteristics which give him the skill in building sufficient controls to prevent loss of the momentum, and backward movement, once the surge has been stemmed momentarily in order to consolidate the gains.

This double objective of getting action for innovation and improvement and holding onto them are the minimum requirements of the leader in management positions.

"As any industrial society advances it becomes increasingly dependent upon the brains and much less upon the brawn of its working forces."
S.E. HILL AND F. HARBISON

How to Identify
What Needs Improvement

F or the management with a desire for constant improvement the problem isn't primarily one of technique, but first of identifying what particular job, product, or project, should come first. This requires some techniques for spotting what needs improvement.

Six rules for identifying areas for improvement. Setting priorities requires some standards for picking targets for improvement. Studies of managers with records of accomplishment in making things happen would tend to show that they usually have intelligence to discriminate between the many types of activities going and focus down upon those that would produce the greatest gains.

Here are six rules of finding these areas for improvement that will get the manager into most of the key areas where improvement efforts will pay off soonest and with the greatest results:

1. *Fix your eye on costs.* Whether the organization is a company which is in business for profit, or is an institution operating with a budget such as a government agency, school or hospital, the good effect of starting with cost reduction is immense. Cost has the quality of being a universal measuring instrument that responds to improvement; in most instances by going down. This doesn't mean that a narrow attention to pennies and the elimination of necessary services is an indicator of good management. It doesn't mean, for example, that you cut away income-producing activity in order to save the money which produces the income. It means you try to spend your cost dollars in such a way that they are producing more service or more income for each dollar spent.

One paper company during a recession attacked the problem of cost reduction by asking every factory employee to suggest savings which would be allocated to advertising and marketing to boost sales and preserve their jobs. The results were a great improvement. Not only did the factory people cut their own cost, but the marketing and advertising staff, knowing that their expenses were coming from pennies squeezed out of operations, worked harder to make them more productive.

The organization which is flourishing and blessed with a rising sales curve and rising profits, may find that excess expenses are less important than getting the goods out and meeting deadlines and schedules. In such periods it's the professional who is able to capitalize on the favorable situation and cut costs.

2. *Is it a bottleneck?* One of the key indicators that management action is needed is if one thing is causing delays which holds up several other things. These vital spots comprise a fertile field for improvement since they pay larger dividends in releasing the productive efforts of other machines, processes, or people who have been held up by the offending spot.

3. *Is it taking too much time?* One management man found after some study of his personal time that he was spend-

ing an inordinate amount of his time on the phone calling and checking travel reservations. By passing this chore to his secretary he was freed for more productive work. The principle here can apply on a wider scale as well. The things which are taking up too much of anyone's time are probably costing more than they should, and are a fertile area for improvement.

4. *Has it drifted imperceptibly in the wrong direction?* One large sales organization found that it had stopped its growth in customers and number of orders from old customers. In checking on the reasons for this declining rate of growth the sales manager discovered that *service* to the customer had slipped in the haste of gathering orders, and a distinct advantage which the company had held in the beginning was sliding away in the urge to get big. By concentrating on reestablishing the quality of service rendered his customers, he was able to start the trend upward once more.

5. *Have outside conditions changed?* Often the world changes and the company stands still, with the result that the company which was pioneering when it began is now left far behind. Henry Ford pioneered in the manufacture of automobiles of which you could "get any color as long as it was black."

Many companies today have expanded into international operations in an attempt to capture foreign markets. Those companies which continue only to sell their domestic customers often find themselves faced with a statistic of a relatively shrinking market for their products.

6. *Is it being done the same old way?* In the light of the dynamic nature of business it becomes a fairly safe conclusion that if a job or process is being done the same old way it was done ten or fifteen years ago— or even last year— it may be ripe for improvement. The facts of innovation and change are that competition in new ideas is increasing and once they've been introduced it's often too late to catch up. Therefore the only safe course is to assume that the other fellow is improving

his methods and products, and that doing it the same way year after year is courting disaster.

Cost as a basic measuring instrument. There's no necessity that a manager become an expert in cost accounting in order to effectively use cost as a measuring instrument for identifying areas for improvement. It is a good idea however for every manager, from president to foreman, to have a working knowledge of cost accounting theory in order that he can rightly identify the major areas of cost reduction and cost incidence in his business.

Quite simply put, the cost cycle begins with money and ends with money. There's no secret funds or reserves which can protect a business from ultimately going broke if it doesn't control costs in every aspect of the business. These costs are usually identified as follows:

Prime costs:

Direct labor (work done on the product)

Direct materials (materials appearing in it)

Burden:

Indirect labor (labor not done on the product)

Indirect materials (supplies used in making it)

Factory overhead expense (utilities, plant management, staff, etc.)

Administration:

General Office

Officer's and staff salaries

Research

Sales Expense:

Salesmen's salaries and commissions

Salesmen's expenses (car, meals, travel)

Advertising (art, copy, media, agency fees)

Merchandising (display, premiums, etc.)'

Profit:

The budgeted surplus which is added to the cost of goods sold.

These terms, which should be as familiar as his own office to every manager, will vary slightly from company to company in terms of how they are defined and classified. Beyond this every manager in the company should be able to identify where the heaviest weight of cost falls for his business and his product. Every manager should know whether or not his business is one which has high labor content relative to total cost, or whether he is in a high selling cost industry.

Discovering the place where the costs are greatest is a ready-made way of discovering where the greatest improvement is possible. Top management normally begins with a hard look at the profit item, and works back from there. For the directors and officers of the company it becomes vital that this be their major *situs* of attention.

Non-financial steps to goal-setting. Merely identifying the cost areas isn't enough, however. The means of reducing costs, no matter where they appear, is more than reading a figure. It requires that new objectives for that part of the business be established. At this stage we've left the figures behind and get into the management action phase. Customarily this involves letting the people in charge of the area where improvement is needed know of the situational need, and getting their active support and efforts for improvement.

In several companies, such as General Electric, Merck, Inc., and General Mills, this takes the form of "objective setting" by top management with the subordinate management of the activity. In Merck, for example, the manager sits down with his subordinates at least annually and jointly they work out a set of objectives which are: (1) organizational improvement, (2) profit improvement, and (3) personal development for the manager. The man and his boss hammer out these objectives for the organization under the manager's jurisdiction, and each retains a copy of the written objectives for the period ahead. At the end of six months, and again at the end of the year, these are reviewed. This comprises the performance review for the manager, and is couched wholly in the terms of his accomplishments against the goals he and his boss have agreed upon.

Within such a framework each manager is made aware of the need for identifying specific things that need improving (including his own personal skills and abilities) and in collaboration with his boss puts himself on record as identifying the areas that need betterment.

This procedure for identifying change is supplemented by the boss asking his subordinate, "What can I do, do differently or refrain from doing that will help you meet these objectives?" This serves to identify the needed improvement in the man-boss relationship required to accomplish the job and get the improvement into effect.

Outside conditions impinging upon business. Such a procedure as management by objectives works admirably in identifying areas for improvement within the cost structure of the firm. It doesn't always take into account the outside forces which are impinging upon the business that needs improvement. Since these outside effects often have a greater effect than internal inefficiencies, they too require clear identification. Unless they are identified before it is too late they may be insoluble problems for management. Let's look at some of the major ones:

1. *The community.* Businesses operate inside the institutional environment of a community. The "community" may be local, regional, national, or global. It draws its employees from the surrounding labor markets, and pay taxes, and obtains services from local, county, state, and federal governments. It also is restricted and bound by the federal government which, under the constitution, serves to maintain commerce between the states and in world trade. This puts the government squarely into the business in the form of regulation, of service, and of advice.

Permitting executives to take part in civic and community

activities, to hold offices in associations and organizations, to lead civic betterment campaigns, or to hold public positions, are often a result of identifying problems which exist in the community that need good men's effort for solution.

2. *The corporate image.* As often as not this overseeing attention to community affairs grows out of habit or imitation among the majority of those who participate. Occasionally it takes the form of justification of the corporate activities— "creating a favorable image" in the eyes of the public upon which the firm depends for its survival. Such philosophies are the latter day descendants of the old style philanthropy wherein the economic pirate distributed a mite of his ill-gotten gains to charity as evidence of his basic generosity. While this is less and less frequently true in practice, the experiences of the past are not sufficiently dead for this sort of image to remain in the public mind.

The important point to be made here is that restraints upon the behavior of companies and corporations will hardly be based upon ephemeral images of corporations, but must ultimately be traced back to the behavior of executives. The actions taken by them in support of impingement into business can normally be traced back to their attitudes toward individual managers— especially those at or near the top.

Images and opinions of business which have an all too immediate impact upon their success will be built up piece by piece from the selected images of executives. Perhaps the more fundamental fact is that images are seldom based on press releases, or upon publicity campaigns, but upon solid works and accomplishments in betterment of the community and nation. Even more basic is the conclusion that such actions must inevitably be personal actions by important officials acting both personally and officially.

*"The world is cluttered up with unfinished business
in the form of projects that might have been
successful, if only at the tide point someone's
patience had turned to active impatience."*

ROBERT UPDEGRAFF

Overcoming Obstacles

The ability to overcome obstacles is more than a random collection of techniques and routines. It's part of an attitude toward obstacles which prods the obstacle-solver onward to accomplishment of his goals where others with less satisfactory attitudes will fail.

This attitude is the nucleus of actions which prove successful in overcoming obstacles and are far more important than the steps themselves, since the steps are created out of whole cloth in order to accomplish the goal. This attitude, dissected, looks something like this:

1. *A strong goal orientation.* The person who will probably have the greatest success in overcoming obstacles have established some clear cut goals for himself, and is determined to achieve them. The fact that he's faced with the same red tape, difficulties, and suggestions for delay that have stopped others, doesn't faze him in the least. All of these blocks diminish in importance in the bright light of the goal which he has fastened his eye upon.

2. *A callousness to defeats.* The good obstacles hurdler normally has a built-in optimism that makes such things as inertia, opposition, confusion, timidity, and ignorance mere details to be brushed aside or otherwise managed.

3. *Decisiveness.* The most pernicious trait a manager can have when faced with obstacles is indecisiveness. Very often this is explained away as a need for mature consideration of the situation, but actually indecision is the result of the mind slipping away into inappropriate or trivial matters. He may find that ordering a new desk or settling a squabble between two secretaries is much more intriguing than writing the order, or picking up the telephone to announce the decision. The obstacle hurdler makes his decisions when he can— and the sooner the better.

The qualities of the obstacle hurdler. Armed with such attitudes, the obstacle breaker or hurdler has several further qualities which distinguish him from the people who don't make the grade. Most of these he's developed through experience and practice.

Interviews with a number of general managers to discover these qualities show that often he's objective about himself and his qualities in much the same way an actor is. Actors often refer to their bodies as "the instrument" and take calisthenics, or alter diet or personal indulgences without regret in order to protect the tool by which they practice their trade. This is likewise a characteristic of action-getting, obstacle-busting managers. Not that they pay as close attention to their physique as actors would, since in their case the instruments are different.

The qualities become instruments which seem to characterize obstacle busters and are highly personalized skills in doing things. Occasionally these are closely allied to the actor's, and include dress, mannerisms, and poise under stress. Yet many less successful managers, who have graduated from the right university, affect the same manners without having any of the same qualities. More frequently than the outward accoutrements of success, the quality of *earthiness* in the fundamental things appears.

A variation of this is the immense ability to carry details in his head, or a carefully cultivated memory for names and faces. In the early stages of a man's career he will use this facility to amass a great array of names and faces of all levels in the organization. He'll have a speaking acquaintance with as many of the great and successful as he can achieve, and by making sure that it covers a decent spread of those of more lowly station he can avoid the reputation of being an apple polisher or boot licker. Then too, he'll want to make these acquaintances among the lesser ranks, especially among the promising ones, for they may in turn become important.

The executive conscience and sense of honesty is a commonly cited quality for a successful manager, which is perfectly sound for a manager to develop since it helps him otherwise fail to reduce. Simply put, it eliminates the necessity for maintaining a tangled fabric of distortions or misrepresentations which must be constructed in order to bolster up the first lie. The truth, however bad, is always preferable to the slight lie which looks more favorable since it requires nothing by way of extraneous and superfluous effort and psychic energy to recall in an instant.

Equally vital among the qualities of the obstacle breaker is that of using people without becoming sentimentally over-involved with their successes or failures. All of these qualities however are subordinate to the manager's ability at problem-solving, of the lock-picking, maze-solving type. This is a function of his powers of adjustment to different and changing circumstances.

Various ways people adjust to obstacles. Adjust he must if he is to overcome obstacles, for problem solving and overcoming difficulties is a process of adjustment that stems from the goals the man has, his urgency in wanting to reach them, and his ingenuity in eliminating or neutralizing the things that block him from his goals. The process for every human looks something like this:

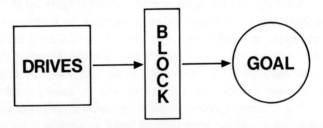

He's driven by the desire for wordly goods, for prestige, for reputation, for self-expression or one of the other multifarious goals that impel people into action. Yet in every day affairs— including those of business— blocks occur. Two people want the same goal which is available to one only. Other people's cooperation is required, and they are reluctant or violently unwilling to offer such assistance. What happens when a goal-seeking man reaches the block is dependent upon his ability to adjust. These forms of adjustment take on a wide range of alternate forms.

Direct attack. Some people find that the normal reaction for them when faced with an obstacle is to lower their head and charge. Where this pattern seems to work for them once they'll try it again. They'll continue as long as it works, and will only try another attack when they finally run into a block that won't topple when it's hit. Since most people run into such an obstacle at one time or another in their life, most good obstacle overcomers use direct attack along with *other* methods of arriving at their goal. Knowing when to attack and when to look for a better way is the first step in adjusting the blocks.

Substitute goals. Another form of adjustment is to replace the goal from which you're blocked with another which *can* be attained. In some cases this may be a goal which is just as satisfactory as the first one, or it may result in lowering the standards of what's expected. While this may be disappointing and even result in a loss of face, such adjustments are often required in business as elsewhere, and the important thing is that the manager not let the fact of having to change goals ruin his ability to adjust well in the future.

Trial and error. Still another way managers adjust to obstacles is to continue a wide range of trial and error responses to overcome or otherwise get around the block. Perhaps one of the greatest mistakes one can make in adjusting to obstacles is to rely too heavily upon a single response. Efficiency in adjusting to obstacles depends upon the ability of the individual manager to continue varying his responses until success is achieved.

Skill in overcoming obstacles in management requires that the executive become a student of the arts of overcoming blocks to avoid being thwarted by them. For one thing he must know something about the nature of the obstacles. Usually these obstacles to getting what he wants are one of several types:

Environmental obstacles. Those are the blocks which are created by the material circumstances in which he functions. For example, the manager of an international division may find that he's blocked by a shortage of skilled labor in the country. It may be that he's barred from installing some improvement in his factory in his country because the union has a set policy of opposition to changes in work rules or methods. He may find that certain materials or facilities are unavailable. Yet these environmental obstacles seldom are the heart of failure in obstacle solving.

More often he's faced with some *personal defect* in himself that prevents him from attacking the problem properly. Such a defect may be a habit of giving up, or it may be a lack of skill, experience or training in the kind of data that the problem requires for solution. In many instances these personal defects are more imaginary than real, and can be either effectively ignored, or in the case of lack of training can be overcome by hard work and practice. People of little ability are more apt to let an obstacle throw them than people of great ability. These abilities aren't necessarily ones with which the person is born, however; their lack implies a self-development program for the manager as an aid to his obstacle-solving ability. Physical vitality and energy are often at the root of poor obstacle solving, and on more than one occasion a physical check up and corrective therapy has transformed a so-so performer into a successful action getter.

Conflicts of motives are less often, but nonetheless important sources of delay and ineptness in obstacle solving and adjustment to blocks in a manager. These consist of situations in which he finds himself between two desires which are mutually exclusive. The normal desire to live a full family life, and the desire to move ahead in the organization which requires that he give extensive time traveling away from home, are typical of such conflicts. Unfortunately the two conflicting urges don't cancel one another and leave the man bland or neutral. Rather, they create tensions which feed on one another, and result in vacillation and "neutral," non-productive activity.

Such words as "worry" and "indecisiveness" are apt labels for the situation in which the manager is torn between desire for the goal and fear of failure, or simple tension caused by the pressures of two strong motives pushing him from either direction.

G. S. Kennedy, board chairman at General Mills, has pointed out that decision-making at the higher levels of management is like walking a girder high above the street. The iron worker is able to walk the narrow girder forty flights up because he has overcome "worry" or fear of falling. The top executive makes decisions which are no more difficult in terms of pure decision making techniques than that of the foreman. It's simply the fear of failure and the enormity of effect if he does so that causes him to tighten up and grab for safety.

Much nonsense has been written about the techniques of decision making as though the failures in this vital area were a lack of understanding of the process. Far more often than inability to handle the data and arrive at the solution, is the fear of failure and the conflict between desiring to get the decision made and that worry about making the wrong one. This puts decision making as an obstacle-busting method into the area of adjustment and only in part into the realm of techniques of collecting, sorting, and analysing data.

Good versus bad ways of obstacle licking. *Satisfactory ways of adjusting are those which help the manager arrive at his goal within the framework of the ethical and value systems in which he works.*

To a large extent then, the manager who is successful in overcoming obstacles is the man who successfully avoids those things which keep him from achieving it. For the preservation of his ego it's possible to relieve his tensions at levels lower than the goals which he has set. If this weren't true then every person who didn't reach his goal in management— or a satisfactory substitute— would be "off balance" mentally. What are some of the less satisfactory forms of adjustment?

Adjustment by withdrawal. Although there are many occasions in life when the manager must recognize that discretion is the better part of valor, and he must retreat from his stand, this can't be termed unsatisfactory. From the action-getting viewpoint, such withdrawals are merely regrouping for the next attack. Such retreats become unsatisfactory from the viewpoint of management action when the manager never returns to the attack but sits down before the block and vegetates. In some cases he may become publicity-shy when publicity would be the best thing for the situation. In others he becomes timid and respectful where boldness and brass are called for. Occasionally he will plead ignorance greater than he actually should, as justification for inaction. In some instances the withdrawal turns into a form of negativism. In still others he simply retreats before opposition or even a tough hurdle which doesn't move toward him, but stands implacable and seemingly immovable. In other situations he engages in daydreaming about irrelevant things, but which proves a successful substitute to him for action.

Perhaps one of the more interesting forms of withdrawal which every normal person engages in at some time, and which managers do too, is fantasy. This is a form of daydream. Rightly oriented, these daydreams can become the plans for achievement, and are part of the goal-forming process for the manager. The manager who dreams of a new plant may have his fantasy become so firmly fixed that he exerts himself tremendously in order to achieve it in actuality. Such daydreams are a positive aid to the action getter, and he needs a good supply of unfulfilled daydreams to keep him alive and moving forward.

When daydreaming and fantasy are a form of substitute for actually accomplishing something which he wanted to do but couldn't reach because of some obstacle, then it's probably harmful. These daydreams often run into several forms in their undesirable aspects. The manager may flop in his efforts and retire to his office and enjoy his reveries in which he is the conquering hero. When a manager slips into the habit of fantasy of an undesirable kind he not only fritters away his time, and instead of actually doing, planning, and analzying which the situation demands, he wafts away into a haze of imagined pleasures and accomplishments.

Adjustment by defensiveness. When a manager hits an obstacle it's also a common thing for him to adjust by building up defenses against the real reasons for his failure. If the results of hitting an obstacle have been especially painful to him it may result in a resolve not to get caught so severely again, and he erects barriers around himself to protect his sensitivities. One president of a small company, for example, led his firm into a new product line quite radically different from the traditional lines it had been in before. The effort fizzled badly, and for many years after that nobody dared mention the words of the product, which had been the focal point of the fiasco, in his presence. He often took personal affront if any slight reference to this product were made in normal conversation with him.

Another manifestation of defensiveness in managers is that they will seek out and be overly responsive to flattery. A company officer of my acquaintance, of limited formal education, found that his limitation caused him some difficulty early in his career. By dint of great drive and native intelligence he overcame this handicap and went on past many of his better educated friends. Yet he never fully shook his defensiveness to this seeming defect, and was especially subject to any form of flattery which bolstered his reputation as a thinker, scholar, or well-informed person in the arts and sciences.

For the manager to handle his adjustments to obstacles by establishing defense mechanisms isn't usually a conscious process. Defense mechanisms are learned through blind trial and error, and often grow out of the fact that the manager isn't clearly aware of his own drives in the first place.

Adjustment by compensation. When the reasons for failure to overcome obstacles are rooted in some personal defect in the manager, the kind of adjustment which results in overemphasis of a trait to overcome a feeling of deficiency in it, may occur. The supervisor who really feels inferior to many of his associates may effect a lordly and overbearing manner to compensate for his inward inadequacy.

Other ways of adjusting. To describe these forms of adjustment doesn't necessarily imply that they are all neessarily bad. There are some forms of adjusting however which are usually unfortunate for the possessor in management since they arouse reaction against him which keeps him from succeeding in future attempts at overcoming his obstacles. *Egocentrism* is such a form. Just as the defensive man may retreat from the press, the attention getter may seek to get his name before the public on every occasion, and retain expensive retinues of press agents to "build up" his reputation. In its worst forms it turns into pathological lies, or self accusations. *Rationalization* is another form of adjustment to hitting an obstacle that stops a manager. The man who fails will go to great lengths to give socially acceptable and rational explanations of his failure. Blaming the tools, the bankers, the workmen, or his luck are such rationalizations. Occasionally this becomes a system of projecting low motives to others, deprecating the goal which he really wants, or more commonly among organization men, is declaring that what he accomplished was "exactly what I had hoped for in the first place." Two danger signs in such adjustment are in seeing conspiracies among others as the cause of his failure, and delusions. The latter two are fortunately uncommon, and are symptoms that the person may be in need of professional assistance in his adjustment problems.

Ends versus means in a free society. All of this is of course couched in terms of the long-run *effectiveness* with which a manager adjusts to the obstacles which confront him in carrying the organization onward toward the goals he— or others— have set for it. These really are some standards by which the directors might appraise its officers' and executives' ability to get things done for example. Or perhaps it might be a standard by which the vice president of manufacturing judges a plant manager's actions, or a general foreman evaluates the results and actions of his foremen. But they aren't the only standards.

Criticism of management methods as it proceeds to demolish the obstacles to profitable operation and corporate growth take a number of forms. These assume some importance since they automatically— in the eyes of the modern professional manager— become further restrictions upon his methods of overcoming blocks to progress. To clearly understand these criteria it's necessary that management identify them more clearly than being that of other classes of people. It means that the modern manager is constrained from violating certain value systems in which the business systems must function if he is to avoid the reverberations which come back to him from his own superiors. These value systems have several facets.

1. *Management gets action inside a human value system.* This human value system provides for the dignity of people, respect for their rights to move freely and serve voluntarily in the market place. The use of tangible force is long outlawed. The use of naked economic coercion must be used sparingly in coercing people into lines of conformity with management goals. A hint of behavior which conjures up the image of the corporation with all its economic might, using its power to squelch the economically inferior individual, will always result in strong disapproval from the wider public and ultimately from the owners.

2. *Management gets action within a system of ethical values.* Management, the prevailing folklore holds, must be ethical and achieve its profits honestly and in a forthright manner. Integrity is a minimum requirement of the manager, and its absence results in retaliatory action by those whose ultimate power is in the political processes which govern all the institutions and people.

3. *Management gets action within an institutional value system.* The roles of free enterprise and private corporations are not only circumscribed by law, but also by prevailing sentiments about them. Managers who hope to accomplish their goals as leaders in such organizations, must recognize the role— and respect it— of other institutions. The labor union, the government, the civic and social institution, the educational system, the church, and other institutions have a status in the eyes of the public. The relation of the corporation to them takes certain broad forms which are really expectations which the public at large charges them with. For the manager who attempts to overcome his personal obstacles, respect for these institutional values are, by and large, impossible to ignore.

Unfortunately for the manager who wears blinders to these respective value systems, the ultimate power to control his own actions is not his. It rests with government, and under the proddings of a populace dissatisfied with means of management, restrictions upon management can— and have been— imposed without compunction. Often these expectations go beyond simply disapproval of certain practices. They are enlarged to expectations of things that he should voluntarily do. He should actively support the national defense. He should pay taxes without evasion. More than this he should contribute of his profits to educational institutions and of management's personal time and money to good causes. He's now expected to take an interest and active part in international affairs of the nation through properly attending to international relations, and behaving altruistically over foreign trade. Such things are part and parcel of overcoming obstacles to business success.

"No sooner said than done— so acts your man of worth."

Five Tests of Initiative

The process of moving quickly to get things into action is sometimes called initiative. It's compounded of a variety of properties and skills which the action getting manager seems to have that his less effective competitor lacks.

A study of the qualities which go into making up this among men who make things move, shows five basic qualities. These are major characteristics and are compounded of a lot of little habits and skills which the man may have been born with, but most often he acquired them in his career. Only a few of these qualities are innate or natural. The rest are acquired, and can be taught to others.

Let's look at each and see how the men who make things happen overcome this obstacle and how we can learn to be like them.

I. Inner drive. Some people with this trait are endowed with an overactive thyroid, or an abundance of animal energy, but this isn't always the case. The big difference isn't mainly physiological. It's a habit of vigorous and positive approaches to everything, of restless unhappiness with things as they are, and a roving eye toward the possibility for improvement.

The doer has developed the talent for picking a single goal out of the millions available and mustering all his talents, knowledge, powers of persuasion, and leadership to reach it.

He may pause while he's choosing a plan or mapping his strategy, but, once it's selected, his energies concentrate in a controlled form of organizational fury. More than simple activity, it is directed energy guided by an intelligent and well-disciplined mind.

Building or training this inner drive into a man isn't done through pep talks. It's a combination of coaching the man to peak personal effectiveness in his daily work habits. When he's reached that level, the next step is to give him big challenges which test and prove his skills.

II. Pick the important things. In terms of skills which a manager can develop to function as a result-getter, one of the key abilities is to pick out the important things for action. The doer's desk gets piled with the same assortment of trivia as yours and mine. He gets as many requests for his time. He is invited to as many meetings and has as many opportunites to dawdle as the next fellow.

The first step in becoming an action-getter is to learn how to wade through the underbrush to find the really important things and do them first. This means that he has mastered several difficult steps along the way. He has trained himself to scan the whole range of things that are pressing upon him and quickly evaluate the importance of each.

First, he more often than not go to the top man in the customer company— at least as high as he needs to go to set things right. As one such executive put it:

"I find it better to deal with the chief of the tribe than with one of the Indians."

Second, he is not afraid to admit his own mistakes and

failure. The important point again isn't that we must have a natural whirlwind to start with. Everybody has capacities which he may or may not be using. Guided experience and coaching in sorting out the facts before making decisions, and an opportunity to practice in real situations, is the key training method.

III. Tough-mindedness. Despite his concern with meeting the needs of others and meeting the basic needs of people, the action-getter has developed a tough-mindedness. For one thing, as Chris Argyris, management researcher of Yale, has put it, he has "a high tolerance for frustration." He can plug through all sorts of red tape without blowing his top when he has to. He frequently endures the delays and runarounds of committees and clearances with spartan endurance. He is patient where such patience is the only possible way of getting the final payoff that he seeks.

This patience isn't submissiveness, however, and when the time for patience is past and more direct action is called for, the action-minded manager is willing to be ruthless. When the choice is between maintaining old relationships and getting the job done he is always ready to decide in favor of the job. Stepping on people's corns isn't his frist choice, but he does it firmly if the occasion demands.

This tough-mindedness sometimes looks a little like inflexibility. Once he's decided what action is best, he'll stick to it no matter how the weather blows. This is partly because he's constitutionally dogged, but mostly because he knows that vacillation will be worse than picking a specific tack and holding his bearing. He knows that pressures for change are inevitable no matter what course he sets. He accepts them as part of the price for making headway.

The action-minded manager is probably tough-minded in his relations with people, too. He's willing to stick by his people through their honest mistakes— or to chop off heads as the need arises. He assumes that men are made of tough stuff and will work hard and take heavy blows as a price of making a living and contributing to the success of the business.

He will urge on a man who is working at less than his best abilities. He is liberal with recognition for good work, and equally liberal with a reverse kind of recognition for the people who aren't performing up to their capacities.

He's tough-minded, too, in being willing to pay the prices for personal success. Long hours, hard work, and man-killing travel schedules are the way of life for him. He concentrates on his job with a fury and singleness of purpose that reduces other things to a lesser role. This doesn't mean he's inhuman or a dull grind. His pleasure and his recreation are often found only in work. As one such executive put it:

"I think people in positions like mine have found a secret weapon which really isn't a secret at all— we don't quit. As I look back over forty years and see the fellows who didn't go as far as I did, I think it's probably because they took a good look at the price you pay in family life and so forth, and decided to settle for less. I can't say they're wrong, it's just that they didn't make the same decision I did. They were willing to let themselves be outworked. Add a little luck to that, and it's a secret formula."

How do you get all of these qualities? First, they aren't learned in a course. They are learned in tough situations. This becomes a matter of assignment of men to places where they take pressure.

In developing the men who make things happen, major emphasis, it would seem, should be on careful selection of people who are willing to pay the price— people with hides thick enough and frames sufficiently durable that they can learn by being tossed against problems bigger than themselves.

Although conferences and courses can help, most observers agree that major emphasis should be on systematic coaching and carefully planned job assignments. In essence, a program to produce a manager who makes things happen must grind in some habits. The ingredients in this program will vary to meet the needs of the man but they will include:

• Early identification of the people who have the native equipment. This isn't much different from what we're doing at present.

• Assignments that give him these three major advantages for development.

1. Tough problems to solve and big jobs to do where he can see the results of good— or poor— performance early.

2: Assignment under an action-getting manager. One action-getter can strike off several copies of himself. If several go-getters are assigned to an action-getting manager, they'll strike sparks off one another, too. Healthy competition is a good force for bringing out the "will-do" factors and causes people to bring out their best abilities.

3. Work with the manager to help him coach and guide these people.

Once you've got an action-getter in a spot where he can do some good for the company and develop his own talents, get out of the way and let him move.

IV. Instilling a desire to excel. The action-getter can use initiative because he's done most of the ground work in advance. He knows that nobody in the company, especially himself, has all of the good ideas. He builds a climate in which a good ideal will get itself into application without a great deal of clearances and approvals all up and down the line.

This implies that the action-getter is more than a self-appointed genius who swings his weight around to get people scurrying. He gets them to initiate by making certain they are ready and able to start things in motion. He does this by listening patiently, asking questions, probing deeply into half-formed ideas to help the initiator develop them more fully. Not only that but he makes it worthwhile for a man to excel in his job, and to pay dividends for people who move quickly and skillfully in their job. When he sees a half-baked idea he doesn't kill it summarily but listens to hear the whole story. If it's off the beam he explains carefully to the originator why it can't be used. If it's good he gives the initiator sincere credit for having thought of it and put it into application.

He's probably created a climate in which people are scrambling hard for new ideas and better ways of doing things. He's also made it plain that he's tolerant of mistakes, and won't hand a man his head for the first or even the second one. The organization which is initiating ideas will have to make some errors in judgment. They aren't afraid to generate and try out a few of their own. They know that an occasional mistake won't cost them their scalp.

The interesting part of such growth is that it hasn't in many cases decreased the agility and vigor with which the organization tackles its problems, not its speed in solving them. The small company which is dominated by one man is often slower than the corporate giant. This seeming anomaly grows out of the place where initiative rests.

As a rule, initiative in an organization should be pushed down to the lowest possible level where decision can be made through instilling a desire to excel at every level.

V. Initiating intelligent action. Simply getting the ball in motion isn't enough. It requires *intelligent* action if the best results are to be achieved. This requires two things:

• *a goal* which is realistic, attainable; at the same time it's hard enough to attain that it challenges people.

• *a plan* which spells out in an orderly fashion how the organization will arrive there.

This requires more than simply getting things into motion. It means movement toward the objective. Managers who have "initiative" or the ability to start moving, based on emotional drives or instinct, won't be as successful in the long run as the one who acts upon reflection, thought, and conscious planning. A lot of initiative is based on such instincts and reflexes, which sometimes lead to self-cancelling or inconsistent action.

The best kinds of initiative are those which are based on experience, and pre-planned procedures. *Pressure* alone isn't properly showing initiative.

Another key ingredient in intelligent action is taking initiative that will carry the unit or department toward the larger plan for the whole company. A plan which makes one department look good at the expense of another, or adds to another department's cost isn't good initiative.

The following case illustrates the crafty type of initiative which doesn't do the overall organization any good. It's from *Time* magazine of July 29, 1957.

"The dominant theme of Soviet railway transport policy" writes one expert in the jargon so dear to experts, "has been that of maximizing the volume of services provided while devoting the minimum possible resources to them". As freight traffic manager on the Vladivostokection of the Trans-Siberian Railway, Comrade Vorobiev was a man with a mission to fill, and the imagination to overcome obstacles. His job was to move a specified tonnage of freight. But what if there was not enough freight to move? The latest issue of *Gudok,* the Soviet railway journal tells how Comrade Vorobiev met his problem.

In 1955 traffic manager Vorobiev's line was in grave danger of falling behind its monthly norm in tank car loadings. Desperate for something to transport, and finding no petroleum, alcohol, milk or other useful liquid available, Comrade Vorobiev gazed about him, cast his eye upon the liquid in a nearby river, and quick as a flash filled 50 of his cars with water and sent them rattling off from Voroshilov. At a siding of the Trans-Siberian line the water froze solid in the cars and it took a month for workmen to chip it out with pickaxes. But no matter— Vorobiev had made his quota. □

EXECUTIVE TIME MANAGEMENT

Getting 12 Hours' Work Out of an 8-Hour Day

H. Reynolds & M. Tramel

Helen Reynolds is an internationally known management consultant in the areas of time management, leadership and communication. She is listed in *Who's Who in Training and Development* and in the *Organizational Development Network*.

Mary E. Tramel is a writer and consultant in time management, communications and modern office procedures. Her writings have appeared in publications in the United States and Canada.

Wise Control of Your 8-to-5 Time

To bring about change, whether it be a wiser use of time or a better functioning office staff, there must be a catalyst—an agent of change, something or someone injected into the situation to bring about the desired change.

If you want to change the way you use your time so that you will use it more wisely, you are the catalyst to bring about that desired change.

If you are going to put yourself into your job situation, into your boss's arena, or into your organization for the purpose of creating a change in the way time is used, you are going to have to know yourself.

Know Yourself

Here are some questions to ask yourself. Your frank answers will reveal thought and work habits that you need to be aware of in order to bring about a wiser use of time. There are no right or wrong answers to these questions. They are meant to help you analyze your habits, good or bad.

A. How organized are you?

1. Do you work at a cluttered desk? Or at an orderly desk with a place for everything and everything in its place?

2. Do you plan ahead?

3. Are you a list maker?

4. How much time do you spend on list making? Do you list only what you need to list to help you remember and keep on schedule? Do you spend so much time making lists that you don't have time left to do what you have listed? Do you avoid making lists altogether and try to keep mental notes that get all jumbled up in your mind and cause you to lose time trying to remember?

5. Do you do tasks in priority order?

6. Do you have many active interests? Or do you concentrate your efforts on a few vital ones?

7. Do you do everything you do with a purpose?

8. Have you learned how to say no?

B. What are your habits?

1. Are you a chronic complainer?

2. Do you begin each day with a conscious effort to be enthusiastic?

3. How punctual are you? Do you make an effort to get an early start?

4. Do you habitually comply with the status quo, or do you look for a better way?

5. Do you procrastinate?

6. Do you relegate and release?

C. What are your personality traits?

1. Are you an optimist or a pessimist?

2. Do you like to work with people, or do you prefer to work alone?

3. Do you have empathy? Can you see yourself and your position through the eyes of your superior? Through the eyes of your subordinates?

4. Are you a perfectionist, dotting every *i* and crossing

every *t*?

    5. Do you worry a lot?

    6. Do you put off making decisions?

    7. Are you aware of your personal rhythm? Do you know when your *up* cycle is likely to be and when you will be feeling *down?*

    8. Are you a quick starter or a slow starter? Do you know your most creative time of day?

    9. Are you motivated to change the way you use your time?

Know How You Are Spending Your Time

Your value as an executive is measured in degrees of effectiveness. It is not so much how efficiently you perform your function as it is how effectively you move toward the attainment of the organization's primary goal.

Efficiency is doing the job right.

Effectiveness is doing the right job.

Peter F. Drucker, author of several management books, says in *The Effective Executive* that effective executives start out by finding where their time actually goes.

To do this, you should keep a Time Record and Analysis for each day for a week. (Figure 1.) Select a week that is normal, not one in which some other unusual occurrence is expected.

    1. Put the date at the top.

    2. Enter on the appropriate line what you are doing every fifteen minutes during the day. (Yes, this will take time; but after you have made the analysis, it will save you many future productive hours.)

    3. At the end of the day, and with all the hindsight you can muster, check each activity in Column 1, 2, or 3.

Column 1: You did the right thing at the right time.

Column 2: You did the right thing but at the wrong time. (Maybe something occurred later in the day that would have

TIME RECORD AND ANALYSIS SHEET Date: _____

Time	What I Did	1	2	3	Time	What I Did	1	2	3
7:00					2:30				
7:15					2:45				
7:30					3:00				
7:45					3:15				
8:00					3:30				
8:15					3:45				
8:30					4:00				
8:45					4:15				
9:00					4:30				
9:15					4:45				
9:30					5:00				
9:45					5:15				
10:00					5:30				
10:15					5:45				
10:30					6:00				
10:45					6:15				
11:00					6:30				
11:15					6:45				
11:30					7:00				
11:45					7:15				
12:00					7:30				
12:15					7:45				
12:30					8:00				
12:45					8:15				
1:00					8:30				
1:15					8:45				
1:30					9:00				
1:45					9:15				
2:00					9:30				
2:15					9:45				

Figure 1. **Time Analysis**

made it easier for you if you had waited until then to do it.)

Column 3: You did the wrong thing (something that didn't have to be done at all— at least not by you).

A careful analysis of your daily charts over a week's time will give you a good idea of how you are spending your time. You may find that productive managerial hours are being displaced out of your workday in fifteen-minute segments devoted to such nonproductive tasks as sharpening pencils, adding figures, dictating routine correspondence, making copies, redoing tasks because of insufficient preplanning, and so forth.

Spend Executive Time More Effectively

Plan your work and work your plan daily is good advice for the executive who wants to use time wisely. You should not only plan your work mentally, but also get your plan down on paper. This will help to keep you on target so you will not be sidetracked by lesser items coming to your attention during the day.

Figure 2 is a sample form for a daily work plan. Whatever format is used, it should be one that will stand out from other papers on your desk.

How To Use The Daily Organizer

1. Establish a system for denoting priorities.

 Priority A = Must do today
 Priority B = Should do today
 Priority C = Could put off
 Priority D = Can delegate

2. In the *To Do* section, list your paperwork goals for today, assigning each one a priority, A, B, or C. If one of your goals can be delegated to an employee, list it as an A/D, B/D, or C/D.

3. In the *To Phone* section, list each person you plan to call that day and the subject. Again, assign a priority to each call.

4. In the *Appointments* section, list the time, the person

DAILY ORGANIZER

Date: _____

TO PHONE:

Person	Regarding	P

APPOINTMENTS:

When	Person and Place	Time

TO DO:

Task	P

TO FOLLOW UP:

Figure 2. **Daily Organizer**

you will be seeing, and the place. In the *Time* column put the maximum amount of your time you think this appointment warrants. A minute or two before that amount of time is used up, start to bring the conversation to a close. You will not always be able to do so, but with a time goal before you, you will find it easier to keep appointments from dragging on unnecessarily.

5. Appointments must be taken care of as they are scheduled. However, on your *To Do* and *To Phone* lists, complete all A priorities before going to B priorities. Complete all B priorities before going to C priorities.

6. During the day enter any task or phone call on which you need to follow up in the *To Follow Up* section. Put down enough detail so you will know exactly where you have left off and what the next follow-up step is. Consider this section as you prepare your Daily Organizer for the next workday.

7. Schedule one hour of uncommitted time each day to take care of the unexpected. If you do not need the hour, use it to catch up on desk work.

Some Reasons Why Schedules May Not Work

You will find it nearly impossible to complete everything on your *To Do* list each day. The important thing is that what you do accomplish are your highest priorities. The reason you cannot accomplish the entire list could be any of the following:

1. You may be trying to accomplish too much.

2. You may not be ready to do some of the things you listed or your goal is not clearly formulated. Consequently, you are jumping into a task in the middle without sufficient analyzing of the task step by step.

3. You may not be paying attention to task priorities.

4. You may be failing to complete decision-making tasks if you find it difficult to make a decision.

5. You may not have all the needed information to complete the task.

6. Your self-discipline may be failing you and you are:

- Neglecting to plan because you are feeling pressured.
- Not staying with the task because you are finding it difficult or boring.
- Allowing a contrary desire to weaken your principal purpose.

7. You may lack self-confidence to achieve your goal.

8. You may be testing the water around the edges of a task instead of plunging in.

9. You may be dwelling on past failures instead of optimistically working toward success.

10. You may be thinking, *I probably won't finish it* instead of *I can and I will.*

A Time to Plan

There is an old Spanish proverb that says, *If you build no castles in the air, you build no castles anywhere.* Successful executives find that controll daydreaming is an absolute *must.* It is called *planning.*

Planning cuts down on unproductive activity and procrastination. The process can be compared to looking through a camera with two kinds of lenses: a wide-angle lens and a telescopic lens.

Wide-Angle Planning

Wide-angle planning gives you the large picture. This is when you rethink your long-range goals and establish short-range objectives for them. This is a time to reminisce on the past: to learn from mistakes and build on successes. It's a time to explore ways to increase your personal contribution to the organization's goal. It's also a time to increase your professional awareness through study and reading of literature related to your field. Reserve an hour or two on your weekly schedule for wide-angle planning. If possible, do it away from your office where your thoughts will not be inhibited by the pressures of the day. Find a quiet place at home or some other spot where you can feel comfortable and relaxed.

Wide-angle planning is easy to neglect because it does not demand your attention. Don't neglect it. It's a wise investment of time that pays high dividends.

Telescopic Planning

Telescopic planning zeroes in on specific problems and tasks. This is a time to:

- *Plan* your day using your Daily Work Organizer.
- *Think* through people problems.
- *Schedule* time.

Establish a quiet hour sometime during each workday for telescopic planning. Choose a time when you can have solitude, when you can give concentrated attention to your thoughts without being interrupted by phone, caller, or secretary.

If possible, pick the same hour every day so people will get to know you are not available for that time.

Don't be concerned about your superior's thinking you are wasting time because you are seemingly doing nothing. Your superior probably has a quiet hour too for his or her planning. And even if this is not the case, your effectiveness as a result of your planning time will soon convince your superior of the wisdom of your allocating such a time.

Record, Manage, and Consolidate Time

You already recorded time when you made your Time Analysis. You have begun to manage your time if you relegated and released tasks that don't belong there. You should repeat this recording and managing of your time at least every six months. Unproductive activities have a way of creeping back into your schedule and you need to periodically search them out and dispose of them.

After you have recorded and managed your time, you will know how much time you have left for tasks that only you can do. The problem is that this time is scattered in small segments throughout the day. Small bits of them, although they may add up to one or two hours, are not sufficient for most executive tasks. You can spend hours in fifteen-minute segments on a task that requires executive-level planning and never get it accomplished. What you need is a system for blocking time so you will have large chunks of it instead of small segments. Here are several ways you can accomplish this:

1. Work at home one day a week.

2. Schedule all meetings, conferences, problem-solving sessions, and the like for two days a week, say Monday and Friday. Set aside either the mornings or afternoons of Tuesday, Wednesday, and Thursday for executive tasks.

3. Schedule a daily work period at home in the morning, say an hour or hour and a half. This is better than taking work home to do in the evening. By the end of the day you are not as productive as you are earlier.

4. Consolidate phone calls.

5. Eat a late breakfast and work through the lunch hour.

Having scheduled some large blocks of time for executive planning, you need some tools to help you use this time wisely. Here are some that other top executives have found to be useful.

Appointment Calendars

Executives need to have three appointment calendars: a pocket calendar, a desk calendar, and a daily plan.

Pocket Calendar. Carry a small pocket calendar with you at all times. If it becomes necessary to make an appointment or schedule a meeting while you are away from your office, a glance at your pocket calendar will tell you what time you have available. Your desk calendar should remain at the office on your assistant's desk.

Cautions. (a) Be sure to schedule a few minutes (five at the most) once or twice a day for your assistant to coordinate the two calendars. (b) Always make entries on both calendars in pencil. Then if revisions are necessary, the original entry can be erased and the revised entry written in its place.

Desk Calendar. Your desk calendar, which is kept by your assistant, will contain on the appropriate date and time line:

- Person or persons appointment is with.
- Place of meeting.
- Subject of meeting (reason for appointment).

Your assistant uses this calendar to schedule appointments for you as requests for appointments come in. She will know how much time you have available and when. That is why it is important that you allow your assistant to have your pocket calendar once or twice a day so both calendars can be kept current.

Daily Plan. Your third calendar, the daily plan, is the one that will save you time and make your appointments productive. It is prepared by your assistant first thing in the morning before your arrival or last thing the day before. It contains: time, name(s), subject, and any other pertinent information you need to facilitate the appointment. The following are typical entries on the daily plan:

10 A.M. Mr. Burton— to discuss your participation in Civic Fund. (You told him previously you would consider serving on the Board of Directors.)

11 A.M. Mrs. Goodal of Chamber of Commerce— to discuss upcoming membership drive. (The strategy outline you requested is being typed now.)

1 P.M. Mr. Brown and Mr. White of Black and Co.— to discuss architectural services. (Their correspondence is attached.)

Your daily plan can be typed on 8½ by 11 paper or on 5 by 8 cards; the date could be used for the heading. You can use this daily plan to complete your Daily Work Organizer (Figure 2).

Pointers for Calendaring

1. Avoid too tight scheduling. This has a tension-building effect on you and your visitors. Time pressure cuts down on your effectiveness.

2. Have your assistant post regular recurring meetings at least three months in advance so that you don't get double-scheduled for those times.

3. Schedule long-winded callers at psychologically strategic times— just before their lunch time, just before a meeting. This will give you an excuse to bring the appointment to a close.

4. Have an understanding with your assistant that s/he is to call or come in to remind you of another appointment. Then say, "We'll only be another three minutes"— and hope that your guest will take the hint.

5. Consider going to an employee's office instead of having the employee come to yours. This will give you a chance to get out and see what's going on and make it easier for you to close the interview.

6. If a person is late for an appointment, tell the caller your time constraint and ask if the business can be finished within that period or if the appointment should be rescheduled. One late appointment can put you behind for the remainder of the day.

7. Remember that other people's time is important to them. If a delay on your part is absolutely necessary, have your assistant or someone else explain the delay, offer some refreshments, and, most important, check back with the visitor frequently.

8. Blocking time is an excellent technique for assuring completion of high-priority projects. When laying out your weekly schedule, block out enough time for high-priority projects that require a lot of time. Schedule enough time in a block so you can build up momentum. Reserve certain days of the week for such projects. When you leave a project unfinished,

PROCRASTINATION RECORD

Item	Date In	Review Date	Future Action

DELEGATION PLANNING GUIDE

Instructions: 1. Enter "D" in month task is delegated.
2. Divide projected completion month diagonally.
3. Enter "C" in top triangle of projected completion month.
4. When task is completed, enter "✓" in lower triangle if completed as projected. If not completed as projected, enter "✓" in actual month of completion.

TITLE OF TASK	Delegated to	Month task delegated/completed					
		JAN	FEB	MAR	APR	MAY	JUNE
Equipment Inventory	Bill Jones		D		C/✓		
Stock Inventory	Fred Smith			D		C/	✓
Budget Report	Mary Brown			D	✓	C/	

Figure 3. **Procrastination Record**

Figure 4. **Delegation Planning Guide**

make a note of what the next step is so you will not have to
waste time reviewing when you return to the project.

Procrastination Drawer

Procrastination is a time-consuming habit; but calculated
procrastination can save time. Some problems, if left alone,
will resolve themselves. Why not keep a desk drawer for such
problems?

If a problem in your procrastination drawer becomes
urgent, you can always say you've had it under study, pull it
out, and go to work on it. It's risky but, on the other hand, you
may save hours not doing some jobs that will never need to be
done anyway.

Keep a Procrastination Record (Figure 3) in the front of
your procrastination drawer. This will save time when you are
looking for an item in the drawer and will be a reminder of
when to review or take action on the item.

Caution: Avoid using your procrastination drawer to put
off a task that you know you should do.

Delegation Planning Guide

If you have projects with due dates spread over several
months, a Planning Guide will keep you on target. (Figure 4).
It will also reveal to you at a glance the major projects that are
in the hopper— vital information you need to schedule your
department's work.

Responsibility Chart

The Responsibility Chart (Figure 5) is a tool to keep you
from overlooking someone who should be in on a specific task
or problem solving. Leaving out a key person will often result
in having to backtrack or start over. It could also result in
miscommunication, which is one of the biggest time displacers.

Suppose your company has added employees and the
employees' lunchroom is now too small. The company's Board

RESPONSIBILITY CHART

Goals: 1. To place responsibility
2. To include all involved persons

TASK: To develop a plan for enlarging the employees' lunchroom

Persons Involved

Components of Task	Your Name	Jim Jones	Betty White	Sarah Cane	Al Franks	Alice Black									
	D														
Determine size and Capacity	S/W CO			CO											
Kitchen facilities	S	W													
Location	S		W												
Lunchroom personnel	S W														
Draw up plan	A W														

(After you have finished filling in the chart, re-think all persons who are involved in each category. If all involved persons have been assigned, place
a check mark in the box for that category.)

Code:

✓	D	- Director (has general responsibility, sets policy, establishes limits, etc.)
✓	S	- Supervisor (supervises and assigns work, sees that job is done)
✓	W	- Worker (does the work)
✓	CI	- Consultant/Imperative (must be consulted)
✓	CO	- Consultant/Optional (may be consulted)
✓	NI	- Notify/Imperative (must be notified)
✓	A	- Approver (must approve or disapprove completed task)

Figure 5. **Responsibility Chart**

of Directors has decided the lunchroom should be enlarged and has commissioned you to bring them a plan for accomplishing this. So your task is to develop a plan for enlarging the employees' lunchroom.

The first step would be to break the task down into components.

List these components on the Responsibility Chart.

Next, list the persons who will be in any way involved in this task. List your own name first and place a D in the square immediately under your name. This will indicate to all concerned that you are the director of the task. Under each person's name, place the appropriate code letter opposite any component of the task that involves that person. The code letters are listed on the lower part of the Responsibility Chart.

After you have filled in the upper portion of the Responsibility Chart look at each symbol listed in the lower portion of the chart and place a checkmark in the box opposite the symbol if you are satisfied with the assignment you have made in the upper portion of the chart.

A Time to Do Paperwork

What to Do About Accumulated Paperwork

Even if you set your priorities for each day and follow your Daily Organizer, there are times when paperwork will pile up on your desk. It is inevitable. Here is a system for wearing down that pile of accumulated tasks.

First, find the time to work on accumulated paperwork. If you can, schedule a day or half-day for it. You can accomplish much more in a block of time than you can in little bits and pieces of time. If you cannot schedule a block of time, an alternative would be to work one, two, or more paperwork tasks in your Daily Organizer. Make a point of picking out one or two of the highest priority tasks from your accumulated paperwork every day.

How to Keep Paperwork from Accumulating

There are few executives who do not have a backlog of paperwork to do; but there are habits you can develop to help you keep your paperwork from getting completely out of hand.

Never handle a piece of paper more than once. Every time you pick up a piece of paper, whether it is a letter, a report, a phone message, do something with it other than putting it in a "to do" pile. If it is a letter that requires your reply, answer it *now*. If it is a report that you need to read and digest, do it *now*. If you don't have time to read and digest it now, delegate the task to someone else who will be able to pick out the highlights and give you a brief summary. The main thing is to get the report off your desk *now*.

Train your professional assistant not to bring you every piece of paper that comes into the office. Make your assistant responsible for routing mail to your support people, answering routine mail, discarding mail of no use such as advertisements that are of no interest to you, filing mail containing information that needs to be kept but that you don't need to see now.

Work out a sorting system with your professional assistant for mail that you need to see. One technique would be to have a folder marked *urgent* for mail that needs your attention today; another folder marked *important but not urgent;* and another marked *information only.* You may want to use a different colored folder for each category.

Have your secretary read letters, reports, periodicals, and so forth, and underscore the main points. Now when you pick up the letter you see at a glance what is needed and you have the information available.

Cut down on mass copying and routing of magazine articles. If an article is routed, have your assistant underline the key points so that those receiving it can skim it quickly.

Make marginal notes on incoming mail. Your professional assistant can then reply for you.

Reply by phone rather than by mail. Using the phone may take less time.

Ask your colleagues not to send you "for information" copies of letters and report if you can do without them. It is often not essential for you to see such material.

Insist that a recommendation be submitted along with any problem statement that comes to you. This will assure you that the person who has the problem has given some thought to solving it and is not merely passing the buck to you. Sometimes all you will have to do is approve the recommendation if it seems logical to you.

Require that reports of more than three pages carry a cover page. A cover page with the subject of the report, the date it was prepared, and the name of the reporter will save you the time you would otherwise spend looking through the report to find this information.

If possible, form the habit of processing routine paperwork at the same time every day. It will become a habit and you will not be likely to procrastinate your paperwork. Also, others will become aware that this is the time of day when you are not apt to be available to them.

Remember: A place for everything and everything in its place. This old adage can spare much wasted time.

Make a periodic check on reports you prepare. Follow each report through to its final destination.

- Who really reads it?
- Who uses it?
- Is the same information being compiled in another department?

Take a critical look at your correspondence, especially intraorganizational letters and memorandums.

1. Is time being spent dictating, transcribing, and delivering intraoffice mail when:

- a phone call would suffice?
- a handwritten note would be enough?
- a printed routing slip or attachment memo could be used?

2. Does your correspondence contain complete information the first time, thereby eliminating a whole file of letters back and forth in order to accomplish what one letter should have accomplished in the first place?

Save time on once-in-a-while tasks by cataloging pertinent

information that you can use the next time you do the task. Such information as person to contact, phone number, prices, schedules, travel arrangements, and so forth can be recorded in this manner. This will cut down on repetitive detail work.

Use a mail summary. Have your secretary record each day's mail on the Mail Summary. Train your assistant to use judgment in what to record; not every piece of mail need be listed. Do not record mail that requires no action. The Mail Summary keeps track of important mail until necessary action has been completed.

A Time To Write

Clear Composition

Clear composition conserves the time of both the writer and the reader. As you form the habit of writing clearly, you will accomplish more writing in less time. Clarity is shortness, simplicity, and strength. But before you can put these into a piece of writing, you must know your purpose for writing. To paraphrase Plato: *Wise men write because they have something to write about; fools write because they have to write about something.*

Shortness

Do not burden your reader with too much data, nor leave out important information that would make your message clear. Careful outlining will ensure proper length of your letter. One-page letters are more quickly read and digested than letters of two, three, or four pages. Edit for any irrelevancy and your letter will probably be the right length for the subject on which you are writing. Be sure to watch out for the following space and time wasters:

78

1. *Repeating unnecessary data.* If you are answering a letter, don't repeat in your letter what has already been said in the letter you are answering. And don't review your previous correspondence.

2. *Excessive qualifying words and phrases.* For example, in *absolutely complete, absolutely* is unnecessary. What is complete is complete. Another example is *misposted in error:* if it was misposted, it was in error, so *misposted* is all that is necessary.

3. *Phrases that have the same meaning as verbs.* Use a direct verb when possible, rather than a longer phrase. *Reached a decision* means *decided. Make a presentation* means *present.*

4. *Say-nothing words and phrases.* In the sentence, **"It is believed that the sum of** *$600 should be spent* **in the interest** of this program," the phrases in bold face are superfluous. *We should spend $600 on the program* is more direct and saves ten words.

5. *Repetition.* What is gained in emphasis by the writer is lost in boredom by the reader. It is time-wise to make the point clear the first time.

6. *Adjectives and adverbs—* unless they are necessary for understanding the message. Adjectives and adverbs are like the noodles in Hamburger Helper: They make the letter last longer, but the meat of the message is often hard to find.

Simplicity

Here are some time-saving ways to achieve simplicity in writing:

1. Avoid ambiguity. For example, *He said today the report is three days past due.* Which meant: that he said it today, or that the report is three day past due as of today? Be sure your meaning is clear on the first reading.

2. Avoid technical language unless you are certain your reader understands it. The same is true of excessive abbreviating.

3. Don't be formal. *In reply to yours of the first instant*

and *I beg to remain humble servant* have long ago found their places in the archives of our language.

4. Write conversationally. It's more quickly understood. An occasional contraction, as in the previous sentence, is acceptable in business letters.

5. Avoid tired words and phrases such as the following:

Feel free to call me	*Call me* is enough
Be kind enough to	*Please*
For the purpose of	*For*
In view of the fact that	*Because or Since*

6. If you have a choice between a familiar word and an unfamiliar one, use the familiar word. If you have a choice between short and long, use the short.

7. Write more short sentences than long ones. Few sentences should contain more than 21 words.

8. Paragraphs should be short— three or four to a page— and contain one main point. Make the point of the paragraph apparent in the first sentence.

9. Connect paragraphs with each other smoothly. Strive for continuity of thought throughout the message. You can gain continuity by:

a. Repeating a word, phrase, or thought from the last sentence of a paragraph in the first sentence of the next paragraph.

b. Using connective words such as *therefore, nevertheless, so, also,* and the like.

10. If you have to mention several items, it will save the reader time if you tabulate them. The items will register more quickly in the mind of the reader.

Decrease Dictation Time

Longhand or Shorthand? If you prefer to write letters in longhand to be copied by a typist, we suggest you try dictating. With practice you can become proficient and you will find your new system displacing far less time than your old method.

Machine or Human? Machine dictation is preferred by many executives. They can organize their thoughts and express them better without the distraction of another person present. There are other time-wise advantages to using dictating equipment: (1) You and your assistant can work independently. (2) Both of you can schedule work at the most productive time. (3) You can carry a portable dictating unit with you to dictate thoughts as they occur to you.

On the other hand, many executives prefer to dictate to a professional assistant. A time-wise assistant can be helpful in a dictation session. S/he can be a sounding board. You might ask your secretary for an opinion concerning the tone of a letter you have dictated. If you have a team relationship, s/he will be able to be frank about the tone of your dictation. An alert secretary can also help you when you are stumped for the right word to express a specific thought and can suggest persons who need copies of certain letters.

Pointers on Dictating

1. *Know what you want to say before you say it.* If you are an inexperienced dictator, take time to jot down a brief outline before you start. It will help you organize your thoughts.

2. *Enunciate clearly.* Speak slowly enough to make every syllable clear and use correct pronunciation.

3. *Don't compete with the shorthand taker.* Don't race ahead of the shorthand taker. Let her/him catch up and wait for you if necessary. You can be a time-wise team and have a cooperative spirit. If your stenographer is so slow that you lose your train of thought or the slowness makes you uncomfortable, suggest that s/he improve her/his shorthand— or hire someone more proficient.

1
8   2
7   3
6   4
5

A Time to Converse

Conversation consists of two parts; talking and listening. Listening is as important, if not more so, than speaking. Approximately 70 percent of your workday is spent in communicating, and 45 percent of that is spent in listening, according to a University of Minnesota study. "Know how to listen," said Plutarch, "and you can learn even from those who speak badly." Wise listening is wise use of time.

Listening is more than hearing: it is perceiving. All you need in order to hear is a pair of ears. To perceive you need not only ears, but eyes, heart, and mind. Webster defines "perceive" as to attain knowledge through the senses.

Ten Quick Ways to Perceive a Person

Perceiving a person, no matter who it is, will displace less of your time if you observe the following suggestions.

1. Give undivided attention. Don't be thinking of something else while the person is speaking.

2. Don't hurry the speaker by looking annoyed, glancing at the clock, or shuffling papers on your desk.

82

3. Don't react negatively to unpleasant news. It is hard for a person to say what you don't want to hear if you show a negative reaction. Although unpleasant, it may be extremely important news for you to have.

4. Avoid reading into the message something that is not there.

5. Be patient with the slow speaker. Give the speaker time to get it out. Help by indicating interest and understanding, by restating in your own words what is said, by acknowledging that the person's feelings are reasonable, and by encouraging him/her to continue.

6. Don't allow the speaker to ramble. Gently but firmly direct the conversation back to the subject.

7. Don't get snarled by minor facts. Pay attention to the overall gist of the conversation. Listen for key thoughts.

8. Jot down notes of important facts to remember (dates, figures, etc.).

9. If the speaker is giving you detailed instructions, make notes. Don't rely on your memory even if you listen well.

10. Don't let your mind wander to what you are going to say when the speaker is through.

How to Manage Conversation

Rule 1: Keep a small notebook with you at all time. You can index it with key persons' names. Jot down in this notebook subjects you want to discuss with any of these people. Look at it several times during the day and whenever you leave your office. Then, when you meet one of these people unexpectedly, you can make the meeting worthwhile by accomplishing one of your objectives.

Rule 2: When you have a complaint, grumble (if you must) to some one who can do something about it.

Taking out your frustrations on any available person is an unproductive way to displace time from your workday and from the workday of others.

Rule 3: Know what you want to say, say it, and omit everything else. Stick to your main point with only enough detail to make the point understood.

Rule 4: Organize your thoughts. If a conversation is not impromptu, take time to jot down on a 3 by 5 card key words to help you present your thoughts in logical order without overlooking important points.

Rule 5: Visualize your ideas for other people. Many people can grasp an abstract idea more quickly if they can relate it to something they can see. Sketch pie charts, stick figures, and action arrows.

Rule 6: Discuss, but don't argue. If the point of your conversation is to persuade someone to your point of view, you will arrive at your goal sooner if you keep your conversation factual, objective, and impersonal. Always attack the issue, not the person.

Rule 7: Check your tone. It is not what you say, but how you say it that determines the result of your conversation. Hours can be lost through misunderstanding, not of the words that were spoken, but of the tone or manner in which they were said. In conversation what is said *between the lines* is more quickly understood than the actual words that are spoken.

Rule 8: Make and maintain contact with your listeners. Practice developing empathy for those with whom you speak.

Rule 9: Avoid socializing too much. Some socializing on the job can have the opposite effect when you return and find too much time has been displaced.

Rule 10: If possible, know the person with whom you will converse. There are two kinds of hearers: readers and listeners. Readers have difficulty following a great deal of oral detail; they prefer to see it in black and white. Listeners won't read long written reports; they prefer to hear it, with a brief note to remind them if necessary. If your hearer is a reader, approach him/her orally with the bare facts and leave your detailed message written out for digestion later. If your hearer is a

listener, plan to give him/her all the details orally, leaving only
a brief reminder of the conversation.

How to Say No and Make It Stick

If executives responded affirmatively to all demands on
their time, there would be little time left for administering. And
yet, when to say yes and when to say no can be a real dilemma.
Whenever someone asks you to displace some time, remember
the three "Be's."

1. **Be selfish.** Ask, "Will the time displacement carry me
closer to my goals? Is the request, task, meeting, duty, project
important to me?"

Ask yourself if saying no will create future problems. Ask
yourself if saying yes will create future problems. If you are not
sure of the answers to these questions, buy time. Tell the request maker that you will have to think it over. Give him/her a
time when you will have decided.

2. **Be firm.** Having decided to say no, be firm. Be definite
about it and don't waver from your decision. It is not necessary
to qualify your decision, but it would tend to keep a good relationship if you gave a reason. If you do, be sure it is sincere and
logical. And don't argue the reason. If the requester attempts
to break down your reason, repeat your no and don't discuss it
any further.

3. **Be pleasant.** Say no as pleasantly as you can. You may
be able to suggest someone else. Express appreciation for having been thought of. Express your regrets. But don't overdo
your regrets because that would be insincere. If you really
regretted it that much, you would find a way to do it.

The Telephone

The ten rules for managing conversation earlier in this
chapter also apply to telephoning. Here are some additional
ideas for changing your telephone into a time tool.

1. Instead of using separate *While you were out* or similar

memos for telephone messages, use a bound phone memo book. Several copies are printed to a page, with carbon. The original page is perforated so it can be torn out and given to the callee, and the carbon copy remains in the book as a permanent record of the call.

The time advantages of this system over separate memos are:

a. Copies of separate messages tend to get misplaced. Bound in a book they are kept chronologically, no filing is necessary, and specific messages are quickly located.

b. If the name or phone number of a person who called is needed several days or weeks later, your professional assistant has the information in the permanent record book.

c. You have a record of the frequency of calls from the same person.

d. You have a record of the frequency of calls on the same subject.

e. You have a record of how many incoming calls are being received by your office as a whole and by individual staff members.

f. Having such records on hand saves the time of having to make a survey whenever this information is needed.

2. Keep a similar record of all outgoing calls you make. Jot down the date, time, the person's name, phone number, and a brief summary of the conversation. You may want to use the same kind of phone memo book mentioned above for incoming calls. Keep this book on your desk near the phone. The originals can be torn out, stapled to any memos from the same person or on the same subject, and filed for future reference. It would be a good idea to have each staff member follow the same procedure.

3. To make your phone messages brief and to the point, think of TEA.

T: Tell the person, in one sentence, if you can, the purpose of your call.

E: Explain briefly.

A: Action. Say what you plan to do or what you want the person to do.

4. Cut down on your incoming calls by educating your callers to phone your support people instead of you. When someone calls you for information a support person could handle, say "Jim is knowledgeable in that. May I have him call you back in 30 minutes?" Then explain the situation to Jim and be sure he calls back at the specified time with the information the caller asked for plus any other helpful information available. Soon, most of your callers will learn they can get what they need quicker by going directly to the subordinate.

5. Train your professional assistant to screen your calls. Your assistant should know the organization well enough to know who can handle which calls, and should be skilled in making time-saving suggestions to callers. However, if your assistant does not know who should take a call, have her/him take the caller's name and phone number and have the proper person return the call. This procedure is better public relations than taking the caller on an unasked-for tour of the organization by phone. Caution your assistant to be thoughtful of the caller's time. A caller should not be kept waiting on the line indefinitely. If delay is unavoidable, a return call should be suggested. If it is necessary to put a caller on "hold," your assistant should make a reassuring check with the caller every minute or two at the most. Eliminate "still busy" and "hold on" from your assistant's vocabulary. Instruct him/her to say a complete sentence, such as, "I'm sorry for the delay, Mr. Smith" or "Mr. Hunt will be right with you, Mr. Smith," and wait for a second or two before leaving the line again in case the caller wants to say something.

6. When you leave your office for any length of time, it is time-wise to tell your assistant where you can be reached and approximately how long you will be there.

7. Let your caller know your time constraint. If you have

only three minutes to talk, say so at the beginning. Then it will be easier to close the conversation when the three minutes are up.

8. Keep a three-minute egg timer by your phone. When you begin the conversation, turn it over. If you turn it over more than one more time before the call is ended, the call may be dragging on too long.

9. Place your outgoing calls in priority order. If you cannot complete them all, you will have completed the most important.

10. Keep a list of frequently called numbers by your phone. Be sure also to include emergency numbers. Your assistant should also have this list handy.

11. If you are making a call and are about to be put on hold, find out who you are talking with and the extension number in case you are cut off.

12. Don't play Ping-Pong on the phone. If you return a call to someone and s/he is out, let the secretary know when you will again be available, or ask the secretary when is the best time to reach the other person, or make an appointment to call at a specific time.

13. Always identify yourself when you call or answer the phone. The game of "Who am I?" is a wasteful time displacer.

14. If you are unable to reach the person you call, you can make an appointment through the secretary to call back at a certain time, to avoid another time-consuming, unsuccessful attempt to reach your party.

15. If it is feasible in your situation, limit the time you will accept calls, say from 1:00 to 3:00 in the afternoon. Reserve the first hour of the day to make outgoing calls.

16. You may be getting calls that are prompted by a lack of information. Your business letters may not be giving enough information, thus prompting a phone call for more detail. Your organization may need to update price lists, schedules, etc.

17. Could job titles of people in your organization be made to more clearly reflect their function? Callers who are confused about who to ask for will usually begin at the top.

18. Keep a pad and pencil next to your phone at all times.

19. Have the appropriate reference material ready for each of your outgoing phone calls.

20. Group your outgoing calls. Make as many calls as you can at one time.

21. Place your own calls when you are reasonably sure you will reach the other person. If your assistant places your call, it is time-wise to stay around to take the call when the other person is on the line.

22. Your local telephone company can arrange conference calls for you. This saves the time of several people's having to assemble in one place for a conference. If they are widely separated, it would also save on travel expense.

23. Use an amplifying device if it is agreeable to the other person. In this way a colleague can hear the conversation and you will be saved the time it would take to brief your colleague later.

24. Occasionally stand up when you call. It will help you relieve tensions and make you sound more enthusiastic.

25. Tell your secretary not to put calls through to you during specific periods throughout the day. This action allows you to accomplish other assignments without interruption.

26. Gesture when you speak on the phone. Even though your gestures cannot be seen, they can be heard through your voice. Your voice will pick up their tone and inflections and you will be more quickly understood.

A Time to Confer

Meetingitis
Meetingitis is a disease that overtakes professionals and businessmen alike. Meetings are necessary for a healthy organization, just as food is necessary for a healthy body. But too many meetings, like too much food, can have the opposite effect, causing a breakdown in the healthy functioning of any organization.

Its Causes

Meetingitis seems to be a disease that is both contagious and infectious. That's why it is so hard to escape. Here are some reasons why an organization catches meetingitis.

1. Many meetings are merely frills that contribute very little to the healthy functioning of an organization. People seem to get infected with a desire to meet and "talk it over."

2. Having a meeting every Thursday afternoon (or some other time) becomes a habit. You find yourself in a meeting simply because the day of the week calls for it.

3. Sometimes the contagion spreads from other departments. The Sales Department meets weekly, so why shouldn't the Accounting Department?

4. Some department heads feel that the number of meetings held is indicative of the contribution of the department to the organization's goals. Too often the time spent in a meeting could be more productively spent elsewhere.

5. Sometimes meetings are security blankets for those who call them. It is easier for some people to call a meeting and expound to a group than to have one-to-one encounters.

Another thing about meetingitis is that individual attacks of it sometimes last and last. A meeting that should take only one hour may go on for three hours. If ten people attend a meeting that should take one hour but goes on for three, then twenty hours are uselessly displaced out of the organization's time bucket. Multiply this by the individual's hourly rates and it is obvious that such meetings are costly in money as well as time.

Its Treatment

Fortunately there are effective treatments for meetingitis.

1. Have a definite reason for every meeting. Think "reason" first, then "meeting."

2. Cancel a regular meeting occasionally to test the need for it.

3. Question every item on the agenda before calling the meeting. Could the items be handled just as well without a meeting?

4. Adopt a rule that all meetings must have top executive approval.

5. Schedule meetings as the last thing before closing time or before lunch to encourage their ending on schedule.

6. Begin on time, regardless of late arrivals. If you wait until the tardy ones come, the on-time ones will begin to be tardy, and the tardy ones will get tardier.

7. Experiment with meeting away from the office to eliminate interruptions. This is especially good when there is a long agenda or if a work is planned.

8. Pay attention to effective conduct of the meeting itself.

9. Train employees in effective conference leadership.

10. Plan the meeting in every detail. Be sure you know who, what, when, why, where, and how.

11. Be sure participants know the purpose of the meeting in time to prepare for it. Have them bring relevant material with them.

12. Keep a folder of agenda items and, instead of having regularly scheduled meetings, don't call a meeting until your folder has sufficient items for a meeting. You will find that some of the items will take care of themselves without a meeting.

13. Limit attendance at meetings to those concerned with the topics on the agenda. The larger the crowd, the more discussion and the longer the meeting.

14. Schedule some participants to attend only that part of the meeting that they can contribute to.

15. Set up a time limit for each topic on the agenda and stick to it. Appoint someone to be the timekeeper.

16. Occasionally have a stand-up meeting. This is a good idea if there are only one or two items to discuss and no writing is necessary.

17. Provide a positive motivation for being on time, such as conference attendance at agency expense for each person who makes all meetings on time during a given period.

18. Discourage tardiness by having the minutes of the meeting show not only those present and those absent, but also those arriving late.

19. Have your professional assistant hold all telephone calls for the duration of the meeting.

20. Plan ahead for all equipment that will be needed in the meeting room, such as flip charts, projector, screen, chalkboard, chalk, markers, pencils, paper, tape recorder, enough chairs, and so forth. It's wise to have an extra projector bulb.

21. Arrange tables and chairs so that all participants can see each other.

22. Have the recorder sit where the faces of all participants are visible.

23. Have a folder with you containing all the information you will need at the meeting.

24. If you have several different evening groups to meet with, schedule the meetings piggyback.

Time-Wise Delegation

T ime-wise delegation is a method of stopping the displacement flow of your executive time on nonexecutive trivia. It is not merely dumping distasteful tasks onto subordinates for the sole purpose of getting rid of a task, but rather a method of developing your support staff.

Why and When to Delegate

When you are running out of time and your support staff is running out of work, it is time to delegate. If you don't, you will continue to be in a time bind. Never put off a task until tomorrow if you can delegate it today. One hour spent training, during a quiet period, will save many executive hours later on. Delegate when your support person is ready take on a new challenge.

What to Delegate

Delegate from your daily routine:
1. Duties that can be assigned on a temporary basis.
2. Fact-finding assignments.

94

3. Preparation of rough drafts of written material, such as reports, résumés, policies, procedures, and so forth.

4. Problem analysis and possible solutions.

5. Routine tasks.

6. Collection of data for reports and/or presentations.

7. Tasks that will challenge the subordinate.

8. Tasks to test your subordinate's ability in a specific area of responsibility.

9. Small units of work assignments from your responsibilities and functions.

How to Delegate

Develop skill in delegating to achieve time-saving results.

1. Consider gradually increasing authority and responsibility.

2. Set clear, realistic goals for the task to be delegated.

3. Communicate the assignment clearly.

4. Give your support person complete information on organizational policy and procedure as it relates to the assignment.

5. Define the limits of responsibility as it relates to the assignment. After the delegatee thoroughly understands the limits of authority, allow him/her to go ahead.

6. When a subordinate has the responsibility for a decision, allow him/her to make it. Resist making decisions for your support people.

7. Take enough time to help a delegatee solve an emergency problem, so when it comes up again s/he can go ahead without interrupting you.

8. When a support person comes to you with a question concerning a delegated task, don't answer the question but help your support person think it through.

9. Set up a system that requires interim reports or checkpoints so you can review progress.

10. Establish a realistic completion date.

11. Delegate to the lowest level that can do the task, within your jurisdiction. If a subordinate of your subordinate could do the task, say so, but delegate to your own subordinate. Let your subordinate redelegate the task if s/he chooses to do so.

12. If a subordinate's decision must be reversed, permit him/her to reverse it. Never openly countermand your subordinate's orders. Back up your support people in their relations with their subordinates.

13. Give the delegatee the authority needed for carrying out the assignment, and inform others that s/he has this authority. This will lessen the resistance of co-workers when the delegatee seeks information and/or help from them in carrying out the assignment.

Cautions Relative to Delegating.

1. Resist perfectionism. Even though a support person may not be able to do a task as well as you can, delegate the task anyway if it can be done passably well. Your support person will never be able to improve unless given the opportunity to do, learn, and grow. This is time-wise delegation.

2. Don't make yourself indispensable by hanging on to all your work. If you have not trained others to take over for you, you are not ready to move up in your career when the opportunity comes. You will not get a higher assignment if you are irreplaceable where you are.

3. You are only as effective as your support staff is effective. Make it easy for them to be effective by delegating challenging tasks to them.

4. Don't accept reverse delegation. If you have delegated a task to one of your support people, don't let the task be delegated back onto your shoulders. If a problem arises in the course of doing the task, insist that the problem not be brought to you without several alternative solutions and a recommendation. Help the subordinate think through the recommendation, but don't make the decision.

5. When a subordinate occasionally fouls up on an assignment, don't make it a big issue. Even the best employee will botch a job now and then. Assign tasks where success is probable, because success is what builds self-confidence. Keep training and delegating until every one of your support people knows how to do one or two of your tasks.

Instructing to Save Time.

Delegation requires instruction in new work.

1. Find out what the delegatee knows about the task. You have become so familiar with the task that you may be assuming others know much more than they do about it.

2. Start teaching the assignment from where the delegatee is in his/her knowledge concerning it.

3. Explain the "why" of every aspect of the assignment. Knowing the purpose of each aspect will enable the delegatee to take the right action if unforeseen circumstances occur.

4. If possible, give an example or illustration of what the result will be. It will help to clarify the task goal in the mind of the delegatee.

5. Have the delegatee explain back to you what the task is, the delegatee's limits of responsibility and authority, the key checkpoints when progress is to be reported, and the time limit for completion of the task.

6. Release the delegatee to do the task. Don't oversupervise. Instead, enjoy your newfound executive time doing more important tasks.

A Time to Take Stock

One-Day-At-A-Time and Three-Months-At-A-Time Webster defines motivation as an urge to push on. If you are motivated to use time more wisely, *now* is the time to push on. The time when you are motivated is the worst time to procrastinate. Begin now to live one day at a time and three months at a time.

Use the time tools you have read about in previous chapters and some others we will cover in this chapter to compile a three-month executive time planning book. It will help you get started using time management tools. As you use these tools to manage your time, you will develop effective time use habits. Here's how to compile your three-month executive time planning book:

1. You will need a thick three-ring binder.

2. Begin with Goal Worksheets, Figure 6, one for each major goal. Use this form for your three-month time planning book.

3. The next page is a Planning Guide for one year. See Figure 7. You don't have to wait until January to begin. Start

GOAL WORKSHEET

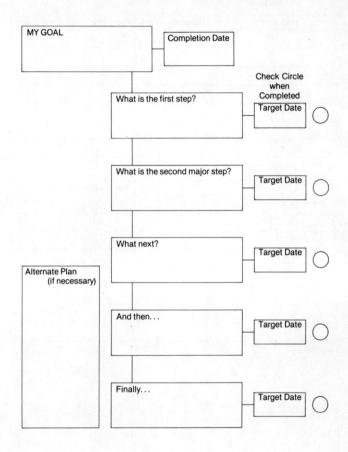

Figure 6. **Goal Worksheet**

PLANNING GUIDE

PROJECT	Report to	Jan	Feb	Mar	Apr	May	Jun
		Jul	Aug	Sep	Oct	Nov	Dec

NOTES:

Figure 7. **Planning Guide**

your wise time management year with the current month. *Report to* refers to the person you report to concerning the proj ect.

Write the task in the project column and put a checkmark in the month when you will have to reserve time for the task. This will point out the months when you will have several projects and the months when you will be relatively free of projects.

4. The next three pages of your planning book are monthly calendars for the next three months. See Figure 8. Use these pages as reminders of appointments, projects, due dates, and so forth.

5. Then comes a series of Weekly Organizers, one for each week in the three-month period you are working on. See Figure 9. List the things you will do each day during the week.

Figures 8 and 9, Reference Calendar and Weekly Organizer, are memory joggers so you will not have to keep a lot of tasks, beginning dates, and due dates in your mind. Record them on these forms, and as the months, weeks and days come along, you will be automatically reminded.

6. Behind each Weekly Organizer, put seven copies of your Daily Organizer. See Figure 2.

7. Behind each Daily Organizer, put a Time Monitor, Figure 10. Fill in the left-hand column from your Daily Organizer. As the day progresses, fill in the right-hand column. This will give you a record of how well you are able to keep on schedule.

8. Behind the Time Monitor, put a Paperwork Summary, Figure 11. Fill this in from your Daily Organizer, and complete the right-hand column as you complete each task.

9. The Year Ahead comes next, Figure 12. Use this page to remind yourself of plans for the coming year.

The Planning Guide in Figure 7 is for non-delegatable projects. The Year Ahead (Figure 12) is a memory jogger to help you complete the Reference Calendar (Figure 8), and the Weekly Organizer (Figure 9). □

REFERENCE CALENDAR

19____   Month: _____

Sunday	Monday	Tuesday	Wednesday	Thursday	Friday	Saturday

Figure 8. **Reference Calendar**

WEEKLY ORGANIZER

The Week of: _____

MONDAY	TUESDAY	WEDNESDAY	THURSDAY	FRIDAY

Figure 9. **Weekly Organizer**

TIME MONITOR

Date: _____

	SCHEDULED	PERFORMED
7:00		
7:30		
8:00		
8:30		
9:00		
9:30		
10:00		
10:30		
11:00		
11:30		
12:00		
12:30		
1:00		
1:30		
2:00		
2:30		
3:00		
3:30		
4:00		
4:30		
5:00		
5:30		
6:00		
6:30		

Notes:

Figure 10. **Time Monitor**

PAPERWORK SUMMARY FOR

_____19____
date

Subject of Paperwork	Action Due	Disposition

Figure 11. **Paperwork summary**

THE YEAR AHEAD

Plans and Appointments

JANUARY	FEBRUARY	MARCH
APRIL	MAY	JUNE
JULY	AUGUST	SEPTEMBER
OCTOBER	NOVEMBER	DECEMBER

Figure 12. **The Year Ahead**

CREATIVITY FOR EXECUTIVES

Eugene Raudsepp

Eugene Raudsepp, psychologist and author, is the president and co-founder of Princeton Creative Research, Inc. He conducts workshops and seminars on creative problem-solving and decision-making in management for major multinational corporations. He was educated in psychology and sociology at the University of Stockholm, Bate College, the State University of Iowa and Princeton University. He is the author of six books on creativity and over 300 magazine articles. Among his books are *How to Present and Sell Your Ideas, Motivating and Managing Creative Individuals,* and the two volumes from which the selections in this Special Section were made— *Creative Growth Games* and *More Creative Growth Games.* The last two books are available from Princeton Creative Research, Inc., P.O. Box 122, Princeton, New Jersey 08540, U.S.A.

Are You
A Creative
Executive?

Condensed from **Management Review**
Eugene Raudsepp

The creative executive has more energy, is more impulsive, and is more responsive to emotions and feelings than the less creative manager. He or she has something researchers call "flexible repressions," which means that the creative person can bring a lot of material buried in the subconscious to conscious awareness.

The real well of ideas is the subconscious, and someone with a distinct lack of inhibitions, such as a creative executive, has a relatively uncluttered pipeline to this source. As psychologist A. H. Maslow put it: "The really creative person is one who is not 'afraid' of his unconscious. This is the person who can live with his unconscious . . . his childishness, his fantasy, his imagination, his wish fulfillment, his femininity, his poetic quality, his crazy quality. He is the person . . . who can regress in the service of the ego . . . voluntary regression. . . ."

Both fluent and flexible in their thinking, creative executives can generate large numbers of ideas rapidly. They can choose and investigate a wide variety of approaches to problems, discard one frame of reference for another, change approaches, and adapt quickly to new developments.

Management Review (February 1978). Copyright 1978 by AMACOM, a division of American Management Association, Inc., New York, N.Y. 10020. All rights reserved

Your less creative colleague probably suffers from "hardening of the categories," which is a lack of flexibility that often results from overfamiliarity with objects or ideas. The really creative executive allows his thoughts to mill about without categorizing.

Youthful curiosity

Creativity is contingent upon how much of our innate curiosity and youthful sense of wonder has remained intact. Unfortunately, these attributes are educated out of most of us by the pressures of conformity and conservatism. Very few adults retain them, but the creative executive holds on to an intense curiosity about everything. An interested, expectant, responsive attitude toward life keeps the creative mind well stocked with all kinds of information that can be drawn on when engaged in creative activity. Creative executives are not content just to see how something works, but they delve into the whys, the cause-and-effect relationships of what they see and perceive. Their curiosity is not centered just on their own fields; their spectrum of interest embraces disparate areas and generates spontaneous enthusiasm toward any puzzling problem.

Originality and openness

Originality in thought is another trait of the creative executive. He or she can think of unusual solutions and can see remote relationships between phenomena. Such persons are likely to perceive the unexpected, the novel, and the fresh in everything they encounter.

The creative individual's openness to unusual ideas sometimes extends to the point of gullibility. Such managers are usually quite ready to entertain bizarre or crackpot ideas and frequently play around with them seriously before discarding them. New perspectives, new concepts, and venturesome ideas offer an endless source of mental exercise.

Sensitivity to problems

The creative executive not only finds fresh approaches to problems, he also detects problems. The ability to see "need" areas or to be aware of the odd or promising allows this manager to note gaps in his company's products, processes, and applications.

Such executives can also see the significance or possibility in situations that a less sensitive manager might overlook. They are acutely aware of people's needs and of the unrealized potential of their staffs. Always interested in improving upon existing products or situations, these managers are like the Socratic philosopher with a "thorn in his flesh"— perpetually disturbed by something. For the creative executive, there is hardly a situation free of problems; this happy state of dissatisfaction keeps his everpresent problem-orientation alive.

Confidence to dare

Daring to transcend accepted patterns of thinking and to stick to convictions in the face of possible discouragement or censure is very necessary in creative work. Rare indeed, however, is the established creative executive, and, even, rarer, the novice, who can maintain complete detachment from criticism.

Self-confidence is an important attribute that can be developed only through experience and exercise. It has been said that nothing breeds success like success, and this is probably true; but the corollary that failure breeds failure need not also be true. Though fear of making a mistake is a devastating emotional block to creativity, executives should realize that progress is made through failure as well as through success.

Since most executives' career orientations are governed by the premise of success, the specter of failure looms large. In the risk-taking enterprise of creativity and innovation, however, failures do occur. Failure should be regarded as a situation from which new or improved ideas may arise. Almost every area of corporate development has had its history of failures that ultimately led to success. In reality, the greatest failure is not to attempt a new idea at all.

The fear of failure prevents many executives from daring

anything really creative, especially when the element of risk taking is considerable. So the young executive needs encouragement and recognition in order to develop the confidence that he or she will eventually come through, no matter how many failures there are.

High motivation vs. "success"

Some executives, however, blunt their effectiveness by excessive motivation or the desire to succeed too quickly. The overmotivated executive may narrow his field of observation, looking for and using only clues that provide a quick solution to a problem. This person frequently passes up leads to novel or better solutions by picking the first workable solution rather than considering alternatives.

Overmotivation can also result in excessively ambitious goals. Some executives want to tackle only very big and complex problems. Failure to solve such complex problems successfully can undermine confidence to tackle problems well within their capabilities.

A lack of persistence or a feeling of flagging interest is often a signal to get away from a problem and relax for a while. Many creative executives turn to another problem because they find they function best when involved in several undertakings simultaneously, each at a different stage and each affording the chance to "relax" when necessary.

During the creative process, however, the creative executive maintains an uninterrupted rapport with the "proposals" that emerge from his subconscious as he forms them into something that makes daylight sense. This requires great self-discipline.

Toying with ideas

There is often a seemingly light side to the creative executive's involvement in work. He may seem to be lost in an irresponsible play of ideas, relationships, and concepts, which he shapes into all kinds of ostensibly incongruous combinations. However, this apparently purposeless exercise strengthens and, at the same time, loosens the "muscles" of imagination. It enables the person to come up with more unique solutions to problems.

Creative executives have often found that playful sketching and shaping of ideas helps them come upon really valuable ones. Furthermore, this toying serves to get them in a proper mood to start ideas flowing. These quasi-serious exercises relax the ever-present critical and conservative orientation of the conscious. By putting this watchful censor to sleep, they can set the stage for the emergence of novel ideas and solutions.

Tolerance of ambiguity and complexity

One reason for the lack of creative ideas among many executives is their strong preference for predictability and order. Many immediately reject ideas that either do not fit into an established pattern or are too elusive for immediate comprehension and categorization.

On the other hand, creative executives can tolerate a high degree of ambiguity. They are actually suspicious of any pat explanations and have developed a healthy respect for groping around and for the unknown during the creative process. Creative persons can perceive a variety of possibilities and are able to simultaneously consider and balance different, even conflicting and contradictory, frames of reference and concepts.

Selectivity

Likewise, creative executives differ from the less creative or noncreative in the quality they show in their selection of elements when confronting a problem. They are able to choose more fundamental aspects and cast the superfluous aside. In creative problem solving, it is, as a rule, not necessarily the executive who is highly fluent with the problem who shows the highest degree of creativity. Whether fluent in thinking or not, the executive who can grasp the heart of the matter frequently shows the highest degree of creativity. In creative thinking, it is quality that counts, not necessarily the quantity of ideas.

Creative solutions to problems are often simple, elegant, even obvious. Yet it is the obvious that often escapes us in trying to solve problems.

Creative memory

The subconscious is a storehouse of facts, observations, impressions, and other memories. While the creative executive's mind is always richly stocked with these memories, this does not in itself indicate creativity. As a matter of fact, a prodigious memory can act as a deterrent to creativity.

What makes memory creative is the dynamic mobility of the components. Where the uncreative memory files its data and impressions within neat and independent cubicles, the creative memory's boundaries are permeable. All kinds of related and unrelated data and ideas can always be cross-indexed and interrelated.

The creative mind is continuously rearranging, pruning, discarding, relating, and refining these data and ideas. In such a permeably structured memory there is the ever-present possibility for new configurations and combinations.

Creativity requires exact, recallable observations and discriminating use of the senses. Try this simple test: In the margin of this page, draw the face of your watch— without first looking at it.

This test illustrates the effect of overfamiliarity. We look at our watches so often we cease "seeing" them. That's what happens when behaviors become automatic and when we take objects too much for granted.

Here's a similar experiment to try on a friend or yourself. Without looking at your telephone, indicate what letters and/or numbers appear opposite the first finger hole on the dial or on top of the upper-left button of the touch-tone telephone.

Incubation

There comes a time when thinking becomes clogged, when errors pile up, and when no significant insights occur. At this point, the creative executive stops working on that particular problem and turns to something entirely different. According to Dr. A. Schlien of the University of Chicago, "Although he has confidence in his ability, the creative individual also has an attitude of respect for the problem and admits the limits of his conscious power in forcing the problem to solution. At some point, called "incubation" by many who have reported the process, he treats the problem as if it had a life of its own, which will, in its time and in its relation to his subliminal or autonomous thought processes, come to solution."

The creative executive also likes to contemplate, reflect, meditate, or just "chew the mental cud." During these periods he often gets some of his best ideas.

Some managers tackle problems with a dogged effort. Although commendable, keeping busy without time for relaxation or change of activity frequently serves as an effective barrier to novel solutions. The executive who knows when persistence with a recalcitrant problem begins to result in diminishing returns, and who then drops it for a while, frequently finds that on returning to it a fresh approach comes with greater ease.

There is a popular but fallacious notion that the creative individual relies on effortless insight and unforced spontaneity. True creativity requires a great deal of self-discipline and old-fashioned effort.

The majority of creative executives do not know the meaning of an eight-hour workday. Their preoccupation with problems is incessant. Creativity, in whatever field, is generated by hard thinking, prolonged reflection, and concentrated hard work. But creative persons have their moments of joy when ideas start flowing after a disrupting hitch.

Frequently, however, the intense struggle with problems is useless. But these efforts, futile as they seem to be, are not necessarily wasted because they activate the subconscious processes of cerebration and incubation. Without preparatory work, the subconscious can be notoriously unproductive.

Whatever the field, creation is a product of hard thinking, prolonged reflection, and concentrated toil. There is a continuous assimilation of data and observations, a continuing pondering on the causes of regularly met difficulties, and a sorting out of hunches and ideas that flash across the firmanent of consciousness.

Creative executives develop a retrospective awareness of when they have solved problems creatively. They take note of the methods that have succeeded and failed. They try to learn "why" by retracing as far as possible the routes followed and those avoided.

Creative individuals schedule their creative thinking periods for times when they have their most favorable mental set for producing ideas. They are aware of their personal rhythms of output. By keeping a record of the most creative periods during a day, they can establish a pattern and plan ahead, reserving peak periods for concentration, contemplation, and uninhibited thinking, and using the less productive times for reading or routine tasks. But even without a time sheet of productive periods, the creative executive develops a sensitivity to moods that promise good returns— and knows when these moods are approaching. □

Creative
Growth
Games

Selected from **"Creative Growth Games"**
and **"More Creative Growth Games"**
Eugene Raudsepp

1. Draw Your Watch
We don't observe things with which we are most familiar.

Creativity requires exact, retentive observation, the discriminating application of our senses.

The problem: On a piece of paper, draw the face of your watch without looking at it.

2. In-and-Out Letters
We live in a complicated age and look for complicated solutions— when frequently what is simple would work better.

Creative solutions to problems are often elegantly simple, and even obvious— once seen. Yet, it is the "obvious" that frequently escapes our notice because we have been conditioned to look for complicated solutions when solving problems.

The problem: Determine the system being followed to place letters inside or outside the circle (i.e., where does the rest of the alphabet belong?).

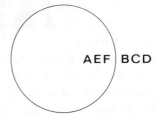

AEF BCD

118 *Creativity for Executives*

3. Like/Unlike

The ability to detect similarities and differences between objects is crucial in creative problem solving. Objects can be grouped together on the basis of common features or attributes. Classification helps us to organize information, and it plays a significant role in strengthening memory. This exercise trains your ability to examine situations from different points of view and be flexible in seeking solutions.

> **PART I:** How many common features or properties can you find in the following 12 letters?
> Z X T S N K H E D C B J
>
> —**Examples**— SDCBJ Contain curved lines
> TNKHEDB Contain vertical straight lines. Now find 10 remaining groupings.

> **PART II:** Explain why each of the 12 letters does not belong with the others.
>
> —**Example**— The "Z" is the only one with two parallel horizontal lines. Now state how each of the letters is different from the rest of the letters (including another explanation for "Z").

ABC
18, 11, 15, 14, 19, 16, 13, 12, 20

4. Spell It Out

Although this problem is presented in numerical terms, consider the possibility that the solution may not lie in the mathematical manipulation of the symbols. We are often misled by the apparent familiarity of the problem "type" into assuming the nature of the answer. With that caution in mind, find the general rule that governs the series:

18, 11, 15, 14, 19, 16, 13, 12, 20

5. A Military Tale

This doodle is attributed to the famous French author Victor Hugo. It illustrates how we learn to deduce the whole of an object or picture from catching a glimpse of one or more of its component parts. This is a skill that can be improved through practice, and one that has a parallel in crossword puzzles and other word games that also depend on this ability. In this case, the key lies in determining the signifance of the vertical line.

6. Arabs and Romans

Here are some matches that are laid out in a pattern.

By moving only one match, make it a true equality. The solution requires that you look beyond the language in which the problem is stated. What other mathematical symbols can you devise by moving a single match? Think visually, and consider the title of this problem. Does it perhaps offer a clue?

7. More or less

Only the creative power of the mind can escape the boundaries that confine us.

Here's another problem that can be solved only if you cast off the unwarranted assumptions that restrict your thinking and hamper your imagination. When solving it, try to rid yourself of any prejudgments.

The problem: Add one line to the Roman numeral XI so as to change it to the number ten. Try for at least three different solutions.

8. The Greek Cross
Creativity is a battle against attitudes.

This puzzle will further train you to avoid restrictions that don't exist but that hamper your mind.

Ten coins are arranged like this:

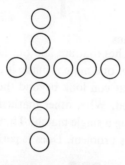

The problem: Move just two coins to other positions so as to form two rows, one horizontal and one vertical, each containing six coins.

9. Breaking Out
You have to free yourself of rules and restraints in order to make discoveries.

This classic puzzle— one already familiar to many— shows how easy it is to read into a problem restrictions that don't exist. We often fail to solve a problem because we impose too many imaginary boundaries and constraints.

The problem: Draw four straight lines through these nine

dots without retracing and without lifting your pencil from the paper.

10. Upended Bottle

This classic parlor puzzle illustrates the difficulty most of us have in freeing ourselves from set notions when dealing with problems. Most people will attempt to yank the $5 bill from beneath the bottle, which won't work, or they will put their fingers under the bill and try to grab the neck of the bottle, which is not allowed.

There are two ingenious solutions to this problem. Try to work out the solutions in your mind, before making any trial-and-error attempts.

Place a $5 bill flat on a table. Turn an empty bottle, Coke or any other kind, upside-down so that its mouth rests on the center of the bill. Without tipping over the bottle— and allowing nothing to touch the bottle other than the bill or the table— remove the $5 bill from beneath the bottle.

11. Part 1. Think of a word that precedes those in the first two columns and follows those in the last two. (You can form compounds, hyphenated words, commonly used expressions, colloquial usage, or slang in some instances.)

Examples:

Break	Strings	Heart	Purple	Take
Sell	Rock	Hard	Work	Hit
1. Rate	Account	_____	Savings	Left
2. On	Head	_____	Lay	Rotten
3. Blame	Gears	_____	Make	Stick
4. Corner	Rope	_____	Sit	Hold
5. Opera	House	_____	Flash	Flood
6. Artist	Clause	_____	Narrow	Fire
7. Jacket	Changer	_____	World	Off
8. Dog	Skin	_____	Herd	Count
9. In	Ugly	_____	Spark	Drain
10. Ox	Bunny	_____	Deaf	Strike
11. Backer	Drawing	_____	Fishing	Telephone
12. Shooting	Door	_____	Shut	Tourist
13. Ware	Foot	_____	Fall	A
14. Step	Flesh	_____	Wild	Cook
15. Up	Guy	_____	Penny	Side
16. Park	Life	_____	Daily	Play
17. Games	House	_____	Like	Make
18. Up	Pocket	_____	Lock	Tooth
19. Polish	Cart	_____	Rotten	Crab
20. Fall	Cap	_____	Good	Christmas
21. Air	Live	_____	Get	Boiling
22. Off	Toe	_____	Hot	Cigar
23. Rank	Over	_____	Have	Push
24. Book	Point	_____	Rain	Double
25. Rage	Look	_____	Wash	Reach
26. Day	Theory	_____	Magnet	Playing
27. Finger	Leader	_____	Bathtub	Key
28. Pudding	Read	_____	Photo-graph	100
29. Pay	Throw	_____	All	Stay
30. Out	Pan	_____	Czar	Saint

Part 2. Think of a word that may be inserted in the blanks below to form new words.

Example: _____ba, _____mage, _____my, _____or, _____pus, _____runner
Answer: Rum

1. _____al, _____boot, _____et, _____frost, _____knife, _____pot
2. _____acid, _____arctic, _____elope, _____ler, _____hology, _____hem
3. _____an, _____bug, _____id, _____bled, _____or, _____us
4. _____cat, _____al, _____uity, _____head, _____igue, _____ten
5. _____alyst, _____atonia, _____ch, _____ty, _____nip, _____skill
6. _____ad, _____ast, _____istics, _____oon, _____ot, _____point
7. _____ace, _____ate, _____ette, _____lor, _____sy, _____try
8. _____er, _____beat, _____ice, _____end, _____ing, _____key

12. Build a Bridge

There is heightening of creative imagination when you are forced to identify your ideas and relate them to one another sequentially. This game enlarges the scope of your associative powers.

Fill the spaces between the words below so that each word is related logically to the word following it. And remember that these associations are examples only. You may find different and equally valid words of your own.

Examples

1. ICE _____ OUT
Possible answer: ice pick out

2. FOLK ____ ____ ____ MATTRESS
Possible answers:
folk music box spring mattress

3. JET ____ ____ ____ ____ ____ AVENUE
Possible answers:
jet engine power play ball park avenue

Now It's Your Turn

1. OLD _____ SHOP
2. FIRE _____ PREMIUM
3. FREE _____ GUY
4. FISH _____ BOOK
5. EXPENSE _____ NUMBER
6. IRON _____ _____BLOCK
7. SLEEP _____ _____ LINE
8. MINUTE _____ _____ MAKER
9. WHITE _____ _____ _____ LAUNDRY
10. BRAIN ____ _____ _____ GAME
11. POWER ____ _____ _____ BRAINS

12. BLACK ____ ____ ____ REMARK
13. SHELL _____ THING
14. NUCLEAR ____ ____ ____ ____ BAG
15. BLANK ____ ____ ____ ____ UPON
16. BODY ____ ____ ____ JAM
17. NOSE ____ ____ ____ ____TIME
18. EAGLE ____ ____ ____ ____ ____ DRUMS
19. FUEL ____ ____ ____ ____ ____ MASTER
20. LAND ____ ____ ____ ____ ____ ____ POWER
21. FOUL ____ ____ ____ ____ ____ ____ ALARM
22. HAIR ____ ____ ____ ____ ____ ____ SCARED

13. Concealed Colors

Almost all creativity involves purposeful play.

This game is also designed to increase your flexibility, your ability to overcome the restrictions of habit. Play it with friends. The one who identifies most of the "hidden colors" wins.

The problem: Name the color concealed (in consecutive letters) in each sentence.

Examples:

1. The newspaper editors decided to go on strike.

Answer: Red.

2. The cab lacked proper brakes to stop at the intersection.

Answer: Black.

Now try these:

1. A big, old, hungry dog appeared at our door every morning.

2. You shouldn't let an upstart like him bother you.

3. He let out a yell, owing to the injury he received.

4. Long rayon fabrics were exhibited in the window.

5. You shouldn't sell this fossil very cheaply because it is a rare specimen.

6. The new law hit everybody's pocketbook pretty hard.

7. Bob's car let out dark fumes when he tried to drive it up the steep hill.

8. The old ogre entered the argument with obvious relish.
9. A huge dog called Lobo ran gently toward me.
10. After you've let the cat in, dig out the buried treasure.

14. Fun With Puns

Several recent psychological experiments have shown that humor, wit, and "playfulness" are directly related to creativity. One type of humor is the ability to pun.

Punning— the association by sound affinity— has manifested itself in diverse cultures and epochs, and is evident in poetry, in dreams, and in the punning mania of children.

Make up a "pun definition" (not a standard dictionary definition) for each of the following words. A pun definition involves the changing of the pronunciation and/or the meaning of part(s) of the word. Make your answers as brief and clear as you can. (Some words lend themselves to several pun definitions.) **Examples:**

Jargon	Glass container missing
Bulldoze	A sleeping animal
Abuse	A motor vehicle (bus)

Now try these:

Illegal	Curtail
Parole	Overtired
Hydrophobia	Therapist
Armature	Kindred
Kidnap	Ferocity

15. Concerned Uncle

The two most common habits or attitudes that block us from solving problems effectively are (1) our natural tendency to latch on to the first notion that occurs to us and then bolt with it— frequently over a precipice; and (2) our tendency not to free our creative deliberation from the restraints of our critical faculties. So ingrained is this habit of simultaneously weighing and judging ideas while in the process of producing them that it takes deliberate, sustained training to separate these two functions.

This exercise asks you not to rest content with the first suggestion that occurs to you, even if you feel that it represents the best solution to the problem, and to produce as many feasible or even offbeat solutions as you can think of. There is always plenty of time later to screen your ideas and weed out the untenable.

You have discovered your favorite 14-year-old nephew (or any other favorite relative or friend) has started to drink alcoholic beverages. What ideas could you think up to induce him to stop?

16. What Goes Down, But Won't Go Up?

This is a classic "story" puzzle that may be familiar to you. Even if it is, and you remember the logical but rather offbeat solution, don't stop there. One of the hallmarks of creative behavior is the willingness to explore alternative solutions— rather than accepting the one that comes most easily to mind. Turn your imagination loose.

A man living on the 22nd floor of an apartment building takes the automatic elevator all the way down to the lobby, but he does not take it all the way up. Why? Give as many possible reasons as you can.

17. The Conscientious Driver

Creative people have the ability to make correct hypotheses that are based on only a few clues or hints. See if you can take a few shortcuts and arrive at the correct solution to the following problem:

Aunt Nellie always followed advice about conserving energy. One day, while driving in her family car, she came to a stop sign and noticed that the odometer showed 25,952 miles. Observant as she was, she recognized the number as palindromic: it reads the same both backward and forward.

"I bet you it'll be a long time before a palindromic number happens again," Aunt Nellie said to herself. Yet two hours later, when she arrived home, the odometer showed a new palindromic number.

What was the new number, and how fast was she traveling in those two hours?

18. The Collected Works

Recognizing the whole problem is half the battle.

Habitual ways of looking at things hamper creative problem-solving, as has already been shown. The more familiar the situation or object, the harder it is to see it differently. Creativity, however, requires a "fresh pair of eyes."

Although this exercise looks simple, it is actually quite difficult. In fact, only one person in a hundred solves it the first time around. It is included because it is so instructive.

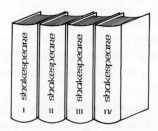

The problem: Four volumes of Shakespeare's collected woks stand on a shelf. The total pages of each volume are exactly two inches thick, and the front and back covers are each one eighth of an inch thick. A bookworm starts eating at page one of Volume I and eats his way through to the last page of Volume IV. Through what distance did the bookworm eat?

19. Joined Together

In order to determine the best method for solving a problem, we frequently need to step back to analyze and organize it. There is a tendency to tackle a problem without considering the alternatives, and as a result, a lot of time and effort are wasted.

Copy this design and keep track of how long it takes you. Tracing is not allowed.

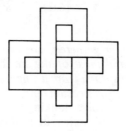

If it took you a minute, or more than a minute, take a different approach, another point of view, and try again.

20. Simple Arithmetic

The creative person spends more time formulating and analyzing his problem before attempting a solution; the less creative person wants to "get on with it."

This exercise is the only one that you solve against a time limit. Although creative thinking usually isn't done best within a specified time, our hurried environment frequently imposes this restriction.

See if you can find a way to beat this problem before you tackle it. Sometimes, you have to be able to step back from a problem to see what's involved.

The problem: In the following simple arithmetic problems, the plus ($+$) sign means to multiply; the divide ($\div$) sign means to add; the minus ($-$) sign means to divide; and the multiply ($\times$) sign means to subtract. See how many problems you can complete in exactly one minute.

$7+2$	$8\div4$	$6+5$	$8\div4$	$6+11$
$20-10$	7×7	$9+3$	5×2	$8-4$
$9\div3$	$2\div2$	$8\div4$	$6+6$	$9+2$
12×2	$15-5$	4×3	$20+2$	$20-10$

6×5	$15-3$	$16 \div 8$	$15 \div 5$	$5 \div 5$
$10+2$	7×5	9×2	$10-5$	$5 \div 1$
$10 \div 10$	$8 \div 2$	4×2	$8+3$	$10-2$
$4-2$	$15-3$	$9 \div 3$	16×6	$8 \div 8$

21. Squares Aplenty

The "germ," wherever gathered, has ever been for me "the germ of a story," and most of the stories strained to shape under my hand have sprung from a single small seed, a seed as remote and windblown as a casual hint. —Henry James

Creativity frequently involves looking at a situation or a problem with fresh eyes and seeing in it something others have missed. This entails the refusal to accept the apparently obvious.

HOW MANY SQUARES DO YOU SEE?

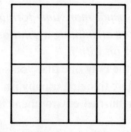

22. Tardy Employee

Creative enegy is never depleted. Progress, in its truest sense, is possible only when there is a surplus of creativity.

This is a useful "real-life" exercise to strengthen and tone up your inventive powers. Try your best to keep your imagination moving, and produce at least five ideas to solve the problem.

IF YOU WERE THE HEAD OF A DEPARTMENT AND HAD A SUBORDINATE WHO WAS HABITUALLY LATE IN THE MORNING, BUT WHO WAS TOO VALUABLE TO FIRE, WHAT WOULD YOU DO TO CORRECT HIS TARDINESS?

23. Occupations
An idea that appears radical, bizarre, or way-out one day, may be readily accepted the next day.

A good creative idea always collides with an old idea, and some individuals find this very frightening.

This exercise will increase your verbal and conceptual fluency within a specified framework.

WRITE THE NAMES OF AS MANY OCCUPATIONS AS YOU CAN THAT BEGIN WITH THE LETTER S AND END WITH THE LETTER R. (These occupations can be formed also with hyphenated or compound words).

Examples: Social worker, Sky-diver, etc.

24. Pie Time
The creative person prefers the richness of the disordered to the stark barrenness of the simple
—Donald W. MacKinnon

This problem tests your perseverance and stick-to-itiveness.
Eleven relatives of varying ages and appetites descend upon your house on a Sunday afternoon. You have only one large custard pie to divide among them.
How can you cut the pie in *eleven* parts— not necessarily of equal size— making just *four* straight-line cuts?

25. Success and Failure
Either I will find a way, or I will make one.

—Sir Philip Sidney

This game is designed to enhance your associational and expressional fluency. Played with friends, it becomes not just useful, but exciting and instructive as well. You are apt to have insight-expanding discussions of the varied meanings which people have for success and failure.

THINK UP FOURTEEN WORDS FOR WHICH THE SEVEN-LETTER WORDS *SUCCESS* AND *FAILURE* WOULD BE THE ACRONYMS. ALL WORDS SHOULD REFLECT IN SOME WAY YOUR CONCEPTION OF WHAT SUCCESS AND FAILURE MEAN TO YOU.

Examples
To me these spell

SUCCESS	*FAILURE*
S— Steadfastness	F— Fickleness
U—Understanding	A—Anger
C—Courage	I— Irresponsibility
C—Courteousness	L— Laziness
E—Energy	U—Unawareness
S— Self-determination	R—Recklessness
S— Soundness	E— Egotism

Solutions

1. Draw Your Watch
Chances are you missed a few important details, or drew them wrong— almost everybody does.

This exercise illustrates the pitfall of overfamiliarity. There are few objects that we look at more frequently than our watch. We look at it so often that we cease to observe it.

Whenever behavior becomes automatic, when we take objects too much for granted, we no longer observe them— and observation is vital to creative problem solving.

2. In-and-Out Letters
The key to this problem lies not in some complex relationship (such as between vowels and consonants, or the place of the letters in the alphabet), but in the simple one of letters with straight lines belonging inside the circle and those with curved lines belonging outside.

One of the secrets of problem solving, and a basic tenet of the scientific method, is that one must always look for the simplest explanation that will account for all the facts observed. Similarly, when a problem is presented visually, it pays to look for simple patterns before "intellectualizing" the data. Always move from the simple to the complex. It's much more difficult to move in the other direction.

AEFHIKLMNTWXYZ BCDGJOPQRSU

3. Like/Unlike

Part I

Straight lines: Z X T N K H E
Horizontal lines: Z T H E
Parallel lines: Z N H E
Open at top and bottom: X N K H
Open at right: Z X T S K E C
Open at left: Z X S T J
Open at top: X N K H
Open at bottom: X N K H

Even-numbered spot in its alphabetical order: Z X T N H D B J

Odd-numbered spot in its alphabetical order: S K E C

Part II

The "Z" is the only letter either at the beginning or the end of the alphabet.
The "X" is the only letter with two diagonal straight lines.
The "X" is the only letter open on all sides.
The "T" is the only letter containing a single vertical and a single horizontal line.
The "S" is the only curved line letter than can be turned upside down and still remain the original letter.
The "S" is the only letter containing two opposite curved lines.
The "N" is the only letter that turned sideways would look like the last letter in the alphabet ("Z").
The "N" is the only letter five letters away from the letter preceding it ("S").
The "K" is the only letter that precedes two letters that make up a word ("HE").
The "K" is the only letter that contains one straight and two diagonal lines.
The "H" is the only letter that contains two vertical lines and one horizontal line.
The "H" is the only letter that phonetically is spelled with "a" (ach).
The "E" is the only letter that has two open areas at the right.
The "E" is the only letter that has three horizontal straight lines.

The "D" is the only letter that contains only one closed half-circle.

The "D" is the only letter that contains only one completely enclosed space.

The "C" is the only open single-curved letter.

The "C" is the only letter that stands for the first note in the scale of C major.

The "B" is the only letter that has two completely enclosed spaces.

The "B" is the only letter that looks like a numeral ("3") when the vertical straight line is removed.

The "J" is the only letter that hangs under the line it is written on.

4. Spell It Out

Solution of this puzzle requires translating the numbers into equivalent words, and arranging those words alphabetically, thus:

18	11	15
Eighteen	Eleven	Fifteen

14	19	16
Fourteen	Nineteen	Sixteen

13	12	20
Thirteen	Twelve	Twenty

5. A Military Tale

People usually make something of these lines: the bare branches of a windblown tree, a part of a street map, a sketch of a tool, or part of a circuit diagram.

If you solved the doodle easily, you probably recognized first that the vertical line represented the edge of an opaque structure concealing most of the other elements of the drawing. It is, in fact, a wall.

The purported story surrounding this drawing is this: A young man had a dog that was very fond of him. When the man entered the army, the dog went along— following his master everywhere.

On this occasion, the young soldier was walking his post on sentry duty with the dog at his heels. What you see is the bayonet on the rifle and the tail of the dog after the soldier has turned the corner of the building. The story, as you can see, transforms the lines into a new structure.

6. Arabs and Romans
Here is the solution:

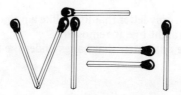

In order to solve this problem, you need to think beyond simple addition and subtraction. But, most of all, you need to be able to see the problem in less literal terms— and to remember the symbol for square root. You need to see the *shape* of the problem, and then be flexible enough to think of translating it from *Roman* numerals to *Arabic*.

7. More or less
The most obvious solution is to add a fractional diagonal:

Other solutions:

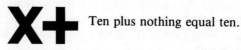

Ten plus nothing equal ten.

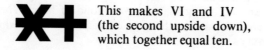

This makes VI and IV (the second upside down), which together equal ten.

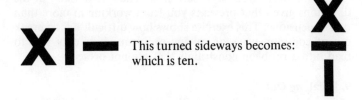

This turned sideways becomes: which is ten.

The foregoing solutions involve adding a straight line. However, the problem statement was: "Add one line . . ." No restrictions were placed as to the shape of the line, and it would be an unwarranted assumption to only solve the problem with a straight line. Almost any mark produced by a sweep of a pencil without it being lifted from the paper would qualify as "one line." Therefore, the following solutions are permissible:

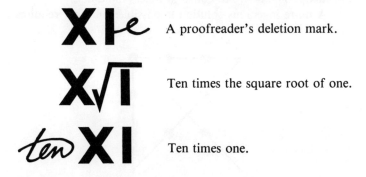

A proofreader's deletion mark.

Ten times the square root of one.

Ten times one.

8. The Greek Cross
The problem can be solved only if you move one coin on top of another:

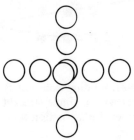

"Not fair," you say? Sure it is. There is nothing in the directions given that prevents you from working in more than two dimensions. This exercise shows how difficult it is to break out of common ways of solving problems, how easy it is to read into a problem constraints that are not present.

9. Breaking Out

This solution illustrates how the "rules" and "restrictions" that we unconsciously carry with us can inhibit problem solving. Note that the restriction of a boundary was not part of the problem as posed.

When children first begin coloring, they often go beyond the lines of figures. Of course, much of this is due to imperfectly developed muscle control. But it may also be because they have not yet become intimidated by boundaries, either real or imaginary. The desire to conform fences in adults.

A more ingenious solution is possible: one that requires not four lines but only three!

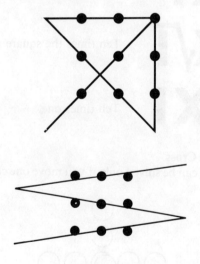

An even-more-astounding solution is possible: one that connects all the dots with a single straight line! It calls for a thoroughly untrammeled imagination and some skillful paper folding.

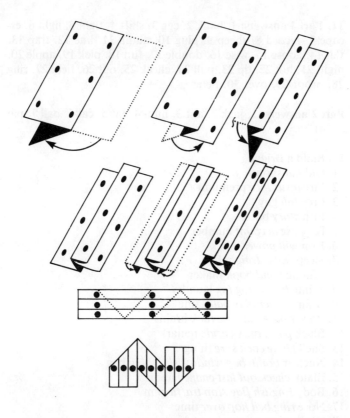

10. Upended Bottle

There are two possible solutions to this problem, both of which are arrived at by lateral thinking. Neither involves moving the bottle in any unusual sense.

The first one is to roll the bill in a tight curl *against* the neck of the bottle, which results in gradually pulling the bill from underneath. The cylinder formed by the rolling bill prevents the bottle from creeping toward you.

The second solution is to set up a rhythmic pounding on the table with your fist. The vibration must be hard enough to separate the bill and the bottle for a series of fractional seconds as you slide the bill slowly toward you. Of course, if you pound too intensely or irregularly, you will upset the bottle.

11. Part 1 answers: 1. bank 2. egg 3. shift 4. tight 5. light 6. escape 7. record 8. sheep 9. plug 10. dumb 11. line 12. trap 13. flat 14. goose 15. wise 16. double 17. fun 18. pick 19. apple 20. night 21. hot 22. tip 23. pull 24. check 25. out 26. field 27. ring 28. proof 29. over 30. peter.

Part 2 answers: 1. jack 2. ant 3. hum 4. fat 5. cat 6. ball 7. pal 8. off.

12. Build a Bridge
1. Old *hat* shop
2. Fire *insurance* premium
3. Free *fall* guy
4. Fish *story* book
5. Expense *account* number
6. Iron *will power* block
7. Sleep *walk straight* line
8. Minute *hand book* maker
9. White *house dog tag* laundry
10. Brain *power play ball* game
11. Power *pack suitcase rack* brains
12. Black *paint brush aside* remark
13. Shell *game cock sure* thing
14. Nuclear *bomb bay window shopping* bag
15. Blank *check out last chance* upon
16. Body *English flag stop traffic* jam
17. Nose *ring bell hop over* time
18. Eagle *scout master hand down beat* drums
19. Fuel *cell wall flower girl scout* master
20. Land *mine gold watch pocket veto* power
21. Foul *play around town house arrest burglar* alarm
22. Hair *shirt button collar bone dry run* scared

13. Concealed Colors
In order to identify the "hidden colors," you have to disregard the signs that say stop, such as word spacing, periods and commas. People who are very habit-ridden find this exercise difficult.

The answers: 1. Gold, 2. Tan, 3. Yellow, 4. Gray, 5. Silver, 6. White, 7. Scarlet, 8. Green, 9. Orange, 10. Indigo.

14. Fun with Puns

Illegal	Sick bird
Parole	The Father role (function)
Hydrophobia	Fear of falling from high places
Armature	Limb of a grown man
Kidnap	Child sleeping; goat sleeping
Curtail	Tail of an animal; bitter beer; short story; short illness
Overtired	Seven tires on a car; outwardly angry
Therapist	A man who rapes
Kindred	Fear of relatives; generous color
Ferocity	City of iron; Egyptian city; city of Pharaohs; fear of city; city plowed up; where gophers live.

According to Arthur Koestler, "The creative process entails— in science, humor, and art— a kind of punning procedure in which disparates are fused." Koestler also observed, "The poetic rhyme is nothing but a glorified pun: two strings of ideas tied in an acoustic knot." Koestler feels that punning involves a temporary, but voluntary and healthy, regression in the service of the ego. In his words: "The capacity to regress, more or less at will, to the games of the underground, without losing contact with the surface, seems to be the essence of the poetic, and of any other form of creativity."

The genius of the Marx Brothers' humor was largely based on their punning ability. In one of their movies, Chico mistakes the word "taxes" for "Texas" and then proceeds to "define" "taxes" as "dollars": "Thatsa right— I gotta uncle that lives in Dollahs. Dollahs, Taxes." Chico's Italian accent enabled him to use a continuous flow of puns: "You gotta haddock? I gotta haddock too. Whatta you take for a haddock?" Or "Sturgeon. Sturgeon. Thatsa doctor thatta cuts you up."

15. Concerned Uncle
Examples:

1. Supply him with literature describing the harmful effects of alcohol.

2. Promise him a substantial reward (*e.g.,* a present or a trip) if he stops drinking.

3. Take him to AA (or Alateen) meetings.
4. Induce him to get treatment at a clinic.
5. Induce him to a see a psychiatrist.
6. Have him make a list of pros and cons of drinking.
7. Promise him a substantial reward at his 18th birthday if he quits drinking.
8. Tell him that as long as he keeps drinking he is not allowed to watch TV and has to retire at 8 P.M.
9. Give him $5 each week that he abstains from drinking.
10. Take him to a hospital ward to see alcoholics who have "wet brains."
11. Have a heart-to-heart talk with him.
12. Suggest to his school principal that they invite the experts to speak on the harmful effects of alcohol.
13. Enlist the help of his nondrinking schoolmates.
14. Take him along to an adult drinking part and show him how stupidly those who drink behave.
15. Compute the money he would save— or could use for other things— if he didn't drink.
16. Tell him that the family car will be off limits for him if he continues to drink.
17. Convince him that it takes real courage not to conform to a fad.
18. Show him skid row.
19. Take him to see the movie *Days of Wine and Roses*.
20. Get him an interview with a famous show-business person or sports hero who has had a drinking problem.
21. Stop drinking yourself to set a good example.
22. Send him to camp or a different school for a while to remove him from his friends who drink.

16. What Goes Down, But Won't Go Up?
The traditional answer is that the man is a dwarf or a midget, and cannot reach the top button. It might also, of course, be a man who is confined to a wheel-chair or who has some other physical limitation that restricts his movement.

But consider some other possibilities that might account for his behavior:
1. He has a sick friend living on the 20th floor whom he visits every night before going home.
2. He lives in a duplex apartment that occupies two floors.

Thus he leaves from his bedroom on the 22nd floor, and returns to his kitchen and living room on the floor below.

3. A habitual drinker, he arrives home late at night. Not wanting to awaken his wife with the sound of the elevator doors, he gets off on the 21st floor and walks up the stairs.

4. He is following an exercise program that requires him to climb a specified number of flights of steps each day.

5. There is a restaurant at the 19th floor, and he stops there every night to have a few "bracers" before facing his wife.

6. He has a mistress living on the 21st floor and he visits with her before going home.

7. In the past, the elevator has frequently gotten stuck between the 21st and the 22nd floor. To avoid this, he gets off on the 20th floor and walks up.

8. He doesn't like his apartment, and in order to prolong his arrival there, he gets off on the 10th floor, and walks up.

9. He is a go-getter. His wife works for a family on the 19th floor, and every night, after a full day of job-hunting, he has to go and get her.

10. His tympanic cavities are badly inflamed, and he has to walk up several flights slowly to get used to the altitude.

17. The Conscientious Driver

26,062   55 mph
Since it would be clearly impossible for the first digit of 25,952 to change in two hours, 2 would have to remain the first and last digit of the new number. The second and fourth digit could not change to more than 6. If the middle digit was 2 or 1, then the car would have traveled 310 or 210 miles in 2 hours. Since Aunt Nellie was a conscientious driver, the middle digit would have to be 0, and the car traveled 55 mph, the speed limit.

18. The Collected Works
The answer: **4¾ inches.**

If you had trouble with this one, you were probably trapped by habitual ways of visualizing. All our lives, we've been accustomed to seeing a book in a certain position: facing us, with the first page next to the lefthand cover, and the last page next to the righthand cover. This is how we hold a book to open and read it.

However, in this exercise, it was specified that the volumes were on a shelf, and you even have an illustration to orient you. With the spines of the books facing you, the order of the pages is reversed.

Truly, the more familiar the object, the harder it is to see it in another context.

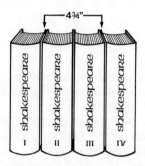

19. Joined Together
This design can be copied easily, accurately, and elegantly in less than 40 seconds. One step-by-step approach is:

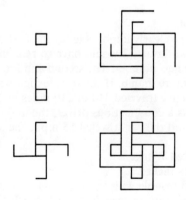

Another imaginative solution begins to take shape when you recognize the pattern as being made up of four identical parts. Drawing them one after another and rotating each successive part 90° makes a speedy reproduction:

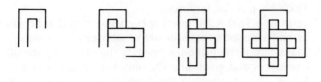

Some people tape two pencils together as a helpful aid in drawing the parallel lines.

20. Simple Arithmetic
If you dealt with the problems sequentially, you probably didn't get very far, because you had to retranslate the terms for each one.

The secret is to do all the plus-sign problems first, then the division-sign ones, etc. This eliminates the need for constantly referring back to the "code." Approaching the exercise this way, many people can complete all the problems in one minute.

21. Squares Aplenty
Answer: 30 squares.

Once you saw beyond the obvious answer— 16, or perhaps 17 (if you counted the square that contains the smaller ones), you were on your way to solving the problem.

There are two important factors of creative problem-solving here. The first is the repressive notion of exclusivity— the idea that once you've identified a unit it cannot be used again as part of a larger unit. There are, of course, squares within squares.

The other quality is persistence. Effective problem-solving is seldom done in a hurry.

22. Tardy Employee
Examples:
1. Offer an office punctuality prize.
2. Institute flexible hours, making it okay to be as much as an hour late as long as eight hours were worked.
3. Offer to drive him to work on your way in.
4. Make his next raise contingent on consistent on-time arrival.

5. Dock his pay for tardiness.
6. Institute a 9:00 A.M. meeting every morning that he would be embarrassed to miss or arrive late for.
7. Make him responsible for opening the office for the other employees and given him the only key besides yours.
8. Make him responsible for keeping track of his subordinates' or secretary's arrival time.
9. Tell him it's okay to be late if he calls you and explains his delay.
10. Serve free coffee and donuts to those there at 9:00.
11. Tell only him that you're changing office hours to 30 minutes earlier. Then, arriving 30 minutes late he'll still be on time.
12. Tell him that he can work on any pet project of his own choosing one day a week, if he arrives on time.

If you produced only a few ideas, perhaps you let your evaluative attitudes intrude? Remember to suspend criticism while you are trying to think up ideas. Failure to suspend criticism is— as was aptly expressed by Dr. Alex F. Osborn— "like trying to get hot and cold water from one faucet at the same time: the ideas are not hot enough; the criticism is not cold enough; so your results are tepid."

23. Occupations
Examples; Saboteur, saddler, safecracker, sailor, saloonkeeper, salvager, sawyer, scalper, scavenger, scholar, schoolmaster, schoolteacher, scoutmaster, screener, scribbler, scriptwriter, sculptor, seafarer, seer, seller, senator, serenader, shareholder, shipper, shipmaster, ship builder, ship chandler, shipfitter, ship owner, shoemaker, shoeshiner, shopkeeper, shoplifter, shopper, shopwalker, shore patroller, shyster, singer, sitter, soldier, solicitor, songster, sorcerer, sparring partner, speaker, speculator, speechmaker, spinner, sponsor, sprinter, squatter, staffer, stage manager, stager, star, starcher, stationer, steamfitter, steelworker, stenographer, stockbroker, stock breeder, stonecutter, storekeeper, story teller, stretcher bearer, stringer, stripper, subcontractor, submariner, surveyor, sweeper, swimmer, swindler, syndicator, etc.

24. Pie Time
Answer

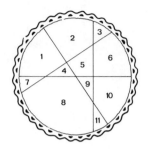

25. Success and Failure
Examples

S— Stick-to-itiveness, skill, synergy, strength, soundness, solidity.

U—Uprightness, unflappability, uniqueness, unity, usefulness, unsuspiciousness

C—Charisma, cash, concentration, considerateness, creativity, character

C—Credibility, cooperativeness, coolheadedness, constancy, confidence, clout

E—Experience, excellence, earnestness, effectiveness, endurance, empathy

S— Surefootedness, study, serenity, self-realization, security, support

S— Serendipity, sharp-sightedness, specialization, staunchness, sobriety, showmanship

F— Fussiness, frustration, foolishness, fanaticism, falseness, frivolity

A—Aimlessness, arrogance, artificiality, abstruseness, automatism, antagonism

I— Isolation, irresoluteness, intolerance, insolence, inflexibility, ineptitude

L—Loafing, lucklessness, low-mindedness, lethargy, ludicrousness, listlessness

U—Untimeliness, unreadiness, unapproachableness, unconcernedness, underemployment, upstartness

R—Rashness, revengefulness, rigidity, resignation, reclusiveness, randomness

E—Envy, exhibitionism, extremism, egocentricity, emptyheadedness, escapism□

HOW TO MEASURE MANAGERIAL PERFORMANCE

Richard S. Sloma

Richard S. Sloma is Vice President for Operations of Qonaar Corporation. He was formerly Division President of ITT and also served as Chairman or Board Member of six international firms. He has written many articles on management and a book on *No-Nonsense Management*.

150

How to Measure
Marketing Performance

Management Marketing/Background Data

1. What is the size of your total market?
2. What share of the market do you have?
3. What is your competitor's share of the market?
4. How effective is your marketing support (on a scale of 1 to 10):
   - Advertising?
   - Promotion?
   - Public Relations?
   - Technical Services?
5. What are the factors that determine your market size and nature?
   - regional
   - national
   - international
   - economic
   - governmental
   - other
6. What are your sales forecasts for your market
   - this year?
   - next year?
   - five years from now?
7. What are the main marketing methods you use?
How effective are they?
How effective are those of your competitors?

8. What are your distribution methods?
How effective are they?
How effective are they in comparison to those used by your competitors?

9. What are your main marketing advantages? Your competitors'?

10. How effective is your sales performance
   - for market or target penetration?
   - in comparison with forecast sales?
   - in comparison to sales expenses?
   - in comparison with customer complaint analysis?
   - in comparison with new accounts analysis?
   - for lost orders?

11. How effective is customer service
   - delivery?
   - scheduling?
   - customer satisfaction?
   - expenses?
   - activity?

12. What is your profitability:
   - by customer category?
   - by type of distributor?
   - by geographical area?
   - by product line?

13. What is the overall "health" of the dealer organization?
What trends are apparent?

Examples of Specific Marketing Objectives

The XYZ company will:

14. Increase sales revenues of product X by N percent within N months by concentrating N promotion dollars in the Y marketing area.

15. Achieve N percent distribution in markets A, B, C and D of X marketing area.

16. Train all area representatives in training program T by N date to market Product X by N date.

17. Complete plans and statements by X date to introduce X new products by X date in Market Y.

18. Upgrade the ratio of sales per employee from X dollars to Y dollars by X date, and to Z dollars by N date.

19. Improve percentages of sales from X, Y and Z percentages within N market area to A, B and C, respectively, by N date.

20. Complete X percent of all follow-up calls for new inquiries within X days of receipt of calls.

21. Contract with N wholesalers by X date to handle N new merchandising by Y date according to marketing plan Z and prearranged schedule A.

22. Increase product turnover from T to X within N months.

23. Maintain sales expense to N percent of total sales while increasing sales force N percent during the fiscal year.

24. Initiate new system X to process orders while expediting the filling of back orders at the rate of N percent per day until N percent of back orders are filled. When N percent of back order levels are reached, then reinstate system Z.

25. Reduce by N percent the average handling time of all customer statements.

26. Increase X ratio by N percent from a monthly ratio of Y to Z percent while maintaining T pricing structure.

27. Reduce the number of complaints in W division from X to Y percent of invoices. Financial settlements applicable are not to exceed Z percent of billings of the division's total invoices per month.

Standards for Sales Promotion Responsibilities

28. Develop specific promotion ideas and detailed cost and work plans identifying the major tasks to be accomplished. This plan will be used as a managing and scheduling tool.

29. Complete public relations and trade relations projects including media contact for specific promotional opportunities. Write and secure placement for press releases and other publicity materials.

30. Develop direct mail campaigns to:
- dealers
- distributors
- agents
- consumers

31. Coordinate promotion tasks with advertising, sales and marketing operations.

32. Develop displays and materials for point of sale.

33. Develop, write and publish annual reports.

34. Produce sales aids including:
- brochures or booklets
- videotapes, films or slide shows
- product literature
- flip charts
- giveaways, samples or other "demonstration" material
- catalogs, reprints or price sheets
- diagrams or models

35. Distribute promotional material to all applicable prospects and media contacts. Develop and maintain media, prospect and other mailing list and list sources.

36. Coordinate trade show or consumer exhibits.

37. Arrange for customer or prospect group hospitality.

38. Develop, write and publish external and internal house organs.

39. Plan and execute:
- New branch openings
- Plant openings, remodelings
- Open houses
- Special events

40. Coordinate promotional work with salespeople and with distributors.

41. Arrange clinics, seminars or educational presentations on the company's products or pertaining to the professional or technical knowledge involved in the company products, designs, developments, or standards.

42. Publish training manuals, training audio visual tapes, training slide shows or training videotapes.

43. Develop sales contests for salespeople, employees, distributors, agents, dealers or consumers.

44. Aid in the development of packaging.

45. Work with coupons, premiums and trial offers to boost sales.

46. Arrange cooperative advertising and promotional efforts or tie-ins.

47. Take charge of sales meetings, conventions and other meeting arrangements.

48. Assume responsibility for upgrading company correspondence, including:

- Check through all departments for letters and redevelop as necessary.
- Develop cover letters for mailings and advertising programs.
- Draft "special occasion" letters.
- Develop model letters for collection purposes.
- Develop sales letters for: introduction of a salesperson before the first call; follow-up after the first call; "thank you" for customer inquiry; maintaining communications between sales call; thanking customer for the first order or repeat orders.

49. Sell all promotion planning, budgets and materials to everyone concerned, from salespeople to corporate management.

**Sales Performance Measurements
for Marketing Management**

50. Total sales of company

51. Projected company sales
52. Sales quotas
53. New account sales
54. Sales of new products
55. New products and new accounts sales
56. Calculated market potential for all sales predicted
57. Calls made by salespeople:
• total number actually made
• total made on new accounts only
58. Quotations made for potential sales:
• total
• new accounts
• new products
• new accounts and new products
59. Number of orders:
• total
• new accounts
• new products
• new accounts and new products
60. Number of accounts:
• total
• number sold in last fiscal year
• new accounts opened and sold in fiscal year
• top potential bracket only
• potential of those in top potential bracket
61. Units sold (product)
62. Gross margin (products & total)
63. Expenses (with and without breakdown)
64. Direct costs
65. Contribution margin

Ration Analysis Data for Sales Management
66. Total sales divided by:
• total quotations
• total orders

- quota
- total expenses
- expense as percentage of sales
- salesperson per day
- total calls
- total potential
- top potential bracket
- potential of top potential bracket

67. Ratio of quotations:
- total quotations divided by total calls
- new account quotations divided by new account calls
- new product quotations divided by new account calls
- new product quotations divided by total calls
- quoted new product sales divided by total quotations in dollars

68. New account sales divided by:
- total sales
- new account calls
- new account orders

69. New products sales divided by:
- total sales
- total calls
- new account calls
- new product quotes
- new product orders

70. Ratio of orders:
- total orders divided by person divided by working days
- total quoted orders divided by total quotations
- total orders divided by total quotations
- total orders divided by 100 calls
- new account orders divided by new account quotations
- new account orders divided by new account calls

71. Ratio of accounts sold:
- number of accounts sold divided by total number of accounts

- number of accounts in top potential brackets sold divided by total number in category
72. Sales expenses divided by total calls
73. Number of calls divided by person per day
74. Units sold divided by man per day
75. New accounts opened and sold in the last fiscal year and the trend shown

Sales Management Objectives by Product Line
76. Market potential to be achieved
77. Total sales volume to be gained
78. Sales as a percentage of potential market to be reached
79. Total marketing costs (quantitative):
- call costs
- service costs
- delivery costs
- marketing administration costs
- marketing research costs
- advertising and promotional costs

80. Marketing costs as a percentage of sales not to be exceeded
81. Gross margin to be achieved
82. Profit contribution to be earned (volume less value added costs)
83. Profit contribution rate (percent of volume)
84. Product net profit to be achieved
85. Gross margin as a percentage of total sales
86. Profit contribution as a percent of total sales
87. Profit as a percentage of total sales
88. Total number of customers to be sold
89. Volume to be sold divided by the number of customers sold
90. Total calls and service and delivery costs divided by the number of customers

91. Net profit divided by sales
92. Inventory to be maintained
93. Cost of goods sold in relationship to inventory
94. Total investment
95. Net profit divided by sales
96. Sales divided by investment
97. Return on investment to be achieved
98. Break even point to be reached
99. Factor for safety to be maintained (volume minus break-even point) divided by break even point.

Marketing Management Standards
for Monitoring Performance

100. Achievement of both short and long-range negotiated goals for profit and for return on investment.

101. Achievement of subgoals for regions, districts and territories for volume, share and profit contribution rate.

102. Achievement of sales performance goals for calls per day, calls per person, expenses per call, order per call and volume per order.

103. Obtain a volume-mix goal by N date

104. Achieve advertising objectives set for coverage, readership, sales, and costs.

How to Measure
Personnel Management
Performance

Background Data for Management

1. Has your organization formally clarified what kind of "people skills" make a difference to your business?

2. Is an active effort made to find and support people who have these skills?

3. Does personnel management actively move into day-to-day administration activities throughout the company? Or does personnel management follow a mode of predicting problems before they occur, discussing them after they occur, but doing little which actually impacts a solution to problems when they actually occur?

4. Does the company have an open and direct environment, or is it all too much tied to the rigidity of the organization chart?

5. Is personnel management responsible not only for finding and selecting candidates but for retaining them?

6. Are employees held accountable for accomplishing specific results rather than simply for doing activities? Are job responsibilities clearly delineated in terms of results or objectives? Is there a close and objective monitoring process in which both supervisor and employee participate and both know the rules and the score?

7. Are training and management development programs keyed to results-oriented performance? Are they designed and delivered by professionals?

160

8. Does the company have a "manpower data bank" in which accurate and comprehensive data about all personnel performance are stored? Is the "bank" continuously monitored, and does each managerial file contain the latest performance appraisal data, job-related strengths and weaknesses, and individual development plan, probable career moves and future potential? Is it used to select candidates for promotion?

9. Do some departments seem to have "traditional" problems with absenteeism or high rates of turnover?

10. What is your company's productivity ratio? Can this productivity be enhanced through greater emphasis on developing the company's human resources, at a minimal cost?

11. Do other executives regard personnel management as hard-hitting, no-nonsense managers with wide-ranging impact on the organization?

12. Do you have a management replacement plan projected for the next two years? The next five?

13. Are managers throughout the company reviewed regularly for progress and especially for signs of "middlescence," "midlife crisis," or other signs of work slowdown or career arrest? What programs do you have designed to make these persons productive once again? How effective have they actually been?

Sample Objectives to Measure
Personnel Management Performance

14. Reduce recruiting costs by N dollars or N percent.

15. Formulate approved incentive system by N date for X department to increase productivity by N percent or decrease costs by N percent.

16. Maintain cafeteria costs at N dollars per month without loss of food quality.

Personnel Management Plan of Action Elements

17. Review of plans of operating departments to determine what service or support they will require.

18. Review of departmental profit improvement opportunities

19. Setting objectives

20. Formulating plans for reaching objectives.

Personnel Management Performance Enhancement Considerations

21. Using recruiting consultants versus internal recruiters

22. Using outside versus inside testing

23. Operating the employee cafeteria versus turning it over to a concession operator

24. Paying personnel on an hourly basis versus an incentive basis

25. Weighing effectiveness of written communications versus personal briefing sessions by supervisors

26. Using on-the-job training versus vestibule training

27. Using in-company versus university management development activities

28. Choosing between manual preparation and maintenance of personnel records versus the use of EDP.

29. If nonunion, what is the cost/benefit tradeoff of continuing nonunion versus going union?

Ratio of Measurement for Personnel Management Effectiveness

30. Personnel costs divided by average number of employees

31. Recruiting costs divided by number of recruits retained

32. Training costs divided by average number of employees

33. Costs of wage increases in excess of industry standards divided by average number of employees

34. Cost of lost production attributed to industrial relations problems divided by average number of employees

35. Number of man-days which were lost, divided by number of man-days worked.

36. Number of man-days lost through absenteeism divided by number of man-days worked.

37. Number of employees who leave divided by average number of employees

38. Number of employees with one year of service divided by number of people employed a year ago.

39. Number of employees with more than one year of service divided by total employed.

40. Training costs divided by training days.

41. Training days divided by trainees

42. Trainees divided by total employees

43. Recruiting costs divided by recruits interviewed

44. Recruits selected divided by recruits interviewed

45. Number of recruits accepting employment divided by recruits selected

46. Number of recruits who remain on job more than twelve months divided by number of recruits who accepted employment.

Areas of Personnel Management
Measurement of Management and Employees

47. Productivity rate of company (compared with rate of leading competitor of industry)

48. Individual performance shown during special work on "task teams"

49. Data in EDP manpower library

50. Performance appraisals

51. Identification of job-related strengths and weaknesses by supervisors and management

52. Promotions, accomplishments and overall "track record" of results

53. Training or educational classes completed along with final "grade" or evaluation

54. Career moves and individual development plans

55. Individually expressed priorities

56. Return on invesment and profit generation
57. Management ranking as a "cost center"
58. Time lost or productivity lost
59. Absences
60. Accident frequency or severity
61. Size of employee work force
62. Number of supervisors and management to size of work force
63. Distribution of work force by training, by experience, by age and by education
64. Intercompany work force mobility and promotion rate
65. Number of "outside specialists" hired for key positions or in lieu of promoting current employees
66. Strike frequency, duration and severity
67. Results produced by strikes or slowdowns or other employee unrest
68. Arbitration costs
69. Benefit costs as a percent of compensation
70. Personnel requirements
71. Recruitment and training costs
72. Retirement forecasts and percentages of work force
73. Work force turnover percentage
74. Results achieved by training as measured in quantifiable, objective testing.
75. Percentage of implementation of performance appraisal recommendations
76. Percentage of objectives actually accomplished compared with those agreed to
77. Understanding of employees about the nature of the company, its competitive status, products, markets, standards and objectives
78. Achievement of individual standards and goals
79. Health problem rates and profile trends
80. Percentage of error
81. Percentage of overtime costs and trends

82. Employee suggestions submitted, percentage accepted, and awards given

83. Requests for transfer

84. Cost ratios for employee advertising, recruitment and selection

85. Costs of testing applicants

86. Ratios for settlement of grievances as well as frequencies and trends

87. Separation analysis

88. Tardiness

89. Break-even performance

90. Performance in maintaining budget costs and deadlines

91. Number of customer complaints

92. Dividend record

93. Cash flow and liquidity

94. Facilities and machine utilization

95. Materials, stock and other expenses

96. Amount of "yield" produced compared with raw materials used

97. Methods and time-and-motion studies

98. New products developed, new ideas attempted, number of patents acquired or applied for

99. Number of sales calls made per sales person and individual salesperson productivity

100. Sales expense per individual, per territory or per product line

101. Sales skills of sales people as quantified in objective testing

102. Conformance to environmental, special interest, and other groups' expressed needs

103. Work sampling and testing against standards and objectives

104. Bonus amounts and percentages

105. Incentive plan performance and measurement

106. Stock bonus and other options

107. Compensation rates and trends

108. Contract negotiations and results

109. Number of hours spent in management training

110. Amount of savings achieved through employee suggestions or innovations

111. Ratio of employees available for promotions compared to total employees

112. Services provided to customers compared with total possible services

113. Measurements of attitudinal dynamics of employees

114. Leadership in professional, business, civic or educational institutions or organizations

Key Psychological, Sociological and Other Needs Analysis as Elements of Employee Motivation for Managers

Each employee, for optimum performance, needs

115. Supportive environment in which to work

116. To know periodically where he or she stands in performance of job

117. Training to learn exactly what results (not activities) are to be achieved on the job

118. Understanding of job standards to be able to measure for himself or herself how well he or she is doing

119. To feel he or she is growing within the company and that this growth will make the future secure

120. A feeling of being needed, that people will listen when important, and that his or her energies, ideas and work are not only heard but are of interest to management

121. To feel the company offers him or her security and protection against uncertainties of life through insurance benefits and, ultimately, retirement with pension

122. To have inputs into the work he or she does and the feeling that the extra effort or "caring" expended is appreciated and will be rewarded

123. To feel he or she is an "expert" at his or her own job

124. To be heard when he or she is annoyed, bothered or frustrated by work which is too simple, routine or boring or, on the other hand, too complex or difficult

125. To feel he or she has an opportunity to grow as much as he or she can grow and thus find his or her own level in the organization

126. Orientation, training and supervisor guidance to feel comfortable in his or her specialized job and to find interest and challenge in it

127. To feel management and the company are dealing fairly with him or her in wages earned, in work to be completed, in standards set and in pay scales in relation to other companies

128. Supportive coaching to use procedures or methods not used often

129. To feel his or her education, personal and professional, continues with work in the organization, and does not end with high school or college

130. To feel he or she is a valued member of the organizational "team" and has good communications and inputs as a member in good standing.

131. To feel he or she is earning advances in salary based on extra effort or output, that the company rewards this extra effort quickly and with gratitude

132. Direct feedback from his or her supervisor or manager to determine how well the company ranks his or her performance against standards, and, moreover, receives specific coaching to do better

133. Recognition for his or her effort, so as to have some identity within the group or within the community

134. To feel worthwhile in the organization and to have direct involvement in setting standards he or she is expected to accomplish

135. To feel that the company is progressing and that he or she is progressing with the company

136. To feel that change is the inevitable result of growth

and that growth, and thus change, is generally beneficial

137. To know his or her place within the group and the group's position within the organization; to have the flexibility to move from group to group as new and more challenging positions become available

138. To feel a respected member of the organization, with important individual strengths and with specific contributions to be made

139. To feel his or her potential is recognized and encouraged by management

140. To feel always that he or she is being treated as an "adult" and a competent "individual"

Monitoring Standards of Personnel Management

141. All jobs within the company have been described and classified within the last two years.

142. Key entry jobs are analyzed to determine exact and "real world" basic functions. These data are used to determine realistic job qualifications so that applicants are screened to meet the *actual* needs of the job.

143. Personnel monitors the company work force through EDP, including qualifications of the "manpower library" to determine advancements based on skills, job experience and company track record.

144. Personnel levels, expenses, turnover (particularly by department), injury, absenteeism, recruiting performance, training costs, and ratios of performance, etc., are carefully monitored, trends noted and acted upon.

145. Personnel has developed a five-year management replacement plan whereby positions within the company, such as president, executive staff, general staff, etc. are identified as to number of positions, vacancies, retirements, or early retirements so as to determine the total number of promotions needed up the managerial pyramid. From this chart, Personnel determines how many new top executives will be needed, how

many department managers, how many middle managers, and how many new people are to be hired and retained to begin grooming for management-level position.

146. Job standards for each position have been developed, and an applicant knows and understands what is expected, based on these data prior to hiring.

147. Applicants are screened to meet the actual needs of the job, to be able to perform work to meet minimum needs. They are not over-qualified nor better skilled than needed to meet standards and minimum needs

148. Pay scales for all employee categories are reviewed by compensation specialists so that employees' pay, overtime, and benefits are in line with current trends and meet competition.

149. Standards are in effect for hiring new employees. An applicant's past records with other companies are checked, individual tests are completed, and, the manager who will be accountable for the employee's performance will have input into the hiring process.

150. All new employees receive an orientation on the company, how it operates, what its goals and objectives are, how the work force is managed, what work standards are as well as company personnel policies, procedures and benefits. This orientation is accomplished through the issuance of a corporate employee "handbook" to the employee after he or she is hired, but prior to the employee's starting work. A brief written "quiz" at the end of the handbook is to be filled out by the employee and submitted to the supervisor, who then reviews the "answers" to be certain the employee has correct orientation, information and assumptions about the company.

151. New employees receive a copy of individual job standards, which stress results to be accomplished rather than activities.

152. Each new employee receives a personal orientation by his or her supervisor on the department, the work performed by the department and the objectives and standards of the de-

partment, the "accountability" system of the department to other departments, the company, and to customers. The methods by which the individuals, and the department are rated, including regular reviews of performance and feedback on *both* strengths and weaknesses, are detailed along with specific information on earning more pay tied to performance.

153. Regular reviews of performance against standards occur each six months in such a manner that each new employee and his or her supervisor know, openly and realistically, what has been done, what's right and what's wrong, where each stands and, most important, what needs to be done to improve performance.

154. Supervisors and managers are trained extensively in management techniques for good manpower utilization. These techniques include: basic insights into human motivation, basic "needs of employees," methods of behavioral "reinforcements," as well as how to conduct interviews, how to rate employee performance, how to conduct open, professional and frank performance appraisals as well as separate counseling sessions to minimize weaknesses and maximize strengths of individuals.

155. Adequate training programs are carried on to meet the needs of skills levels for employees as well as management and performance data for supervisors and management

156. Management development training is based on the needs of management, enhances company performance goals and is presented by competent professional trainers.

157. When managers or staff attend an outside training program, they bring back an assessment of the effectiveness of the program, the practicality of the material and the professionalism of the trainer. Personnel maintains a file on the preferred training programs and makes an assessment of their worth as demonstrated by the attendee. Inadequate, poorly structured or delivered, or primarily esoteric programs are identified, and no more personnel are scheduled to attend.

158. A library of business, professional and technical books, tapes and audio manuals is maintained for the benefit of those who wish to utilize this information for home study.

159. Exceptional information, such as books of outstanding interest, professional articles of pertinence or classes of more than routine impact, are summarized in written brief form, and this information is duplicated and made available for home study

160. Personnel management is actively concerned with the daily operating activities of the company and their impact upon the overall management of the human resource and its performance.

161. Personnel is responsible for the retention as well as the selection of employees. It aids in determining the total requirements of jobs when an employee is to be promoted and in deciding on whether the employee has the capabilities for the job, including skills, duties, reporting interrelationship, responsibilities, authorities, standards, objectives and planning so that the right people are always being groomed for the right management position. Personnel monitors individual career progress.

162. The track record of individual work on each "task team" is monitored since this will allow Personnel to determine individual manager's ability prior to being placed in a line or staff responsibility.

163. A "systems approach" to management is promoted so that the focus of the work is on achieving specific results.

164. Standards for open and honest communications are set by top management and reinforced by Personnel communications, including corporate newsletters, memos or employee bulletins. Such communications talk "real world" facts about the company, sales or markets, corporate developments, personnel changes and problem solving. They are intended to keep an employee abreast of what he or she actually needs to know about the company and the company's progress and problems.

165. All legal requirements for hiring and employment, including minorities and women, are being observed and monitored.

166. Checks are made periodically to be certain that employees are receiving the skills and professional training they need to meet standards.

167. A supervisor's handbook details methods of handling problems common to all supervisors and includes conducting interviews legally and correctly, handling appraisals, methods of systematizing potential discipline problems, handling grievances, dealing with problems in a systematic manner and how to maintain open, two-way communictions with employees.

168. Employees are encouraged to make suggestions which will benefit the company's efficiency, profitability or productivity. Rewards for suggestions are quickly given, based on a "task team's" prompt evaluations.

169. Objectives for the Personnel Department are set with the aid of personnel management, which is called to answer for meeting objectives or to determine why objectives have not been met. Rewards are tied to outstanding accomplishment of objectives.

How to Measure
Controllership Management
Performance

Background data for Management

1. What is the average "age" of your accounts receivable? Has this age been increasing?

2. Have your inventory levels been going up and your cash levels down?

3. Have overall costs been escalating?

4. Are your financial operating reports prepared in such a manner that variances are highlighted — or hidden?

5. Are all major expenses and costs under strict budget control?

6. Do your financial controls include a variable budget?

7. Is return on investment measured at regular intervals by product or by project?

8. Does the company calculate and analyze its break-even point by product line or project?

9. Are systematic methods being employed to reduce costs?

Controllership Functions and Overall Objectives
(As defined by the Financial Executives Institute)

10. Planning for Control: To establish, coordinate, and administer, as an integral part of management, an adequate plan for the control of operations. Such a plan would provide, to the extent required in the business, profit planning; programs for capital investing and for financing, sales forecasts,

173

expense budgets and cost standards, together with the necessary procedures to effectuate the plan.

11. Reporting and Interpreting: To compare performance with operating plans and standards, and to report and interpret the results of operations to all levels of management and to the owners of the business. This function includes the formulation of accounting policy, the coordination of systems and procedures, and the preparation of operating data and of special reports as required.

12. Evaluating and Consulting: To consult with all segments of management responsible for policy or action concerning any phase of the operation of the business as it relates to the attainment of objectives and the effectiveness of policies, organization structure and procedures.

13. Tax Administration: To establish and administer tax policies and procedures.

14. Government Reporting: To supervise or coordinate the preparation of reports to government agencies.

15. Protection of Assets: To ensure protection for the assets of the business through internal control, internal auditing and the proper insurance coverage.

16. Economic Appraisal: To appraise economic and social forces and government influences continuously, and to interpret their effect upon the business.

Objectives for Controller Management
Performance Measurement

17. Reduce clerical accounting costs by N dollars by installation of approved EDP by N date within capital budget of N dollars and expenses of N dollars.

18. Reduce monthly closing cycle by N days.

19. Reduce by N days the cycle time needed to prepare cost follow-up reports.

20. Reduce printing and copying costs by N dollars.

21. Hold auditing expense to no more than N dollars.

**Controllership Management Plan
of Action Elements**

22. Review plans of operating departments to determine what service or support they will require.

23. Review departmental profit improvement opportunities.

24. Determine objectives.

25. Set plans for reaching objectives.

Monitors of Effectiveness of Financial Controls

26. Break-even point for product of project

27. Return on invesment, overall and per product line

28. Inventory costs, age, count and turnover

29. Cash and working capital liquidity, current and forecast

30. Current ratios:

- operating expenses to gross sales
- current assets to current liabilities
- cash liquidity compared to best competitors or industry averages
- capital expenditures to budget
- cost of sales to actual sales
- profit by unit and by product line
- actual sales to planned sales
- debt to equity

31. Variance analysis:

- expenses
- prices
- sales
- time
- product volume
- cash requirements
- gross profits
- per share earnings
- inventory

- budget performance
- per unit or product line profitability

32. Productivity:
- man-hours per production unit
- units produced per machine
- operating time in comparison with down time

33. Accounts receivable, turnover, age collection stats and "problem" accounts.

34. Make-or-buy analysis and decisions

35. Working capital current ratios, loan restrictions, line of credit utilization, lease obligations, temporary investment opportunities

36. Short- and long-range financial planning

37. Money market developments

38. Purchase vs. requirements

39. Discounts on purchases

Guidelines for Management in Budget Formulation

40. Budgets should be a control as well as a planning tool.

41. Budgets should measure performance by providing the basis for that measurement through specific and quantified plans.

42. Each manager should have clearly defined departmental objectives.

43. Plans and budgets should be prepared not only for departments, divisions, etc., but for overall corporate operations.

44. Variances from budgets are analyzed and variances corrected on an ongoing basis. Managers are called to task for continued deviations from planned budgets.

45. People who need to achieve specific, quantitative objectives are involved in the setting of the objectives. Responsibilities and standards are set.

46. The budgetary process is integrated within overall corporate planning.

47. Controllable and noncontrollable expenses as well as

normal and abnormal expenditures are separated to account for planned deviations. Variable budgeting also indicates direct expenses for each item at its stage of production.

48. Specific review at specific periods, or when major changes in operations occur, allow for revising the budgets upward or downward.

49. Budgeting is a major managerial effort extending over a period of time. It is not only an important control tool for expenses and costs, but establishes standards and goals for the measurement of managerial performance.

50. Financial rewards and compensations are tied to performance goal.

**Managerial Steps and Procedures in
Formulating a Budget**

51. The sales forecast is the beginning point, and it determines production, inventory levels and costs.

52. The production budget is calculated in the following manner:
Units to be produced = Planned
ending inventory of
finished goods
plus (+)
planned sales
minus (—)
beginning inventory of
finished goods.

53. Material usage and purchases budget is determined: Purchases in units = desired ending material inventory quantities plus (+) usage minus (—) beginning inventory quantitites.

54. Direct labor costs, factory overhead costs are determined next. These usually can be calculated from existing engineered data. Target inventory level is the inventory level at the end of the cycle.

55. Cost of goods sold budget is calculated.

56. Marketing, selling budget as well as general and administrative budgets, are factored into the master budget.

57. The cash budget provides an estimated effect on the cash position of the operations. Correctly used, it provides cash control and planning to avoid cash deficiencies or surplus. The cash budget is factored with the cash receipts budget, which shows collections of receivables and other sources, as well as experience with bad debts and lag between sales and collections. Cash disbursements budget consists of material purchases averaging, outlays of direct labor wages, costs and expenses and disbursements such as purchases of fixed assets.

58. A pro forma balance sheet is thus reached.

Management Ratio Analysis for Corporate Financial Effectiveness

59. Net profit after tax divided by equity capital

60. Net profit before tax divided by total capital

61. Corporate tax divided by net profit before tax

62. Total profit divided by total capital

63. Interest paid divided by borrowed capital

64. Borrowed capital divided by equity capital (leverage measurement)

65. Total profit divided by interest paid

66. Total capital divided by borrowed capital

67. Current assets divided by current liabilities (quick ratio)

68. Stock divided by average daily cost of sales (stock turnover)

69. Debtors divided by average daily sales

70. Creditors divided by average daily purchases

71. Fixed expenditures divided by total expenditures (profit vulnerability)

72. Long-term capital divided by fixed assets

73. Income after tax divided by the value of the investment

at the beginning of the period

74. Gross dividend receivable divided by the value of the investment at the beginning of the period

75. Capital gain divided by the value of the investment at the beginning of the period

76. Tax on dividend divided by gross dividend

77. Tax on gain divided by capital gains

78. Dividend (gross) divided by market value of ordinary shares

79. Profit after corporation tax divided by market value of ordinary shares

80. Market value of ordinary shares divided by profit after corporate tax

81. Profit after corporate tax divided by gross dividend

82. Profits after corporate tax divided by number of ordinary shares

83. Profit after corporate tax divided by equity capital

84. Net assets at book value divided by number of ordinary shares

85. Preference shares divided by total borrowed capital

86. Loans divided by total borrowed capital

87. Overdrafts divided by total borrowed capital

88. Trade and expense creditors divided by total borrowed capital

89. Corporate and/or income tax provisions divided by total borrowed capital

90. Income tax reserves and deferred taxation divided by total borrowed capital

91. Investment grants divided by total borrowed capital

92. Amount outstanding on hire purchase accounts divided by total borrowed capital

93. Amount outstanding on lease accounts divided by total borrowed capital

94. Debts factored divided by total borrowed capital

95. Bills discounted divided by total borrowed capital

**Management Standards for Maintaining or Assessing
Corporate Liquidity Status**

96. Current ratio is a primary test which looks at assets available to pay liabilities falling due. It is calculated

$$\frac{\text{Current assets}}{\text{Current liabilities}}$$

(Normal "standards" are a two-to-one ratio.)

97. The quick ratio is a more selective standard. It concentrates on assets which can be turned quickly into cash, such as marketable securities and cash itself, but no stock:

$$\frac{\text{Quick assets}}{\text{Current liabilities}}$$

(Most managers hold that one-to-one is "standard" for most norms.)

98. Conventional ratios are backed up by "secondary" tests of liquidity, including:

• Vulnerability of the company's profits during a slowdown of turnover (fixed costs/total costs). In general, the higher this ratio the higher the company's ratio of current assets to current liabilities must be to survive any recession.

• The speed at which the company is turning its stock over (stock/average daily costs of sales). A rapid stock turnover will "excuse" a lower ratio of current assets to current liabilities.

• Rapidity of debt collection (credits/average daily sales). A fast debt collection will "explain" a low current asset to current liability ratio.

• Credit amounts (credits/average daily purchases). Higher rates than normal will tend to lower the ratio of current assets to current liabilities.

Higher rates than normal will tend to lower the ratio of current assets to current liabilities.

• Long-term liabilities coming due in the near future. The extent of these liabilities determines the current asset to current liability ratio that needs to be strengthened.

• Capital expenditure plans. Proposals for these plans will tend to run down the current asset to current liability ratio, unless there are immediate new plans also afoot to raise new finance soon.

99. Liquidity ratio calculation. This ratio calculates the effect rising inflation has on corporate liquidity:

$$\frac{\text{Stock plus debtors minus creditors}}{\text{Long-term capital}}$$

Monitors of Controllership Management Performance

100. Analyses of cost variances are routinely and regularly performed so that factors causing differences between standard and actual costs are identified and eliminated. Reports are printed and distributed.

101. Standards for variance analysis are based on engineered or other scientific data, rather than "historic" information.

102. Estimates for costs of a job or a process are within N percent of actual costs or time involved.

103. Variances are pinpointed as to material, labor or overhead variables in production areas.

104. Cost variances generate specific managerial action toward the accountable person as well as the accountable department.

105. Cost accounting systems apply to all departments of the company, including administrative and clerical areas.

106. Return on investment and other ratios are measured routinely on each project or product by line.

107. Cost control programs are prioritized.

108. Cost standards are no more than N months old; after reaching N months of use they are automatically out of date and must be replaced before use.

109. Cost control responsibility is shared by all employees, who are aware of these standards and goals.

110. Company employees who produce specific techniques to aid cost reduction through savings of time or material are rewarded in a company-wide program. Rewards are based on a

task force's estimate of savings per year involved, and the employee is compensated on a percentage basis.

111. Budgets are set up for use at an appropriate user department level to show directly the interrelationship of the budget, actual cost and cost control reports:
- Material usage reports show not only material budgeted but a report of actual material used during a specific time span. Variance from standard is shown along with units produced and units budgeted to be produced.
- Labor efficiency reports show not only the direct labor actually used by the direct labor budgeted. Any change is shown in a "variance" column.
- Overhead budget variance reports show the budgeted costs and the actual costs and break out the variance.

112. Variable budgets show how each cost or expense will change with changes in volume or activity for each product or division of the company.

113. Cost controls are set prior to cost incurrence, rather than after cost incurrence, by providing supervisors with cost standards or objectives for scheduled work.

114. Cost controls are realistic, attainable and quantitative, and the people responsible for meeting controls have been actively involved in the planning process.

115. Cost controls are seen as positive factors, and employees have understanding of cost-consciousness.

116. Employees understand the standards involved, can measure cost constrols by comparing actual costs with the standards set and thereby can gauge their own performance.

117. Cost control responsibilities have been affixed throughout the company. Each cost is the responsibility of some one individual, and he or she is held accountable.

118. Incurrence of cost is keyed to production activity.

119. Process costs systems, in which all costs are placed into "reservoirs" or "cost centers," have been investigated for usefulness and cost controls.

120. Determination has been made as to the best use of the LIFO or FIFO cost accounting system.

121. Standard costing sytems, using set standards instead of attempting to determine an "actual" cost per unit in a period, is always double-checked with the use of variance analysis so that actual cost can be compared with predetermined costs and inefficiencies can be highlighted and eliminated.

122. Capital budgeting is an ongoing concern, not just "one shot."

123. Capital budgeting takes into account the timing of the cash flow through the use of present value methods.

124. Rate of return is calculated prior to a capital budgeting decision and return on investment is calculated after investment is undertaken to measure performance.

125. Mortgage financing, using the plant as collateral, has been investigated.

126. All borrowings are done by predetermined, systematic methods and are authorized by the board of directors.

127. Accounting is separated totally from other departments such as sales, purchasing, etc.

128. An internal auditor reports to a senior manager other than the controller.

129. Operating management reports are prepared to highlight variances as well as to report routine facts.

130. Major expenses and costs are under budgetary control.

131. Employees who work in ultrasensitive areas are routinely rotated, and all employees are required to take full vacations.

132. Accounting manuals are in use, and books of account are kept up to date and are sufficient to the company's business.

133. Accounts receivable with customers are routinely confirmed by company personnel.

134. The credit department is independent of the sales department and operates on its predetermined standards for ope-

rations. These standards determine which companies will have credit. Credit performance is monitored so that operations suggest that all who meet standards have credit, and the bad debt ratio is not so low that it might suggest lost sales because of too-tight credit policies.

135. Employees who authorize credit do not have access to cash.

136. The credit department is consulted prior to the payment of a credit balance to a customer.

137. Customer accounts are balanced with control accounts by an employee specifically charged with this responsibility. He or she does not also handle the accounts receivable records.

138. Delinquent accounts are reviewed at stated frequencies by an accountable manager.

139. Trends of accounts receivable to days of sales are monitored closely for changes in aging.

140. Customer's orders of more than N dollars are subject to review and authorization prior to shipment.

141. Sales invoices are used. These are prenumbered, and all invoices are checked for accuracy.

142. Preparation of the company payroll is done within a system which involves a number of employees and which has a manager for final authorization and accountability.

143. Payroll accounts are reconciled every N days.

144. Investigations are made when unpaid employee checks are determined.

145. A separate manager is responsible for hearing employee grievances or questions about payroll checks or procedures.

146. All salary rates are in writing, along with any changes or additions. These have been signed by the appropriate managers or foremen.

147. Cash and currency are deposited daily in a bank account which pays interest.

148. A system for authenticating deposits as well as handling cash, particularly those coming in through the mail, is in use.

149. The bank has instructions not to cash checks made payable to the company but only to accept them for deposit. The bank has a list of only a few names of executives who can sign these checks for the company.

150. A policy has been developed for check cashing by employees.

151. Petty cash is handled by a system which restricts amounts and which controls responsibility for the money. Vouchers are used, books kept, and the funds are audited irregularly but often by an auditor independent of the fund or the department.

152. The ratio of costs of credit department, auditing department, etc., is calculated as a percentage of sales.

153. Inventory is closely monitored for levels, uses, costs and particularly timing. Cost records are tied to the financial records.

154. Inventory records are maintained no matter where in the plant material purchases are delivered. These records show the amount delivered and other pertinent checks. Discrepancies are immediately noted and action is taken.

155. Ratios for inventory have been calculated for best company use at various points in the company's production cycle. Purchasing's records are monitored to determine that purchases are neither more nor less, than what actually can be used during a predetermined period so that company investment in inventories is maintained at the lowest level possible.

156. Inventory records are checked against physical inventory every six months. Systematic checks to be made are detailed in written instructions.

157. An employee has the responsibility for maintaining controllership overviews on inventory, particularly if the company has large amounts of investment in this area.

158. Quantity, unit conversions, prices used, additions, extensions and summarizations are double-checked on inventory management.

Controllership Management Performance Objectives

159. Reduce fixed assets to a level not to exceed N percent of tangible net worth in N years.

160. Improve profits to gross sales from N percent to N percent within the next N months.

161. Reduce customer returned material from N dollars to N dollars within N months.

162. Reduce EDP costs by N percent within N months by elimination of N reports to be determined by value analysis and actual use.

163. Reduce the average age of accounts receivable from N days to N days.

164. Reduce bad debt losses to less than N percent of all sales.

165. Increase working cash by N percent in each of banks utilized within N months by limiting inventory levels to N percent of those currently carried.

166. Analyze expense trends five years out for each operating department based on the past five-year trends and set projected anticipated expenses. Then set a 10 percent reduction of those projected expense trends beginning with the first projected year.

167. Complete a cost manual and checklist and distribute this to each appropriate manager by N date.

Cost Accounting Management Checklist

168. Determinations of cost control responsibility.
   a. within the organization
   b. organization of Comptroller's function
   c. relationship with operating departments
169. Work authorization and flow checks
   a. production requirements determination and order issuance procedures
   b. material procurement determination (explosion) procedure (inventory check and open commitments procedure)

    c. parts manufacturing determination and procedure (economic lot and inventory check and prior usage procedure)

    d. factory scheduling and loading procedure (man-hour and equivalent man determination)

    e. production control follow-up procedure

    f. expediting procedure

    g. inventory control on orders in process as related to new requirement

    h. departmental flow and inspection points

    i. inventory points

    j. physical inventory situation

Note: Have work flow and authorization been charted?

  170. Direct labor

    a. basic direct labor defined (source by operation or by complete part?)

    b. handling of auxiliary direct labor and inspection direct labor

    c. method of arriving at direct labor standards and inclusion of items other than "pure" effort

    d. plant and expense labor handling (burden application)

    e. distinction between direct and indirect labor and reporting of diversions of direct labor

    f. relationship of work standard to pay standard and effect on rate used

    g. computation of work standard (used in cost standard)

    h. computation of pay standard

    i. (1) determination of rates used (use of standard rates or actuals dependent on feasibility)

    (2) base for recovery of burden from D/L (Standard hours, including re-work, standard dollars, etc.)

    j. flow of effort and identification with work standard (piece part) and operation or operator

    k. scheduling and loading procedure

171. Direct material
a. identification of direct material — basic and auxiliary
b. costing of direct material and inclusions thereof (taxes, duties, incoming transportation, insurance, packaging) and development of standard
c. price variance determination
d. plant and expense material
e. material burden inclusion
f. handling of special tooling charges
g. physical flow of material (flow checks) and paperwork support (requisitioning)
    (1) receiving
    (2) raw material stores in and out
    (3) parts stores in and out
    (4) semifinished stores in and out
    (5) work in process in and out
    (6) finished goods in
h. issuance procedure of standard material (minimum issue, open requisitions, etc.) costing on requisition or standard B/M basis, excess material usage procedure and reporting as variance.

172. Shrinkage, rework, scrap, etc.
a. standards content for shrinkage, if any and method used to determine contents (unavoidable engineered only)
b. method utilized to control excess shrinkage through control of material issues
c. handling of shrinkage in labor pay procedures
    (1) at operation discovered
    (2) on cost of prior operations
d. handling of rework
    (1) identification, responsibility determination
    (2) authorization for rework and paperwork procedure
    (3) costing of rework
    (4) use of standards in rework, where applicable, and where economically feasible

(5) reporting
e. determination of scrap
    (1) identification of cost and responsibility
    (2) reporting against allowable shrinkage
    (3) physical handling and sale or reclaim procedures
f. production scrap applicability and costing
g. physical handling and costing of customer returns
173. Packaging and shipping costs
a. inclusion in manufacturing costs rather than sales and distribution costs
b. definition of direct labor and material in packing and shipping costs
c. handling of outgoing freight, cartage and insurance (terms of sale, etc.)
d. determination of Shipping Department burden and allocation to Assembly Departments in budget determination of burden rates
e. entries required
174. Manufacturing expense
a. item definitions
    (1) direct working
    (2) indirect working
    (3) indirect labor
b. use of associated labor benefits burden center
c. handling of maintenance expense (including purchased maintenance) and work order system
d. determination of manufacturing cost adjustments
e. definition of budget centers
f. definition of budget centers and number required
g. *annual* allocation only of service departments to production departments and bases used (for months use per day rather than 1/12) (no reallocation to other service department after initial allocation)
h. burden rate establishments
    (1) determination of normal practical capacity

    (2) manufacturing burden rates and base to be used (standard direct labor hours)

    (3) material burden rates and contents

  i. flexible budgeting and application

    (1) definition of fixed (per work day) and variable (per hour) expenses (budget purposes only), emphasis on physical determinants (head count)

    (2) definition of unit of activity (standard labor hours, machine hours, etc.)

    (3) use of fixed and variable burden rates in studies and variance determination only

    (4) use of indirect manning tables and other physical unit planning documents

    (5) issuance of budget reports prior to the start of a period.

175. Entries

a. cost inputs

b. cost outputs

    (1) standard costs to inventory

    (2) transfers to assets

    (3) plant and expense control balances

    (4) variances, cost adjustments, and their computations (including material burden variances)

c. adjustments to actual costs, where required

d. costing of sales procedures

176. Paperwork flow

a. purchase, receipt, inspection and storage of and payment for purchased material

b. material issuance

c. recording of direct labor and costing and distribution

d. work order system for maintenance, etc.

e. cost accounting procedures relative to above inputs, cost output, control reports and handling of data

177. Standards revisions

a. present procedures, approvals, and causes (when made:

annually or during year)

b. identification of parts in all products on which used (used on file)

c. (1) effect on inventory and valuation   (2) cost of modification and handling.

d. entries used

e. profit implications and their handling

178. Reports

a. departmental control reports by budget center

   (1) off-standard performance labor and material

   (2) direct working

   (3) indirect labor

   (4) rework

   (5) scrap and shrinkage

   (6) manufacturing expenses

   (7) variance reports and analyses

   (8) summary report of variances, rework and other controllable costs

b. segregation of controllable vs. noncontrollable with *all* cost accounted for

179. Pricing

a. comptroller's activity responsibility for a review of sales prices for reasonableness, inclusion of all cost elements, and desirability from the profit and financial viewpoint (standard margin report with sales at catalog price and actual billed price)

b. control of inventory cost through:

   (1) valuation control (at standard)

   (2) usage control through reporting of inventory level vs. usage

180. Implementation schedule

a. steps (including flow chart requirements)

b. time schedule

c. responsibility

How to Measure
Production Management
Performance

Background Data for Management

1. What is your plant's productivity:
- per dollar of plant investment?
- per dollar of wages?
- per employee?
- per man hour?

2. Has the ratio changed in the last year? Last three years? For the better — or worse?

3. How does your plant's performance measure up with your leading competitors? The industry in which you compete?

4. What is production management's degree of effectiveness as measured by the ratio of production costs divided by the sales value of production? Has this ratio changed in the past several years? What is the trend?

5. What is the correlation of inventory with sales levels? Is too much money tied up in inventory for too long a time?

6. What is the ratio of work farmed out to work produced by your production unit? Is that ratio increasing — along with your expenses?

7. What is the frequency rate of rescheduled production?

8. What percent of materials winds up as scrap or waste?

9. Have complaints been heard about designs that cannot be easily produced, designs which change production schedules, decisions that delay production or design changes which are "too frequent"?

10. Is the accounting department computing all costs of manufacturing and supplying these to production management on a weekly product-by-product basis? Is corrective action taken when facts contained in these reports indicate a need?

11. Are machines selected for certain production runs on the basis of best cost per unit and best machine speed? Have specific production standards been set and communicated for each machine and its use?

12. What is your actual material cost in terms of percent of production cost? What is the trend indicating?

Product Management Performance Improvement Goals

13. Determine optimum length and size of production run.

14. Arrange for the most efficient scheduling of production workers.

15. Change production locations.

16. Introduce process changes.

17. Establish optimum organization of production supervision.

18. Maintain proper balance between production scheduling and inventory levels.

19. Increase or decrease maintenance to match actual requirements.

20. Change plant layout and/or workflow.

21. Introduce or expand use of automated equipment.

22. Reduce fixed costs.

23. Alternatives:
- optimum inventory levels.
- adequacy of plant and equipment manufacturing facilities.
- raw materials and labor availability and utilization.
- length of production runs or season.
- annual production required.
- optimum location for manufacturing.

24. Raw materials forecast.

25. Production forecast and schedule.

26. Each manager assumes personal accountability in establishing and maintaining effective working relationships within production and with other divisions and departments.

27. Plans for reaching objectives.

Plant Production Manager Objectives

28. Complete construction and equipping of approved addition to new plant by N date within capital budget of N dollars and expense budget of N dollars.

29. Produce X number of Y products at N cost.

30. Install and have new equipment operational by N date within capital budget of N dollars and expense budget of N dollars.

31. Decrease the plant's quality reject rate from N percent to N percent by N date.

Overall Production Management Objectives

32. Any variances in excess of plus or minus N percent will be explained in writing within N hours of their occurrence.

33. No division will wait more than N working days for action on a production request.

34. Upgrade shipping performance to be on time during N year from N percent to N percent.

35. Reduce "down" time due to lack of parts or materials by N percent.

36. Raw material inventories will not exceed a ratio of N percent to the next quarter's volume as forecast.

37. Complete value analysis of Product X by N date.

38. Rearrange according to plan B the NY assembly line.

39. Study the effectiveness of the NY unit with the objective of reducing facilities and manpower now used to produce volume N or X product.

40. Reduce the accident frequency rate at Plant Y from N percent to N percent during N year.

41. N percent of all customer requests on order status will be answered within N hours after receipt of the request.

42. Back orders never exceed N percent of the plant's monthly shipments.

43. N percent of all orders will be shipped within N hours of their scheduled time.

44. Production is not late on more than N percent of its planned production.

45. Equipment "down" time because materials or components are not at the proper work stations or because of improper scheduling will not exceed N percent of the available machine hours.

46. All data on production are reviewed in depth at least once weekly. Data are distributed in written form to applicable other divisions and management teams.

47. New products and changes are brought into production without disrupting normal production flow and without incurring more than N hours of overtime.

48. Raw material stock for each product will fall to N days' supply at least once each month.

49. Quality control from Product X will be reduced in cost from N percent of sales to N percent during N date.

50. Productive inventory, as measured by dollar value, will not exceed N dollars during N months.

51. The value set on obsolete or salvage materials will not be less than N percent of its original value.

52. Inventory on materials and supplies is handled by EDP, determined by formula and reordered through "check points." Computer printouts are run on items older than N months.

53. Inventory in use is moved within N minutes from station to station.

54. Each manager and his or her department head will review the performance of the unit under the manager's control within N days of the end of each report period. Managers will

be reviewed openly on their performance against plan.

55. Reports of performance against plan are generated daily and in the hands of managers within N hours of the end of the work shift or working day.

56. The plant manager will make a personal tour of the plant at least once a day.

57. Information needs of various department heads and managers are reviewed every N months and judgments of their actual needs against the costs of generating this data are made. Nonessential elements of information are eliminated.

58. Cost of machine A repairs will be reduced from N dollars to N dollars during N year.

59. One technique in work simplification will be developed for Plant A during an N-month period through weekly cost-reduction meetings between affected workers and supervisors.

60. EDP system for N departments will be installed to replace N dollars of clerical labor, with the system's leading and operational costs not to exceed N percent of the projected savings.

61. Inventory lead time will be reduced from N weeks to N weeks while maintaining standards of production.

62. A master schedule of sales will be compared to inventories at N intervals to reduce stock frequency rates to N percentages during N year.

63. Material-handling costs will be reduced to N percent of manufactured costs by new process layouts in the X plant by N year.

64. A vendor-rating system will be completed by N date to establish reliability, price and delivery for all vendors to achieve competitive bidding for materials at or below an index achieved for last period.

65. Stock rejects of product X items will be reduced by N date to N percent of all items in plant A during N year.

66. Heat losses at a certain percentage (N percent) or less of all heat transferred will be achieved when moving Product N

from system X to system Y.

67. Shipping costs will not exceed N dollars per unit of Product N from shipping point A to shipping point B.

68. All subordinates will be met at their work stations briefly once a day to ascertain status of work. Once every N days the manager will hold a work appraisal meeting personally in his office with each subordinate and openly review work performance.

69. While completing Project A, Plant B will maintain overtime hours at the rate of no more than N percent of scheduled hours.

70. Customer complaints because of quality control or incorrectly shipped items will not exceed N percent of all items shipped per year.

71. Orders are shipped according to customer specifications when shipping is paid for by the customer. Otherwise, they will be shipped by the least costly but effective method. In no instance will shipping time between plant and receipt by customer exceed N days.

Production Management Performance Monitors
72. Manpower productivity and performance
73. Value analysis
74. Manufacturing costs
75. Costs per unit
76. Purchasing costs
77. Variances in costs
78. Lead time for production
79. Production backlogs
80. Costs of overtime
81. Standard cost vs. actual
82. Shipping costs
83. Percentage of projects completed vs. planning
84. Equipment obsolescence and depreciation trends
85. Inventory levels compared with sales levels

86. Back order rates and categories
87. Inventory levels compared with back order levels
88. Deadlines achieved in terms of percentages
89. Performance variance as a percentage compared with budgets
90. Percentage of labor capacity's utilization
91. Comparison between machine hours per item and total process items
92. Correlation of output and input between equipment use and labor capacity
93. Percentage of company production compared with work which is farmed out
94. The frequency rate of rescheduling production
95. Work behind schedule aging
96. Ratio of productive output per unit of labor input
97. The ratio of new personnel hired to experienced production workers
98. Ratio of assets to inventory
99. Turnover of inventory
100. Rework percentages and trends
101. Ratio of net sales to inventory
102. Percentage of available floor space actually used
103. Percentage of capital equipment actually used
104. Equipment down-time percent vs. age and profile
105. Percentage of material handling compared to unit cost
106. Scrap, reject or waste percentages and trends
107. Order error percentages
108. Completion rates measured by task-time
109. Correction ratios for defects
110. Scrap and waste percentages and trends
111. Setup preparation time percentages
112. Safety stock depreciation frequencies
113. Ratios of demand time to supply time
114. Levels for minimum lead time reordering
115. Queue ratios

116. Machine capacity and actual utilization
117. Dollars and units of output
118. Dollars and units of shipments
119. Production occupancy of available footage
120. Units and dollars of waste, scrap or rejects
121. Breakdown reports
122. Consumption of utilities
123. Production equipment
• condition
• upkeep costs
• age
124. Usage of shop supplies and nondurable tool consumption
125. Material yields compared with:
• raw material consumption
• material cost
• shrinkage (if applicable)
• direct labor
• manufacturing cycle timing
126. Productivity:
• net output per worker hour
• net output per unit of labor and tangible capital
• net output per unit of weighted tangible capital
127. Percentage of employees on incentives
128. Average earnings as percentage of base rate
129. Number of engineering personnel to number of factory workers
130. Number of production and inventory control personnel in relationship to total plant employment
131. Inventory performance measurements:
• dollars invested in inventory
• turnover rate of inventory
• inventory declared surplus or obsolete
• costs of holding inventories
• actual material costs vs. estimated materials costs

- levels of backup stock
- percentage of shortages of inventory
- inventory items of which no distribution was made, as a percentage
- actual levels of inventories compared with planned levels

132. Number of employees
133. Employees on regular wages
134. Employees on incentive plans
135. Employees on standards
136. Employee overtime in man-hours
137. Man-hours of each cost center
138. Factory engineering: man-hours; dollars
139. Materials handling: man-hours; dollars
140. Factory warehousing and shipping expenses
141. Clerical: man-hours; dollars
142. Quality control and inspection: man-hours; dollars
143. Tool and fixture making: man-hours; dollars
144. Setup time: man-hours; dollars
145. Maintenance and repair: man-hours; dollars
146. Housekeeping and sanitation: man-hours; dollars
147. Production planning establishes workload of each machine and operator with sufficient lead time so that production can adequately forecast and schedule manpower and machine priorities.
148. Production standards include machine speeds and optimum rates of production. The best workers are scheduled to get the most challenging jobs on the best machines.
149. The current status of any order can be readily determined in minutes.
150. Coordination between sales and production allows sales forecasts to be prepared in sufficient detail so that these may be readily translated into specific production planning.
151. Production schedules are widely communicated among persons who will be responsible for them and are also posted and otherwise prominently displayed.

152. Both production and production control double-check the accuracy of records.

153. Customers and others are given a means to communicate their ideas to make production operations more effective, suitable or profitable.

154. Materials availability is always double-checked before production begins so that there are no shortages which will slow down or curtail the production run.

155. The actual cost of the quality control department has been checked within N months and represents no more than N percent of production costs.

156. All major jobs and operations have time standards, machine speeds, work standards, and other data established prior to production runs.

157. Continuous reviews, occurring every N months, analyze methods and operations as well as standards for their pertinence, productivity and effectiveness. Those production methods or standards not meeting the criteria of this review are revised or withdrawn and replaced by new thinking.

158. Actual production is compared with planned production daily and deviations are analyzed so that future production will conform with planning.

159. Time recording data is double-checked for accuracy and reliability.

160. Delays of production are communicated, along with estimated timetables, to all affected departments.

161. All applicable company departments are considered when make-or-buy decisions are encountered. Costs are analyzed and known before contracts are let.

162. Scrap items are recorded and logged. This record is used as a measure of worker effectiveness as well as a method of reducing cost.

163. Equipment performance is inspected at intervals after its installation to be certain it functions up to design and designated standards.

164. Idle-time reports are prepared for machines and workers to be analyzed for causes of idleness and to boost productivity.

165. Delays or interruptions causing idle time are checked and causes are systematically eliminated.

166. Delays or interruptions are compared against planning so that production schedules are consistent with realistic expectations.

167. Steps in all operations are analyzed to determine if certain steps can be modified or eliminated so the process may be simplified and made more efficient.

168. Operations are analyzed to determine which components or production steps can be divided and later combined more effectively with other operations.

169. Small parts used in quantity are weighed rather than individually counted.

170. Materials handling is analyzed for cost reductions through the use of bulk or other specialized methods including pallets, hoists, forklift trucks, conveyors, skids, etc.

171. Repetitive functions which call for little human judgment are analyzed from the point of view of automating the job.

172. New and technically advanced machinery and equipment are analyzed for possible purchase based on economic justification and practicality.

173. Plant work areas are analyzed every N months for needs of modernization and upgrading, including work arrangements, new lighting, painting in bright colors, industrial carpeting, etc.

174. Time and motion studies have been completed on manufacturing and warehousing areas so that all machinery, equipment and materials are placed for most efficient production. These studies have been performed by outside specialists and are undertaken every N months.

175. Efficiency of machines and their conformance to stan-

dards are checked every N months.

176. Warehousing is efficient and well laid out, vertically as well as horizontally, with vertical storage and shelving area used the height of the area and serviced by forklift trucks.

177. Inventory and production records are checked for actual use of materials to determine that all materials are accounted for.

178. Inventory areas are separate from production areas, and systems are in effect to discourage pilferage or waste.

179. Shipping as well as receiving areas are under control systems to safeguard materials from pilferage. No strangers or unauthorized persons are allowed to spend time in these areas without proper supervision, nor is any employee allowed to take materials without proper control authorizations. Valuable portable items are fenced off and under lock and key.

180. Systems are in effect so that all incoming and departing materials are checked against itemized lists.

181. Machines or operations which are critical in the productive cycle have a backup operator trained and ready to take over so that output is not stopped in the event of operator illness or accident.

182. The ratio of workers to supervisors is such that output is high but supervisors can still take care of their work duties.

183. Supervisors are trained to provide job direction to those who need it and have enough time to perform this important function.

184. Systematic training provides attitudes, knowledge and skills in problem solving and cost controlling.

185. There is a "career pathing" program in effect so that employees who have the necesary qualifications and proper motivation can advance in the company.

186. "Job posting" occurs throughout the plant so that all employees have knowledge of every opening in the company and have an opportunity to better themselves.

187. Standards exist and are well understood for the ranking

of every employee in relationship to his or her work. Rewards are given only for accomplishments and results, not for effort, for personality traits, or for activities.

188. Extensive programmed training involving written material and testing is given every employee prior to his or her being held accountable for any job. Employees are thus well trained for the job they are about to perform.

189. Workers and supervisors alike cooperate in "task team" efforts to solve production and cost problems.

190. Positions in supervisory or managerial posts opening up through retirement are identified N years in advance, and suitable replacements are identified and trained.

191. Turnover ratios of workers or supervisors in any department do not exceed the ratio in other departments or for the industry as a whole.

192. Analysis has been made of the suitability and possible productivity gains of such scheduling procedures for workers as "flex time," in which workers schedule their own working hours about a core time in cooperation with their work unit and other departments while meeting standards and department goals.

193. Analysis has been made of the "work team" approach or similar approaches whereby teams of workers handle one process from start to completion while still being held accountable for all production schedules and standards.

Production Management Performance Ratios

194. Production costs divided by the sales value of the production

195. Production contribution divided by the production assets

196. Direct materials cost divided by the sales value of production

197. Production overhead divided by sales value of production

198. Raw material stock divided by average daily purchases

199. Finished goods stock divided by the average daily value of production completed

200. Work in progress divided by the average daily value of issues to production and the products completed

201. Value of factory plant divided by sales value of production

202. Sales value of production divided by the area of the factory plant

203. Value of plant divided by sales value of production

204. Manufacturing plant at depreciated value divided by the plant at an undepreciated value

205. Sales value of production divided by the area of the factory plant

206. Direct labor cost divided by the sales value of production

207. Direct labor cost divided by hours worked

208. Standard hours of productive work divided by total attendance hours

209. Sales value of production divided by standard hours of productive work

210. Standard hours of productive work divided by total standard hours produced

211. Total standard hours produced divided by working time

212. Overtime hours divided by total hours

213. Overtime premium hours divided by overtime hours

214. Machine operating costs divided by the sales value of production

215. Machine fixed operating costs divided by maximum output

216. Machine variable operating costs divided by actual output

217. Actual output divided by maximum output

218. Sales value of production divided by actual output

219. Employee's basic wages divided by maximum output
220. Supervisor's basic wages divided by maximum output
221. Bonus output divided by actual output
222. Overtime payment divided by actual output
223. Maintenance divided by actual output

Production Management: Symptoms And Treatments

Symptom	*Treatment*
224. Low efficiency rate, excesses of essentially nonproductive work or "lost time"	Plan the work well ahead of time; schedule workers as soon as possible at each shift's beginning; transfer workers from one job to another immediately after completion of work or after machinery difficulties; keep a high level of maintenance on machinery to prevent breakdowns, and when they occur, have a system of immediate steps operative to commence repairs; develop accountability standards for each worker along with goals and objectives for each job.
225. Low machine productivity	Establish planning to set a rate of production for each job; set accountability standards for each job; be certain all machines are well maintained and ready to go, and the best workers get the best machines.
226. Low rate of worker productivity	Establish accountability of worker for specific results to

be performed; set job standards; train workers in most effective methods of obtaining results; keep records of these results and keep workers informed and rewarded for special efforts; plan for a minimum amount of manpower for each job consistent with safety and other standards.

227. Not enough output because of lack of hours worked or worker shortages

Plan for higher machine and worker utilization; work as much overtime as is effective and necessary; seek and train additional workers to supplement current crews.

228. Excessive idle time on machines

Use planning and control for larger work batches or more consistent work scheduling so that as many machines as possible are fully manned at each shift's beginning; organize work flow; set job standards; establish worker accountability for results on machine, alert maintenance for repairs and adjustments for as little "down" time as possible.

229. Material quality uneven or poorer than required standards; yield from material less than desired

Keep records of purchasing's standards for vendors and check raw materials against these; inform applicable

persons of significant
deviations for possible
actions; keep checking
material systematically and
frequently; be certain that
process standards are strictly
carried out.

230. Processing is not up
to desired standards

Check the work to be certain
that the workers involved are
knowledgeable in processing
methods and standards and
correctly use them; plan
ahead on how to use the
material for best processing,
including such details as how
to cut lengths; arrange for
checks often of the work
with attention to factors
such as finish and
dimensions.

Production Management: Performance Standards

231. Production management understands and applies financial measurements focusing on return on investment and return on assets calculations as involved in production's purchasing decision, acquisition of facilities and equipment, inventory materials stocking, make-or-buy decisions, as well as production of the product line so that emphasis may be given to those products which will present the better return on the assets needed to manufacture them.

232. Standards of performance and objectives are expressed partly in terms of return on investment, return on asset calculations, as well as other ratios which quantify production management's achievement of results.

233. Objectives for each job are set and they become the

focal point for measurements.

234. A policy of "no surprises" is in effect whereby a problem which can be anticipated is communicated in advance for proper handling or decision making.

235. Production management has established policies for recurring decision-making situations which are repetitive and which require consistency.

236. All production policies are known to all who will make decisions.

237. Participative management policies are used to shape decisions in applicable matters.

238. Production management integrates and controls the resources provided to achieve objectives and the standards of performance required by the company.

239. Production management makes economical use of labor, equipment and materials to manufacture the company's products in the quality and quantity required to meet the company's sales commitments.

240. Production management concerns itself with all facets of production policy, production organization, human resource development, commitments and responsibilities, standards of performance, accountability, facilities and equipment and relationships within the organization as well as relationships with major customers, suppliers and the community itself in which the production plant is a "good neighbor."

241. Company policies are set for inventory levels as well as the record keeping of inventory. Determinations are made for timing, for raw materials, in-process stock, supplies and materials as well as finished stock. Part of the policies also determine standards for categorizing salvage or waste stock as well as how to sell these to reclaim part of costs.

242. Studies are made of competitors to maintain a competitive production stance.

243. Variances in policies are made in writing within N hours after action is taken. No more than N percent of deci-

sions a year will be at variance with company policies.

244. All procedure policies have a "Sunset Clause" in them whereby they automatically lapse after N years unless specifically renewed.

245. An information system has been set up to supply all facts needed for sound production operations as well as for forecasting and planning.

246. Production management has compiled a specific management procedure manual and copies have been distributed to those who will use them. They cover such matters as purchasing determinations, inventory control, production control and scheduling, materials handling, maintenance, receiving and shipping, packaging, quality control, manufacturing specifications and processes, design specifications, product testing and inspection procedures, value engineering, capital expenditures determinations and justifications, machinery and equipment use and standards, make-or-buy decisions, measured work, accountability statements, safety requirements, manpower use, manufacturing audits and measurements, and other procedures.

247. Production management is concerned with the company's good standing in the community of which it is a part. Management is encouraged to take part in community activities and organizations. Each manager is required to belong to at least one community or civic organization which has as its goal the betterment of the community or the business climate.

248. Production management provides community or business leadership by holding office in civic or business organizations.

249. Each plant receives at least N column inches of space in the newspapers representing its community with at least N percent of these published stories having an overall favorable viewpoint to the company or reporting "objectively" of the company's actions or changes.

250. Top production management schedules at least one

lunch period per month with top management of another department with the purpose of exchanging contacts and information. Each meeting is followed by an informal written report sharing needed information with departmental teams.

251. A "master file" is kept of all pertinent inputs to policy matters, including requests for variations. When X requests for variations on policy are received, the policy itself is reviewed for revision.

252. Each policy is reviewed no less than once every two years.

OPPORTUNITIES:

A HANDBOOK OF BUSINESS OPPORTUNITY SEARCH

Edward de Bono

Born in Malta, **Edward de Bono** obtained a medical degree from Malta University, then proceeded as a Rhodes Scholar to Christ Church, Oxford, where he gained an honours degree in psychology and physiology, as well as a D. Phil. in medicine. He also holds a Ph. D. from Cambridge.

Dr. de Bono has held appointments at the universities of Oxford, London, Cambridge and Harvard. He has worked in the Department of Medicine at Cambridge University. He is the founder and director of the Cognitive Research Trust, which develops thinking as a curriculum subject in schools. He is also director of the Centre for the Study of Thinking.

Among his many books are *The Use of Lateral Thinking, The Mechanism of Mind, Technology Today, Practical Thinking, Lateral Thinking for Management, Teaching Thinking, The Greatest Thinkers, Wordpower, The Happiness Purpose* and *Future Positive.* His works have been translated into 17 language.

He is also the author of *Letter to Thinkers,* a publication for those concerned with opportunity development and creative and conceptual thinking. The letter is published ten times a year by Gower Publications, Croft Road, Aldershot, Hampshire GU 113 HR, U.K.

"Opportunities: A Handbook of Business Opportunity Search," by Edward de Bono. Copyright 1978 by European Services Ltd. Published by Associated Business Programmes, L'udgate House, 107-111 Fleet St., London EC4A 2AB England. All rights reserved

"An opportunity is as real an ingredient in business as raw material, labour or finance — but it only exists when you can see it."

Information and ideas. In our management thinking we tend, quite rightly, to rely heavily on information.

Our hunger for information should not, however, blind us to the fact that information alone is insufficient. In addition to information we need ideas. Ideas are the spectacles through which we look at information.

Ideas without information are pretty worthless. Information without ideas can still be useful. The best of all is abundant information supplemented by ideas. The mistake, which so many people make, is to assume that collecting more information will do away with the need for ideas.

Executives are trained to solve problems as they arise. They are not trained to pick out areas in which the generation of ideas could be useful.

But when an executive consciously sets out to find opportunities he quickly finds areas that are in need of ideas. In this way the opportunity search provides a framework that excites and focuses the creativity of executives.

Ideas thrown up for no good reason are rarely used. But ideas generated to satisfy the idea-hunger of an opportunity search are more valuable because they fulfill a need.

We know that market-pull innovation is much more effective than technology-push innovation. So it is with the generation of ideas. The first stage is to generate a need for an idea. The second stage is to generate the idea to fit that need. That is what opportunity search is about.

'An opportunity is a course of action that is possible and obviously worth pursuing.'

What is an opportunity?

To many executives an opportunity is a high-risk speculation. There are better ways of making profits than the pursuit of high-risk speculations. An opportunity does have to be a speculation because it is about the future. In that sense almost all our activities are speculations because we are trying to bring something about and believe that our actions will do this. But the 'high risk' feeling is erroneous. A true opportunity is not a high-risk area. A true opportunity should be obvious in its benefits. What is risked is the thinking time taken to consider an opportunity and to bring it to the stage where it is obviously worth pursuing further.

An executive may have to do a deal of thinking before he

perceives that an opportunity is worth pursuing. It is this appreciation of benefits that motivates anyone to explore an opportunity. As an executive continues his thinking in pursuit of the opportunity the promise of the benefits may wax or wane or go through cycles of either. Further thinking may show the benefits to be illusory or smaller than initially supposed. Further thinking may show that the benefits are as imagined but that the cost and difficulty of achieving them diminish their value to the corporation. All this is thinking time and that is what is being risked.

To turn an idea into a real opportunity requires thinking time and thinking effort. The first purpose of the thinking is to formulate the opportunity idea. The second is to assess the benefits. The third is to work out a course of action that is feasible. It must be self-evident that the better the thinking the less risky is an opportunity.

When an opportunity is defined as 'a course of action that is possible and obviously worth pursuing,' it should not be supposed that the course of action that is worth pursuing refers only to undertaking the whole project. The course of action could just as well refer to getting more information; doing a market study; carrying out further research; or setting up a pilot project. It is the first step that may be obviously worth pursuing and depending on the result of that step the next step may be equally worthwhile. When looking at a large opportunity it is the executive's business to break that down into preliminary steps that are obviously worth pursuing. Even if the only step that is obviously worth pursuing is to ask an expert in the field, that is the step to be taken.

There is no short cut to opportunity search and development. Deliberate thinking time is required. The more of that we can risk the less we risk other resources. Nor should it be imagined that the thinking time is wasted if the opportunity is turned down. That thinking investment may prove useful in another situation later on.

Figure 1 shows in a visual way some approaches to opportunities:

We can look for a simpler and more direct way of achieving what we want.

We may find that by re-thinking what we want to achieve it becomes simpler to reach.

We can look to see whether with our resources and established direction there is something else we could achieve as well.

Direction, destination and means

You can look in a defined direction: north, south, upwards or downwards. Within that direction you may then see several destinations which you may want to reach. It is the same with opportunities. There may be broad directions in which a corporation wishes to look for opportunities or the direction itself may be an opportunity.

The only difference between a direction and a destination is that a direction is broadly defined but a destination can be defined tightly.

Once a destination has been defined it becomes possible to examine the means of getting there. This is a further area of opportunity search. There may be a variety of different routes, many of which are not all obvious until we have discovered them.

Too often it is thought that opportunities only exist in terms of directions that are discussed at corporate strategy level. Far less thought is given to searching for opportunities at the destination level and even less at the means level.

The thinking involved

It is deliberate thinking that will uncover opportunities and turn a fanciful idea into something that is obviously worth pursuing — a true opportunity. Some of this thinking is concerned with information-gathering, assessment and analysis. But a great deal of the thinking — perhaps more than in any other management field — is concerned with perceptual

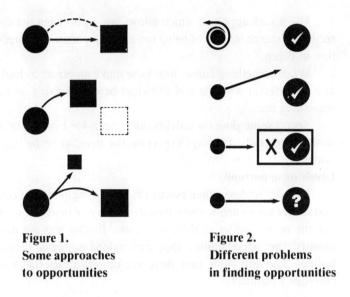

Figure 1.
Some approaches
to opportunities

Figure 2.
Different problems
in finding opportunities

change. Perceptual change involves both what we are looking at and the way we look at it.

Figure 2 suggests that in one case we may fail to see an opportunity that is obviously worthwhile, because we are not looking at all. We are either too content with what we have to bother to look or too busy with our day-to-day survival problems. In the second case there is strong commitment to look for opportunity but the gaze is directed in the wrong direction. In the third case we are indeed looking in the right direction but we cannot identify the opportunity because we are looking at it in the wrong way or because it is lost in the midst of something else. In the fourth case we do see the opportunity but we cannot immediately see its value and therefore have to do some more thinking in order to uncover the value. We can therefore list some simple strategies that could overcome these different problems:

Decide to spend some time and effort in a deliberate search for opportunities.

Use a scan approach which allows you to broaden the direction of search instead of being too eager to pursue one direction in depth.

When something comes into view make an effort to look at it in different ways (lateral thinking) before hurrying on to something else.

Spend some time on a deliberate search for benefits in a situation instead of always expecting the benefits to be self-evident.

Levels of opportunity

In order to discourage executives from imagining that opportunities are someone else's business it may be better to spell out the opportunities at different levels. In this way we can identify the opportunities that are indeed someone else's business and still show that there are opportunities that are everyone's business.

Corporate level

Corporate level opportunities affect the way the corporation is going to behave in the world around it. There may be opportunities for acquisitions, mergers, diversification and such like activities.

Management level

Figure 3 suggests the difference between corporate level and management level opportunities. Management level opportunities are concerned with the running of the organization. Such opportunities may include re-structuring, financial control and accountancy changes, leasing opportunities, personnel policy, cost-cutting exercises, setting up a deliberate opportunity audit structure and all other matters concerned with improving the performance of the organization.

Job level

Job level opportunities arise when a person looks around at the opportunity space created by his own job. It may be a matter of time management, of delegation, of consultation, of simplifying procedures, of changing habits, of developing new

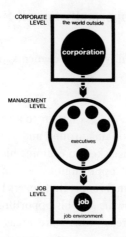

CORPORATE
LEVEL
the world outside

corporation

MANAGEMENT
LEVEL

executives

JOB
LEVEL
job
job environment

Figure 3. Levels of opportunity

strategies, of learning, of putting aside time for opportunity
search. A corporate strategist has two opportunity levels. His
job level allows him to consider what opportunities there might
be for improving his performance as a strategist, whilst at the
corporate level he considers the opportunities for the corporation. The same thing applies at management level where an executive may be looking for management opportunities and also
job level opportunities.

Personal level

Personal level opportunities are concerned with self-
development, self-actualization (in Maslow's terms), promotion opportunities, mobility opportunities, status opportunities
and all the various things which lead to the advancement of a
person.

Elements of the Opportunity Search Exercise (OPEX)

The four Opportunity Search elements are:

1. Opportunity Audit

The Opportunity Audit is similar to a financial audit. It is a survey, a review, a looking around and a stock-taking. Once a year each executive is asked to examine his own opportunity space and to see what opportunities he can find in it. He is asked to prepare a formal report that covers the following matters: description of how he sees his opportunity space; a list of four 'idea-sensitive areas' which are areas in which opportunities can be developed; a specific opportunity objective on which he would like to work, including benefits, plan of action and help needed; opportunities outside his own opportunity space — in other divisions or departments or on a corporate level.

The Opportunity Audit is then followed up at intervals of four months by reports which detail the progress that has been made towards the chosen opportunity objective.

2. Opportunity Manager

The Opportunity Manager is the central organizer of the opportunity search exercise. It is his responsibility to set up, coordinate and orchestrate the whole structure. His role is that of an organizer and liaison officer. He does not try to determine the direction of opportunity search but he sets up the framework within which executives can choose their own directions. He sets the Opportunity Audit in motion and collects the results. He acts as general communication channel, facilitator and ombudsman in the whole opportunity area. He creates communication channels with different departments, senior management, outside consultants and individual executives as required. He does not, however, choose the Opportunity Team nor chair its discussions.

3. Opportunity Team

The Opportunity Team is a permanent body though the membership may rotate. This team has ultimate responsibility for opportunity search, development and coordination within the corporation. The team is independent of such division as R & D or Strategic Planning though it may work closely with them from time to time. The Opportunity Team receives all the opportunity Audits as input. It may also generate its own input from the outside world or from within the corporation. The Opportunity Team surveys, consolidates and evaluates the opportunity objectives put forward in the audits. The Opportunity Team allocates opportunity development resources from a specific budget or may recommend an opportunity to R & D, Marketing or any other department. The Opportunity Team may also provide information, liaison or organizational help as requested by an individual executive in his opportunity audit.

Where more than local help is required the Opportunity Team is responsible for putting together an Opportunity Task Force to tackle an opportunity.

4. Opportunity Task Force

This is no different from any other task force. It is project-oriented and comes into effect to tackle a specified opportunity. An Opportunity Task Force is set up by the Opportunity Team whenever it seems that a specific opportunity, generated by the audit, cannot be handled by the executive concerned even with additional help. The task force should, however, include the executive who has suggested the opportunity. The task force may consist of only one person or of a group of people from different departments. It may include outside consultants or the specific task may be delegated to an outside consultancy in the first place; for example, market research or a feasibility study. The task force may have an information-gathering role, a liaison or negotiating role, a project development role or a focused management role. For example, an Opportunity Task Force may have responsibility for a project that is being worked upon in the R & D division.

Purpose

The purpose of these four elements is to provide two things: focused attention on opportunities and channels of action. For those familiar with matrix management the elements have a staff rather than a line function. The Opportunity Team is, however, more than an advisory body. It must be able to take some action on its own. In a way it is the Opportunity Conscience of the organization.

Value

We can summarize the value of the opportunity search exercise as follows:
1. Executives are given a chance to stand back from daily chores in order to focus upon opportunities.
2. The exercise increases an executive's perception of his opportunity space and can enhance job interest.
3. A formal upward communication channel is provided.
4. The exercise encourages initiative by asking for it.

'Opportunity space is defined by all the worthwhile things we have in our power to do — if only we could think of them.'

Opportunity space

It is not much use tossing out ideas if no one is willing or able to catch them. Similarly, it is not much use dreaming up opportunities if no one is willing or able to do anything about them. The 'receivability' of an idea, or an opportunity, matters as much as the idea itself. That is why the Opportunity Audit starts by asking executives to define their opportunity space. If an opportunity falls within a person's opportunity space then that person can act on the opportunity. So if an executive starts by paying attention to his ability to 'receive' an opportunity he is more likely to think of opportunities upon which he can act.

Definition of opportunity space

'If an opportunity is within our opportunity space then we can act upon it.' That is the simplest and best definition — but it is not much use for describing our opportunity spaces. The opportunity space includes all the changes, decisions and choices that we can make. It includes the assets we are using and the actions we can take:

'I can make changes in these areas.'

'These are the decisions I can make.'

'These choices are up to me.'

'I can take action of this sort.'

'I have the use of these assets.'

Opportunity space defines both our freedom of action and also the assets we have. Such assets may include time, know-how and contacts.

Examination of opportunity space

In carrying out an examination of his own opportunity space an executive should pay attention to the areas listed below.

Areas of activity. List the different areas of activity and consider the available freedom of action, choice and decision within each of them.

Types of operation. Go through the different types of activity or operation that occur within the job description. How much opportunity space is there in the carrying out of these operations? Does one take the stereotyped approach for granted? Has the rigidity of an approach ever been challenged?

Reaction patterns: Examine the reactions that are expected in different situations. If someone swears at you it is within your opportunity space to swear back, shrug or smile.

Attaching importance or assessing priorities usually lies within an individual's opportunity space.

Example of opportunity space

A person whose work involves giving seminars to executives might describe his opportunity space as follows:

'Opportunity to alter the presentation and to try out new methods. Opportunity to collect new examples and stories for future use as illustration. Opportunity to study the thinking of those attending the seminar. Opportunity to carry out simple experiments of a psychological nature. Opportunity to test the reaction to new concepts. Opportunity to clarify one's own ideas as they are explained or defended. Opportunity to have one's own ideas changed or improved. Opportunity to make contacts. Opportunity to make friends. Opportunity to arrange further work of a consultancy or in-house nature. Opportunity to learn about different types of industry. Opportunity to learn about business climate in different types of industry. Opportunity to put people in touch with one another or to provide contacts. Opportunity to recommend or praise a colleague. Opportunity to find out which type of promotion was most effective in bringing participants to the seminar.'

Description of opportunity space

The degree of detail used in the description of the opportunity space is important. Generalities should be avoided because, although they do cover what is implied by them, they do not serve to direct attention.

Purpose of opportunity space description

The first purpose is to increase an awareness of those areas in which there is freedom of action. From an effort to describe the opportunity space can come a consciousness of opportunities. In some instances the description of the space will almost be a list of opportunities.

The second purpose is to define, in advance, the type of opportunity that is 'receivable' so that when one sets out to develop opportunities these can be treated in such a manner as to make them fall within the opportunity space.

Job description and opportunity space

Opportunity space describes the space in which changes can be effected. A job description describes the expected role of the executive. A careful look at a job description may lead to some awareness of the opportunity space that exists in the job. To say that an executive is expected to make buying decisions is to describe his job; to say that he has flexibility in negotiating the price, arranging the payment terms, choosing the seller and choosing what is to be bought is to describe his opportunity space. Opportunity space is space for change and initiative.

'If a situation seems likely to be affected by an idea then we may call that situation an idea-sensitive area.'

Idea-sensitive areas (i. s. a.) and general opportunities

An idea-sensitive area is an area which seems fertile for the development of an opportunity. It is an area in which further thinking may uncover a definite opportunity. It is an opportunity-rich area. The benefits arising from an idea in that area are obvious — all that is required is the idea. A general opportunity is a trend or direction which seems to offer benefits. An idea-sensitive area is an area to look at in order to find an opportunity. A general opportunity is a direction within which a more specific opportunity may be formulated.

An idea-sensitive area (i. s. a) is an area where an idea will make a considerable difference. In other words, it is an area where it is *worthwhile* to try to generate ideas. All idea-sensitive areas are important but not all important areas are sensitive to ideas.

Philosophically the distinction between an i. s. a and a general opportunity would be hard to sustain. In practice, however, the distinction is useful. An executive may be able to focus upon an area where the benefits arising from an idea would be considerable. He has set out to look for an i. s. a. Another executive may prefer to think in terms of general opportunities: by examining assets, circumstances, traditional ideas and attitudes.

With an i. s. a. we identify a worthwhile area. With a general opportunity we start thinking about an area and see if this thinking leads to a general opportunity.

'Thinking is the operating skill whereby intelligence acts upon experience.'

Review of fundamental thinking processes

In this section I intend to review the fundamental thinking processes. Most people regard thinking as a fairly straightforward process: 'Give me the facts and I will give you the logical conclusion.' This is a very limited view of thinking and completely excludes the sort of creative exploration that is essential for opportunity search.

We can define thinking as 'the purposeful exploration of our experience maps.' The excellence of our mind arises from the function of the brain as a pattern-making system that allows incoming information to form itself into patterns that can be stored and used.

We can start by considering some of the basic operations that we carry out when thinking. These familiar operations are really 'intentions' — they are operations which we intend to carry out. In carrying them out we may use a whole range of mental activities.

Focus

This is the most important and the most difficult thinking operation. It is difficult precisely because it seems so simple and so obvious. There are few people who can choose to focus their attention on something and keep it there. That is why 'checklists' of attention areas are so useful as a help to thinking. If an executive is asked to focus on the short-term benefits of an opportunity, he will find no difficulty in doing so, but left to his own devices he might have only considered benefits in a general, rather vague, way. Our language device of the 'question' is there in order to get us to focus. Asking the right question of others and also of ourselves is a key part of thinking. We can also direct our attention by having a defined area in which to look.

Analysis

This is the operation with which most executives will be at ease. Our education system pays a good deal of attention to analysis and so does management training. In order to cope with the world we have to treat it in 'chunks.' We look at a bicycle, or cash-flow, or sales figures. Each of these chunks contains a large number of ingredients; sales figures for each week or for each district or for each salesman; sales figure for the different products, etc. In short, in analysis we look beneath the 'chunk' in order to see the components. In science we look beneath the effect in order to see the interacting causes.

Abstraction

In this operation — also familiar but a good deal more difficult than analysis — we seek to extract the general principles or mechanisms that seem to be operating in a situation. We seek to separate the principle from the particular situation. I prefer to call the operation 'function extraction.' The ability to extract and deal with functions is very important for creative thinking. The difficulty arises because many people can only see things in concrete terms and feel uncomfortable dealing with abstractions which seem theoretical. There is an even greater difficulty in knowing the most useful level of abstraction. For example we might say of a bicycle:

'A transport device.'

'A one-person transport device.'

'A one-person transport device which uses no outside fuel.'

'A one-person transport device with two wheels that is driven by turning a crank with the legs.'

Words like 'device,' 'thing,' 'mechanism,' 'process' allow one to describe the function without spelling out the details. There is considerable skill involved in making the most fertile abstractions.

Alternatives (lateral thinking)

There is no *logical* reason for looking for alternatives unless we are dissatisfied with what we have. And yet in creativity it is vital to be looking for alternatives no matter how satisfied we may be. There therefore has to be a deliberate intention or exercise of will to seek alternatives. The challenge process comes in here. It is often necessary to challenge something that seems perfectly adequate in order to explore alternatives. If we understand creativity such a challenge is indeed logical, but if we do not understand, it seems absurd to challenge something which is satisfactory. Curiously we do not have a verb to describe the need to look for alternatives. That is why it was necessary to create the term 'lateral thinking.'

Synthesis

The opposite of analysis. We put together different ingredients or pieces of information to arrive at a whole. The pieces may themselves have been obtained from analysis. Planning, problem-solving and prediction all make use of synthesis. We construct scenarios of the future from past experience and an analysis of present trends and influences.

Search, judgment and matching

Another very familiar process. We scan our experience to find something that matches what we have in mind. We might have a mental image of the executive we need for some particular role and then we scan through all the executives to see which one matches the requirements. With judgment the situation presents itself and we see whether it matches the requirements or criteria we wish to apply. Matching itself is the operation of putting two things side by side in our minds and commenting upon the points of similarity or difference. It may also consist of constructing something to match a pre-chosen set of requirements. For example, we might set out to construct an opportunity that matches pre-chosen characteristics of cash-flow, time scale, capital needs and so on.

Modification

It involves judgement, analysis, synthesis, abstraction and alternative search but it deserves an entry of its own because as an 'intention' it does not arise from these other intentions. With modification we take something as it is, for example an idea, and proceed to change it by a process of forced evolution. This process may involve removing faults or improving general characteristics such as simplicity or it may involve moulding the idea towards some desired shape.

Provocation

This operation is important for creativity. It is a definite part of lateral thinking. We can summarize the process by the statement: 'There may be not a reason for saying something until after it has been said.' All our traditional thinking is based on the logical reaction to information. The conclusions or statements we derive are soundly based on this information. With provocation this is not so. A provocative statement need have no logical connection with the existing state of affairs. It is used precisely in order to provoke new ideas. The importance of a provocative statement is 'where it gets us ' not 'where it has come from.' A provocation is a mental experiment — in order to see what happens.

'Moving-in' and 'moving-out' as modes of thinking

The difference between 'moving-out' and 'moving-in' is illustrated with standardized symbols in Figure 4. In the moving-out mode we have a starting point. We then move out from the starting point. We do have a general idea that we are looking for situations that could be beneficial but this is only a flavour at this state. We move along from idea to idea until something begins to look promising. We then try to crystallize this idea. When we have a definite idea we see if we can tailor or transform it so that it becomes worthwhile.

In the moving-out mode there is a great deal of exploration and experimentation. We may find ourselves considering ideas we have never thought of before. Each idea we have acts as a sort of provocation towards another idea, just as each mountain scaled enabled us to see the route to the next one.

In the moving-in mode we know where we want to end up and we know what we have to deal with. This is more like ordinary problem-solving. We react to information and analyse it to produce the best answer that is consistent with that information. This is standard management behaviour. In opportunity search, however, we may only know the 'type' of situation we wish to reach without knowing the exact situation.

These two modes of thinking are quite distinct and it is important to appreciate the distinction. In the moving-in mode a line of thought which does not lead towards the desired end-point will not be taken but in the moving-out mode it will be. Yet the two modes are complementary. In the course of solving a closed problem one may have to use some creative speculation in order to open up a new approach. In the course of tailoring a speculative idea towards a useful idea one has to use the moving-in mode.

For the moving-out mode the important thing is to have a starting point. Later in the process a clear definition of usefulness has to be brought in right at the beginning through the acceptance of the desired end-point. So one mode has a starting point and the other has an end-point. Both of them are directed towards finding real opportunities.

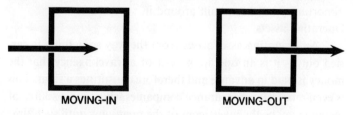

MOVING-IN   MOVING-OUT

Figure 4. Modes of thinking

'In order to get going we need a starting point for our thinking. There is no harm in making a formal checklist of such starting points.'

Starting point check-list

The check-list of starting points set out in this section is not exhaustive nor is it meant to be novel. Some of the starting points are more appropriate to certain businesses and certain individuals.

Intrinsic Assets

Intrinsic assets can include cash, land, capital equipment and plant of any sort, people, a strong brand image, distribution channels and distribution outlets, market position, patents and licenses, know-how, experience, technology, existing services and products, etc. As an illustration, the intrinsic assets of a brand image like Kelloggs can be used to launch other food products. Failure in an area can also be an intrinsic asset because the experience built up in the course of that failure may have a value if applied elsewhere. Market muscle and know-how are assets which can be applied to products which others have failed to launch. The question, 'Where do our strengths lie?' will uncover many intrinsic assets but by no means all, for an important asset may not be regarded as a strength until an opportunity has been built around it.

Operating assets

An operating asset arises from the way something is carried out — it is an operating asset of a travel agency that the money is paid in advance and therefore constitutes a float. This is even more true of insurance companies whose main source of income may be the investment of the premiums until such time as they are paid out in claims. There is often an overlap between intrinsic assets and operating assets but it is useful to keep the distinction as a help towards focusing on the particular way in which something is done. A car and a driving license are both intrinsic assets but the fact that you drive past a certain place each morning is an operating asset.

Situation assets

A situation asset is an asset that depends on the current 'situation' or circumstances. Usually it arises from a change in circumstances.

In looking for opportunities arising from situation assets the trick is to go further than saying, 'How does that change affect us?' It is more a matter of saying, 'What new situation has arisen? Does this new situation offer any opportunities? Are these opportunities of interest to us?'

'Left behind'

As we get better and better at doing something we tend to 'leave behind' areas which could develop as new opportunities.

In focusing on this area of what has been 'left behind' it is important to be honest about what is being done well and about the direction that is being taken. Once this has been defined the next step is to see what has been left behind. The third step is to see whether any opportunities can emerge from what has been left behind. The fourth step is to ascertain the size and profitability of the opportunity.

Synergy

Synergy occurs when two or more assets are combined to give a benefit which is greater than the sum of the separate parts. In practice the opportunity-seeker may look around for complementary activities such as the combination of petrol stations and supermarkets.

Synergy is not the same as simplification. If two parts of an organization are collecting information it may make sense to combine the two collecting functions— this is simplification. There is, however, a synergy between selling and doing market research.

Variable value

The classic instance of variable value is when one person's waste becomes another's source of profits.

An English-speaking person in England has little chance of using his ability to speak English as a source of income. But if he were to go to Brazil he might find that he could make a living just by giving private lessons in English to business executives.

Variable value means that the value resides not in the things itself but in the value to the person who is selling it and the value to the person who is receiving it.

The concept of variable value is one of the most fundamental in opportunity search because in the end all business is based on the concept that the value to the buyer is rather higher than the value to the maker and it is this added value that has to provide return on investment.

Although there is an overlap, this consideration of variable value is not the same as value analysis. Value analysis considers the true value within a fixed context: variable value consideration alters the context to see if the value alters.

Challenge

'Challenge' is a basic mental process which is used to challenge complacency and the taking for granted of existing operations. By applying the challenge process we can make a starting point out of anything. In our minds we say: 'If we challenge the way this is now done might we come up with a different way which will cut costs, increase profits or expand the market?'

Ordinary criticism has its use but it is different from challenge. The reason we need to challenge things which are beyond criticism is that there can be considerable potential in this area.

'De-averaging'

The process of market segmentation is well known. Instead of treating a market as a whole an attempt is made to break it down into different segments which have different needs and tastes and then to cater for each of these. The 'de-averaging' process is very similar.

The Laker Sky-train concept is an attempt to de-average transatlantic airline passengers into those who need to get there on time and in comfort and those who want to get there in the cheapest possible way and do not mind about comfort or schedules.

In practical terms the de-averaging concept can be applied to customers, processes, people at work, products or anything else. The question to ask is: 'What are we dealing with here? Is there an average concept which could be broken down?'

Significant point

It is a very useful exercise when reading a newspaper or a magazine to try to pick out the significant point in the piece that is being read. This significant point is in the general context of opportunities. For example, an article which mentions that fifty-three per cent of married women in England go out to work might have as its significant point the forty-seven per cent who do not go out to work. Is this because they do not need to or do not want to or cannot? This might lead to ideas of developing work which can be done at home or even the Avon lady type of home sales force.

It is a useful exercise to practice picking out significant points and constructing an opportunity context around them. Even if there is not much success at first the opportunity habit of mind that may be developed in this way will prove useful elsewhere.

Disadvantage into advantage

Almost everyone knows the story of the salmon-canners whose product no one wanted to buy because it was much paler than customers expected salmon to be. But sales picked up as soon as the product was advertised as 'the only pale salmon.' This classic tale of turning disadvantage into advantage illustrates a starting point that can be used for opportunity search.

'Under what circumstances . . .'

This is a variation of the preceding starting point. It need not, however, apply only to a disadvantage. It could apply to any characteristic or feature or activity. Under what circumstances would that characteristic become a distinct advantage or open up an opportunity? The 'clearing-out sale' label is often used to give credibility to low prices.

'What business are we in?'

This is a fairly traditional approach. The answer to the question provides the starting point for opportunity thinking.

The question 'what business are we in?' can be transformed to 'what are we trying to do?' when it is the work situation itself that is under scrutiny.

Me-too

The 'me-too' concept is the most obvious and perhaps the safest source of opportunities even though it may not be very satisfying intellectually. The entry of Kodak into the instant photography market in competition with Polaroid was a delayed example of me-too. The success of *Penthouse* magazine was a me-too as regards the concept established by *Playboy*.

The logic of the me-too situation is sound. Someone else has shown that a market exists. Someone else has developed the market and spent money doing so. Someone else has made the mistakes and learned from them. It makes sense to move in with a parallel product and reap the benefits of the experience of others — no matter how unfair it may seem.

The me-too temptations are not without danger. The market may not be big enough for two major suppliers. The result is a price or promotion war which reduces the profitability of the opportunity.

Brought in from abroad

Bringing something in from abroad is a sort of 'me-too' operation except that it is usually done by agreement or licensing.

Obviously it does not follow that a product which has been a success in one country will repeat that success elsewhere. Each market has different characteristics.

A periodic eyes-open trip round the world should be part of the opportunity search process. The large trade fairs help in this respect but do not make unnecessary a visit to the actual marketplace of the shops and stores.

Bringing in something from abroad applies to ideas and processes as much as to products.

Market size

It is usually the growth of a market, in terms of a trend, that is more appealing than the actual size. Size itself is more often used as a reason for not entering a market — on the basis that it is not large enough. Nevertheless where a market is huge there is a temptation to get in there and get a piece of the action.

Paradoxically there are opportunities to be found in a declining market. The major producers may be getting out of the market so fast that there is an unfilled need.

Trends

Another traditional source of opportunities: trends in leisure behaviour, trends in market growth and so on.

Spotting a trend and getting in early with a good product has always been the classic recipe for opportunity.

A trend away from something becomes, in practice, a trend towards something else. A trend away from identical mass production in cars may become a trend towards individualized cars or replicas of famous marques of the past. It can be useful to identify trends as being away from something because the opportunity seeker may then put in his own destination, such as car livery designed by famous artists.

Focus on areas of weakness and areas of strength

'What are the areas of strength in the organization?' We can list those areas and then look at each in turn to see whether there are any opportunities that arise from them. If management services are a strength, there may be an opportunity to take over companies that are less well run. If distribution channels are the strength new me-too products or products from abroad may be fed through the channels.

In the same way it is possible to list the areas of weakness and to generate opportunities from these. An ailing part of an organization may be sold off to someone else to whom it may be more useful (variable value). A multiplicity of unprofitable products can be simplified. Undifferentiated (commodity-type) products can be differentiated. Packaging can be changed. An area of weakness should not be regarded as an area for 'patching-up' but as a high opportunity area that merits focused thinking attention.

Idea-sensitive areas

The concept of the i. s. a. (idea-sensitive area) was introduced earlier. Such an area might be a high-cost area or a bottleneck or a problem area or a high-pay-off opportunity area. Obviously an i. s. a. provides an ideal starting point for opportunity search.

Provocation

Provocation is part of lateral thinking. It is an attempt to switch our thinking channel by taking a provocative jump.

There are many ways of setting up a provocation and the simplest is to take the existing situation and reverse it. The food-processing department of a major company were used to taking the fish bones out of the fish. As a provocation they decided to try to take the fish away from the bones.

There is no way of telling where a provocation will lead. The provocation provides the starting point and ideas that develop are followed. All the time there is an attempt to shape the idea into a practical opportunity. The process has three stages:

'Let's set up a provocation.'

'Where does the provocation lead?'

'How can we transform this into a practical idea?'

Transfer

This is really a special form of provocation. We look at an unconnected operation and see how we can transfer the methods and process to our own operation.

As a starting point procedure the transfer operation is easy to use. You fix your attention on some other industry and then move mentally through its operations noting at each stage what transfer or provocative value they may have. The other industry may be chosen at random or because it seems to be parallel in operation to one's own.

'With a problem we can define, in advance, the desired destination or end-point of our thinking.'

End-point check-list

Idea-sensitive areas

An i. s. a. may be either a starting point ('We have the ability to mould plastic more cheaply than anyone else, how can we use the asset?') or an end point ('We have a very high cost of distribution, how can we reduce that?').

An i. s. a. should not be defined in the same way as a problem. For example, the i. s. a. of the high cost of seminar publicity should not really be defined as: 'How can we reduce the high cost of seminar publicity?' but rather as: 'The high cost of seminar publicity is an i. s. a.' From the latter definition we can think about reducing costs but we could also think in terms of making more profitable use of the incurred costs, by offering seminar packages for example. Within an i. s. a. several different problem definitions, objectives and starting points can be tried.

The 'something' method

In this method we define our end point by defining the characteristics the final idea should have. For example, in looking for a mail order product we might say: 'We need "something" that is small in size, not easily damaged, easy to illustrate, with a high profit margin and with a naturally focused market.' We then set about looking for 'something'.

The words 'something', 'someone', 'some way', 'a device', 'a method', 'a means', 'mechanism', 'a procedure', 'a person' and 'an idea' are all general purpose terms that are interchangeable with 'something'. Rather more specific terms in-

242

clude words like 'a product' or 'an incentive.' On the whole it is better to avoid those. It is better to say, 'We need some way of motivating our salesmen other than by money', than to say, 'We need to look at salesmen's incentives other than money'. This is because the more specific the definition the more it locks out.

Market gaps

The classic type of gap is the 'in-between' gap where two things are being done but there is a gap in between. A classic example is the 'Mastermind' game marketed by Invicta Ltd. It was marketed at about L1. At a lower price range there were any number of small, pocket-type games which were too cheap to be given as a Christmas present. At a higher price range (L3-4) were more substantial games which involved a definite buying decision and were too expensive to give as casual presents. The Invicta game was substantial enough to be given as a present and yet cheap enough to be added on to other purchases.

'Combination-gaps' are useful areas for opportunity search. Two things might be done separately but bringing them together creates a new opportunity — such as, a holiday and organized shopping service in London for overseas visitors; a combined gardening and house maintenance contract; or a good shop and take-away food service.

Doing something no one else wants to do has always provided good opportunities. The new business of 'waste management' or city refuse handling is an example.

Then there are 'transfer-gaps' where we transfer a marketing method from one field to another. Disposable pens to disposable lighters to disposable razors (the Bic Company). The gap is seen as the lack of that marketing method in a particular field.

Needs

The Babycham story is one of the classics of need satisfaction in the UK. Women were beginning to go into pubs with their boyfriends. They did not like the taste of beer and it was still considered unfeminine to grasp large glasses of beer. There was a need for a new 'dainty' mildly alcoholic drink especially for women. And that was where Babycham came in as a perry-based drink sold in elegant small bottles with heavy promotional backing. It provided the needed answer at the moment when the question was asked: 'And what can I order for you?' It could also be seen as filling a gap in the drinks market.

Indirect needs or ancillary needs are an important area for opportunity search. The growth of mini-computers might create a need for advisers, brokers, service engineers or a second-hand market.

Objectives

If we know what we want to do that constitutes an end-point for our thinking. Challenging and altering an objective may provide an opportunity. Finding quicker or cheaper ways of achieving an objective would also provide an opportunity. Setting up an objective is itself a definition of an opportunity.

Sometimes we can go directly towards an objective. At other times it may be possible to move towards the objectives by a route which actually opens up new opportunities on the way.

Wishful thinking

'Wouldn't it be nice if we could keep our order book full by building a unique type of ship which other yards could not imitate,' would be an example of wishful thinking. Once the fantasy objective has been stated, in general 'something' terms, then we can start thinking towards it. Occasionally, having thought the unthinkable it becomes thinkable in the same way as Margaret Thatcher's unthinkable bid for leadership of the British Conservative party suddenly became fact. More often the thinking that takes place towards a fantasy objective will turn up useful opportunity ideas on the way even though the fantasy remains a fantasy.

'Wouldn't it be nice if we could carry out that operation

with one man instead of two.' 'Wouldn't it be nice if we could mould dozens at once instead of doing them singly.' 'Wouldn't it be nice if we could predict the price of coffee for twelve months ahead.'

'Wouldn't it be nice if all my customers became selling agents on my behalf' could lead to concepts of pyramid selling or the Avon cosmetics type operation. It could also, indirectly, lead to the idea of selling kits and so allowing the buyer to be his own manufacturer — from the extracted principle that the purchaser helps the seller in some way additional to just buying.

Defects

A defect implies an assumption about what things should be. It is in questioning these assumptions as well as in remedying the defect that opportunities may be found.

A defect often implies something missing — a gap. As usual it is much more difficult to focus upon something that is not there than upon something that is wrong. The trick is to use the 'opportunities' inherent in the existing situation.

Faults

In practice there is little distinction between defects and faults but it is worth making a distinction so that we can have two entries on our check-list, and hence two opportunities to focus our attention. So we can define a defect as 'something which falls short of expectations.' And we define a fault as 'something which is better removed, something which contributes negatively to the value of what we are doing.' If we are giving in a product much more value than the customer wants or is willing to pay for, then that is a fault. If our advertising turns away certain potential customers even though it attracts others that is a fault.

The simple rule is:

'What does this product lack?' (defects).

'What would we like to do away with?' (faults).

It is best to make a deliberate list of defects and of faults and then to go through this list spending some thinking time at each entry. It is worth discussing such lists with others for what may appear to be an obvious fault to one person may not be a fault at all to another.

Quality improvements

Here we define a direction in advance and then see if we can improve what we are doing towards the direction indicated.

Common quality directions include: customer appeal, cost-effectiveness, reliability, simplicity, efficiency, servicing costs, production efficiency, quality (in terms of apparent value), brand distinction and so on.

Problem-solving

By definition any problem is also an opportunity. A problem arises from our awareness that there is something we want because it would be to our advantage — and that is the definition of an opportunity.

We can consider some basic approaches to problem-solving.

Stock solutions. This is a matter of applying experience. We try to recognize the problem and having done so we search through our repertoire of stock solutions and find the one that fits the problem. Then we apply it and solve the problem. This is the sort of problem-solving that is used by doctors, lawyers, engineers, accountants and business executives. The trouble arises when a problem is mistakenly identified as a classic problem and treated as such when it is different.

Constructed solutions: If there is no ready-made solution, we have to build one. We analyze that problem and break it down into its different components or sub-problems. We then try to find or develop a solution for each sub-problem. Finally these solutions are fitted together to give the overall solution. The major process involved in constructed solutions is analysis in order to create sub-problems for which stock solution can be found.

Working backwards: We take the desired solution and then work backwards from it towards our starting point. When we have reached our starting point the problem is solved. It is important when using the working backwards procedure to work backwards from the desired end state and not from a proposed solution.

Re-definition of the problem. Here we challenge the problem itself. Instead of accepting the problem and solving it, we question whether we are looking at the right problem: 'Is this really the question we should be asking?;' 'Why do we want to solve this problem?;' 'What do we really want to do?' Too often we assume that our first perception of the problem is the correct one and that all we have to do is to solve it.

Provocation. The provocation method has been mentioned above. Provocation involves an apparently unreasonable step which is taken in order to get our ideas flowing in a different direction.

Upstream problem avoidance: Instead of solving the problem we move upstream and take a route which does not allow the problem to develop. This procedure is said to be much favoured by NASA. Instead of improving a faulty component the effort is directed towards changing the procedure so the component is not needed in the first place.

Although problem-solving is an important part of the opportunity search exercise an executive should be aware of the danger of confining his opportunity-seeking to problem-solving. It would be easy to take this line because problems are concrete and staring one in the face whereas other opportunities do not exist until they have been discovered. Since there will always be enough problems to occupy fully an executive's thinking he will need to make an effort to go through the starting-point and end-point check-lists in order to develop other opportunities.

'Like a new born baby a new idea must, at first, be nourished by care and indulgent attention.'

The treatment of ideas

Having once focused on a starting point, ideas usually start to emerge. The two starting-point check-lists provided in preceding sections ought to give rise to some ideas about opportunities. The next stage — and perhaps the most important — is the treatment of these ideas. Very rarely is a new idea born in the full glory of its potential. At first an idea may be weak, dull or even impractical. Like an infant, the new idea needs proper handling if it is to develop its potential. It may be a matter of cosseting one's own ideas or it may be a matter of nourishing the ideas of others.

Paradoxically the best way to encourage a positive attitude towards emerging ideas is to develop confidence in the ruthlessness of one's final judgement. Many executives kill an apparently unpromising idea at birth because they do not want to waste time on it or because they fear they might be led astray by it. An executive who has confidence in the ruthlessness of his ultimate judgement can afford to nourish new ideas because he knows that in the end the idea will be thrown out if it cannot prove itself. To be afraid to play around with a new idea actually betrays a lack of confidence in judgement rather than the exercise of realism.

It is not easy to sit down and pluck a brilliant idea out of the empty air. It is much more practical to take a thought and to work upon it so as to form it into a useful new idea. This treatment of ideas is perhaps the most important part of creativity. In this section I shall indicate some of the problems and processes involved.

The killer phrase

There is one phrase which kills instantly at birth an untold number of potentially valuable ideas. This killer phrase is the expression 'the same as . . .' A person comes up with an idea and immediately another person pounces on the idea and says: 'That is the same as . . .'

The result is that the idea is dismissed and gets no more attention. If it does get attention it is henceforth treated exactly as if it were the old idea (with which it had something in common) and the value of the new slant is completely lost. In either case the idea is virtually killed.

The answer to the killer phrase is as follows: 'Yes, in some respects this new idea is similar to the old one you mention but I invite you to join me in focusing on the points of difference in order to see if we can develop a new idea.' The proposer of the idea should also make an effort to point out the differences.

Function extraction

Function extraction involves taking a concrete example and extracting from it the 'function' or 'general principle.' I shall be using the words 'function' and 'principle' interchangeably. Function extraction is related to the 'something' method that was described in a preceding section. It is a matter of dealing with process rather than with things: 'What is the process here?;' 'What is happening here?;' 'What function is this thing performing?'

The PMI

PMI stands for Plus, Minus and Interesting. Perhaps the commonest fault in thinking is 'instant judgement.' An idea is proposed and the listener instantly judges whether or not he likes it. His thinking is then directed to supporting and rationalizing this instant judgement. Indeed, the more skilled he is at thinking the less chance will he ever have of exploring the idea because his support of the instant judgement will be complete enough.

In practice the PMI means that if a person does not like an

idea he is nevertheless forced to spend some time looking for the plus points and interesting points. It also means that if a person does like an idea he is forced to make himself aware of the negative points.

Provocation and stepping stones

Normally we treat a suggested idea as something to be judged. Do we like the idea or not? Do we like what it would lead to or not? We judge whether the idea would work. We judge whether the idea would be practical for us. Even if we have a positive attitude of mind or are doing a PMI we are nevertheless making judgements.

The 'stepping stone' process means that we make no attempt whatsoever to judge an idea. We use the idea purely as a mental stepping stone to get to a new idea. The purpose of a stepping stone in a stream is to allow us to get across to pastures new. We step on to the stepping stone only to step off it again. We do not even have to keep our balance on the stepping stone if we move off smartly enough.

Tailoring an idea

Generating an idea involves creativity but tailoring that idea so that it becomes practicable involves just as much creativity.

Tailoring may involve simple modification to an idea to get rid of some obvious disadvantages. Tailoring may also involve a change in scale. Sometimes an idea may seem too expensive and yet a change of scale can make the idea feasible. Often tailoring involves extracting the principle of an idea and then incorporating this in a more practical form.

The difference between tailoring and screening can be expressed quite succinctly. 'Is this idea of any use to us?' is replaced by, 'Can we tailor this idea to suit our situation?' In tailoring we cut the coat to fit both the cloth that is available (the opportunity-user) and the wearer (the market).

The DPA rating

Where an idea is concerned with a new way of doing

something the DPA rating can provide a convenient device for allowing people to express their view. 'D' stands for 'difference': how different is the new suggestion? 'P' stands for practical: how practical is the new suggestion? 'A' stands for advantages: what advantages does the new suggestion offer? The rating is given out of a maximum of ten points or a hundred. An idea may be rated ten out of ten for difference if it really is novel. But it may get only two out of ten for practicality and only three out of ten for advantage. Another idea may get a high rating both for difference and for practicality but may offer no special advantages over the existing method. Packaging the three aspects of consideration together ensures that each gets some attention. It also emphasizes that novelty or difference as such do not create an opportunity for change.

Spell it out

This is a request that a person may make of himself or of another. It is surprisingly easy to talk about an idea in a general way and yet never spell it out in concrete terms. Vague ideas evaporate when an attempt is made to spell them out either in writing or verbally.

There comes a time when an idea has to be made concrete in order that the gaps and deficiencies can be seen.

As with some procedures mentioned in this section, the spell-it-out procedure is not meant to be used in a critical or destructive manner. It is meant to help the development of the idea.

Information available and information required

Clarification of what is known and what is not yet known is part of the treatment of an idea. To know clearly what information is still needed is an important part of the treatment of an idea. It is different from mere ignorance. A person who knows that he has to find out the current price of paper is in a different position from someone who has ignored that price even though neither of them knows the answer.

Satisfy and define

There are two types of request which a listener may make

of someone who is proposing an idea. The first request is: 'Satisfy me.'

The second type of request is: 'Define for me.' In the 'satisfy' request the listener wants to know what the proposer can see. In the 'define' request the listener wants to know in which direction the proposer is looking even if there is nothing to see at the moment.

Any effective thinker should be able to use on his own thinking the requests that are useful when used on the thinking of others. He should be able to detach himself from his own thinking in order to treat it objectively.

'An opportunity may be an opportunity if you can hitch a ride — but not if you have to walk.'

Action structure for opportunity

An action-channel is a course of action from which we are only separated by a decision. Once we have made the decision to take the action then we move smoothly along the action-channel.

An action-channel is an action that is in your power to take.

Channels of effort

Channels of effort are very often distribution or communication channels. If they exist it is no great effort to plug a new idea into the system. If they do not exist the potential of the idea would have to be great enough to justify the risks of setting up special channels for it.

In a complex society the existence of effective channels of effort is often more important for the success of an opportunity than is the new idea itself. The term 'market muscle' means that a company with powerful marketing channels can make a success of a product which is not itself so wonderful.

Delegation

The existence of effective delegation makes an effective action structure for opportunity. Without it an opportunity is likely to die because it would be unusual for everyone to be as enthused about it as the originator.

Fashions, trends and bandwagons

The opportunity-spotter plugs into the energy of a fashion or bandwagon and gets carried along with it. He may decide that pollution is going to be a bandwagon and so he sets up a pollution consulting service. Riding a fashion trend can be very effective because the trend both provides the publicity for the service and creates a need for it. Many successful opportunity-takers have paid more attention to action structures such as these than to the basic idea itself.

Tapping existing energy

Many companies have set out to tap the energy of house-wives who cannot leave home because of having to look after children. Often the work provided tends to be rather low paid: stuffing envelopes, painting toy soldiers and the like.

The Avon cosmetics distribution system made very effective use of the energy and motivation of housewives — making stockists and saleswomen of them. The Tupperware concept was somewhat similar.

Trigger

All opportunity seekers love trigger situations where the right input at the right time can trigger a response quite out of proportion to their efforts.

Once someone shows that something can be done an avalanche of action may be triggered off. The problem for the initiator is to be sure he keeps part of the action.

Amplification

If a lot of people are doing your work for you, your efforts are amplified.

In considering an opportunity it is useful to see whether there are any amplification possibilities in the action structure of that opportunity. Public relations is an effort to involve the amplifying power of the media — at no cost.

Positive feedback

Positive feedback is one way of achieving amplification. A publisher makes a promotion effort with a book. The book gets on to the best-seller list. Because it is there bookshops want to stock it and readers want to buy it. That keeps it on the best-seller list. High sales make more money available for promotion so the publicity effort is increased which further increases readership. A scandal involving a person gives that person publicity value so the next thing the person does gets publicized, and so the process goes on until it reaches the point when a number of people are very well known simply for being well known.

A variation of positive feedback is the repeat customer: once he has bought your product he is more likely to buy from you again. Here his purchase feeds back to increase his willingness to buy.

Contact channels

In some areas contact channels are vital. It may be a matter of knowing the person who makes the decisions or knowing the person who knows the mechanics of the situation. It may be a matter of knowing the person who has the information or who knows where it can be found. Many non-executive directors of large corporations are there because they are the custodians of important contact channels.

'Whenever we are dealing with the future we are dealing with risk and uncertainty and whenever any change is proposed that risk and uncertainty is greatly increased.'

Dealing with risk and uncertainty

It is not surprising that much of business is dealing with risk and uncertainty because all of business is dealing with the future. When we concern ourselves with opportunity we are dealing with greater risk and uncertainty because we have to do much more than predict that an already existing business will go on being successful (the minimal prediction anyone has to make — and it is increasingly difficult to make).

We can now look at the various methods we use in order to reduce risk and uncertainty.

Analysis

This is not as useful as it would seem. Through analysis we seek to treat each component of what we are doing and each component of the market as a factor with a likely mode of action. When we put all these actions together we hope to work out the prognosis. The problem is that subtle outside influences may be neglected and also two separate types of action may, when combined, lead to a third type that is not predictable from the first two. In spite of all this we have to attempt an analysis in order to satisfy ourselves.

Recognition

An experienced person would recognize a trend or the type of reception a new idea was receiving. Recognition is valuable because if it is accurate it leads to sound prediction — just as a doctor recognizing chickenpox or measles can predict the outcome. There is of course the danger of false recognition where a new situation is falsely treated as a recognizable one just because it has some features in common — like a doctor mistaking polio for hysterical paralysis.

Comparison

This is by far the most used and most useful method. We can compare the new product to something already existing in the field or in the experience of our company. We can look at what has happened abroad. We can look back in history and compare what we are doing with what has happened before. Comparison is much less certain than recognition because there may be only points of similarity and we have to decide whether these are important points. Will the firlm on killer whales be as successfully received as was *Jaws?* Is the point of comparison that both are about sea monsters or that sharks have a special terror? Or is it that people go to a cinema to be frightened in mass company— something that they cannot get in front of a television set? Most of our thinking is comparison thinking. But in order to use comparisons we may have to use analysis first to isolate points of comparison. We may also have to use lateral thinking to generate new concepts before comparing one thing with another.

Hunch

Some people would work on hunch or their exquisite sensitivity to a situation. This might mean that the complex computer of their mind has taken in a large number of factors and put these together in a special way to give the hunch that is not open to rational description.

Trends

You observe the trend, you plug your idea into the trend and then you predict the success of your idea from your prediction of the trend.

Market research

Market research can be used to give a factual state of the market: how many people have two cars; how many households do not yet have a refrigerator or deep-freezer. There is no quarrelling with such findings. The interpretation put on them may be open to debate. Are the families without deep-freezers potential future buyers or those families whose eating habits have decided them against a deep-freezer? Even so, are such habits likely to change with better education?

Test runs

Instead of predicting you try it out. You advertise your product in a small area and see what response there is. A test run should be more effective than any other means of prediction because it actually creates a mini-feature which can be observed. The difficulty is that the novelty of the trial may ensure more attention than would be sustained if it were a full run.

Extrapolation

Extrapolation and scaling up are full of dangers. And the dangers can work both ways. A service or product tested on a local level may be a failure but when promoted nationally may be a success.

Feasibility study

We consider a favourable scenario and then work out what is actually involved. A feasibility study shapes the risk and uncertainties so that we can react to them precisely.

Spell it out

A feasibility study is a precise form of the exercise of spelling something out. What are the risks and what are the uncertainties? What is the exposure and what is the fallback position? Spelling out something may reveal that even if the response is excellent the market size is too small and the cost of reaching it too high. Spelling out something may show that an attempt to estimate customer satisfaction is pointless if there is no satisfactory way or bringing the service to the attention of potential customers. The more precisely risks can be defined the more they can be by-passed, tailored or reduced.

Wide targets, narrow targets and nearby targets

If you aim at the bull you may easily miss. If you are content just to hit the dartboard you are much more likely to be successful.

The widening of the target in order to reduce the risk is not contrary to the principle of market segmentation. In fact market segmentation is really a form of target widening: we find that market in which everyone is a potential buyer of our product.

A nearby target is not the same as a wide target: it means being ungreedy. If we aim for only a tiny share of the market the risk of getting that is reduced. If we do not rely on a price advantage we may not need high volume sales. If something can be done in small stages the risk is obviously less than if it has to be done all at once.

Degree of innovation

Whether or not we like it consumers, and the world in general, base their behaviour on their experience. So the more an innovation connects up with this experience the less is the risk. That is what is meant by degrees of innovation.

Cumulative effects

When there is a string of 'ifs' in a row and the chance of success in each case is estimated at about even odds, the eventual chance of success is only one in sixteen ($\frac{1}{2} \times \frac{1}{2} \times \frac{1}{2} \times \frac{1}{2} = 1/16$). But if the risks are in parallel ('We would be content if this happened or if this happened or if this happened,') then the chances of success are quite high. This difference between sequential 'ifs' and parallel 'ifs' is important. When a number of things must go right 'ifs' are sequential; when any one of a number of alternative 'ifs' will do then they are parallel.

Any number of damp matches are not as good as one dry match. A number of small reasons, each of which is valid in itself, can reduce uncertainty. A number of half reasons can never amount to a full one. If we are trying to predict what will happen then every clue helps. If we are trying to ensure that something does happen then we need strong, full reasons.

Risk and reward

No one gets a medal for taking unnecessary risks. An effective innovator gets the odds on his side. He makes an attempt to reduce the risks as much as possible. It does not follow that the higher the risk the higher the reward. The man who dashes across the road in front of the traffic is no better off at the end than the man who waits for a gap or moves along to the crossing.

Uncertainty is perhaps the only certainty we have. We cannot shy away from uncertainty and cannot hope to remove it entirely, but we can learn to cope with it.

'If the benefits cannot be spelled out clearly and precisely there is no opportunity. There may be a calculated risk involved in achieving the benefits but the benefits must be clearly perceived.'

Evaluation

In this section I do not intend to go in detail into methods of critical path analysis, cost analysis or cash-flow profiles. I must assume that costing and planning techniques will be available to senior executives who have to evaluate opportunities. What I do intend to do is lay out a simple conceptual framework within which opportunities can be considered.

Spell out the benefits

Benefits should be expressed in as precise terms as possible.

Multiple benefits may be present but a listed mass of lesser benefits may hide the absence of a major one. If a major benefit is present this tends to get diluted by the addition of every conceivable other benefit so these should be firmly separated from the main benefits. Do a number of minor benefits add up to a major benefit? The answer must be no. A number of damp matches do not add up to a usable match.

Approval and rejection

Approval or rejection of an opportunity should also be spelled out. In life we often try too hard to place something either in a box generally labelled 'good' or one labelled 'bad.' Then we react to the label. With opportunities the specific reason for approval or rejection should replace the general label.

A person who puts forward an opportunity proposal has a right to know exactly why it is being rejected. If more information is required then it must be specified. A person who accepts an opportunity proposal has the duty to spell out to himself and to his colleagues his exact reason for doing so.

Benefits

In looking at the benefits we can adopt a very simple check-list approach.

• What are the benefits?
• How do the benefits arise?
• How large are the benefits?
• On what do the benefits depend?
• In what way may the benefits fall short of expectation?
• What are the assumptions?
• What problems are likely to be met?

The time profile

The time profile is inseparable from any consideration of opportunities. Is it a long-term or a short-term opportunity? What sort of lead can be expected over competitors? Is it for this season's fashion shows or next? How long will the negative cash-flow period last before returns start coming in? How long a time is likely to be needed for research and development? Will the full benefits come through in months, years or decades? What is the opportunity life-cycle (on the analogy of a product life-cycle)? The time profile may be related to matters outside the control of the organization but most favourable and least favourable guesses should be attempted.

The choice of one opportunity over another may depend entirely on the time profiles. So spelling these out is as important as spelling out the benefits. Benefits that might arrive too late to save a company are not really benefits.

Goodness of fit

The way an opportunity fits a particular organization is important but difficult to assess. On one hand there is the danger of excessive conservatism which rejects anything new and on the other there can be an over-optimism which assumes that a well-managed organization can tackle anything.

The following are possible questions to assess goodness of fit:

- Does the opportunity fit the type of manager we have?
- Does the opportunity fit our cash-flow situation?
- Does the opportunity fit our market strengths?
- Does the opportunity fit production and research facilities?
- Does the opportunity fit our style of thinking?

In considering goodness of fit the basic question is whether the opportunity is one which especially fits the organization (making use of assets and serving needs) or one that would be open to any organization that happened to think of it. In between are the opportunities that would be open to any organization with enough cash and management resources.

Investment

In the pursuit of any opportunity there is going to have to be an investment of money, time, people, effort and attention. Obviously the investment has to be considered against the expected benefits and against alternative use of the resources.

Resource allocation is very much part of a manager's basic function and the exercise of this skill needs to be applied to opportunity investment. Are the resources available? Can they be obtained? What are the alternative uses? The effects of dilution, distraction and diversion should not be underestimated. It may be possible in terms of time, money and people to pursue several projects but mental energy and motivation may not be spread so easily. Many people work much better if they are single-minded. Attention is a resource like any other.

Test-beds

An opportunity is dealing with the future in one way or another. The risk and uncertainty are dealt with by analysis and comparison and above all by test situations. The possibility of setting up a test-bed and the cost of this need to be considered when the opportunity is evaluated. The test may be a market research test, an information test, a scientific test, a production test or anything else.

Cut-offs

There must be a pre-planned point at which a project can be abandoned. Otherwise, from moment to moment, it will always seem to make more sense to put in a little more effort and money in order to avoid wasting what has already been invested and because the feeling is that the success must be just around the corner. The cut-offs should be considered in advance when the opportunity is being evaluated. Cut-offs may be operated in many different ways.

Target cut-off: Certain targets are set. If these targets cannot be achieved as planned, the project is abandoned.

Cost cut-off: A cost limit is set and when the money has been exhausted the project comes to an end.

Time cut-off: If something has not been achieved by a certain date then it may not be worth pursuing the project further.

Test response cut-off: A test-bed is set up and if the project fails to pass the test satisfactorily it is abandoned.

Disaster cut-off: If things go badly wrong.

Review cut-off: The building into the programme of specified review stages with the abandonment of the project if at any stage the benefits no longer seem sufficient to justify the investment.

Difficulties

When an opportunity presents no difficulties it usually means that it has not been examined in sufficient detail. A properly evaluated opportunity will be accompanied by its list of difficulties and it will also be shown how these are going to be tackled. Yet again it is a matter of focus and spelling things out.

Scenario

A scenario is what the opportunity-proposer expects to happen. If events will not follow your script, it must describe what events will themselves do. For a good opportunity the wishful thinking scenario and the expected results scenario should coincide.

Should the scenario be set at the most optimistic or the most pessimistic level? The answer is that it should be set at the most favourable or optimistic level. A favourable scenario still has to be realistic. A 'favourable' scenario is one in which all things work out as expected. It does not mean setting the actual value or extent of effects at the maximum level.

Once the most favourable scenario has been spelled out in detail and possibly mapped, three other scenarios can be derived from it. There is the worst possible scenario and two intermediate ones.

Value

In the end what matters is the value of an opportunity. The value is the relationship between the benefits on one hand and the effort and risk on the other.

We can therefore end with two questions:

Do we need opportunities?

What are we doing about it?

THE
GELLERMAN
MEMOS

Saul Gellerman

Dr. Saul Gellerman is a recognized pioneer in the application of the behavioral sciences in organizations. He is the author of seven books on motivation, including the award-winning *Motivation and Productivity*. A management consultant for the past fourteen years, he has also made twenty-one management films. He was with IBM for eight years in personnel research and line management. His doctorate in psychology is from the University of Pennsylvania.

FROM : SAUL GELLERMAN
SUBJECT : THE LABOR-COST RATIO

This is the ratio of revenues to all cost attributable to employees. In most companies it lies somewhere in the 20%-40% range. The importance of the ratio lies in the fact that all other cost must be paid, if at all, with whatever is left after the payroll has been met. If the ratio gets too high, something — be it maintenance, research and development, borrowing capacity, or whatever — must be squeezed.

More than just payroll is involved. So-called "fringe benefits" typically add 30% or more to wage and salary costs. To be realistic, add the non-salary costs of training, safety, first-aid, cafeteria subsidies and morale-boosting activities such as internal magazines. Payroll plus 40% is by no means an excessive figure for total labor costs.

Three factors can boost the labor-cost ratio out of sight, and if all three are operating the odds become formidable that it will rise above 60% — beyond which point the chances of the company remaining either competitive or profitable start to diminish sharply. These are:

1) Making too many promises of future benefits whose funding can be deferred;

2) Adding new employees to the payroll at a faster rate than the long-term growth of revenues; and

3) Increasing average pay levels faster than the long-term growth of productivity.

The mathematics are obvious, so each trend is clearly undesirable. But each trend is extraordinarily difficult to resist, and extraordinarily easy to overlook.

a) Promises

The most painless way to settle a union contract, or to contrive to keep unions out, is to indemnify people against risks that they will encounter, if at all, far in the future. Pensions are the most obvious example, but medical and hospitalization costs present the same temptation (because illness is related to age). When the employee population is relatively young and the actuary's assumptions are relatively optimistic, the burden of such promises on this year's budget may be quite mild. But the employee population is bound to get older — declining birth rates have seen to that already. So the piper will be paid sooner, rather than later, on pension funding. Meantime, the costs of insuring medical and hospitalization benefits have blossomed profusely.

b) Hiring

When employment is swollen beyond need, it is seldom because people are hired to do unnecessary work. Rather it is because existing employees are not sufficiently productive to do what must be done. That, in turn, may be due to restrictive work practices, to cosseting loyal employees whose jobs may have out-stripped their abilities, or to management's inability to motivate.

It is all-too-easy to misconstrue additional hiring as a welcome sign of company growth, when the only thing that is growing is the labor-cost ratio. There is much to be said for subcontracting, for temporary or part-time workers, for fixed-term employment contracts-indeed for anything that helps to keep a tight rein on the number of fulltime employment commitments.

c) Pay Increases

Rising pay levels are influenced more by the calendar than by trends at the bargaining table or in the job market. The largest component in most people's raises (including so-called "merit" raises) is the fact that they have been employed for another year. If raises kept pace with productivity, or even with the potential productivity represented by increased knowledge and skill, this would be no particular problem. Alas, that is seldom the case.

Given enough time, most people get about as good as they're ever going to get at a given job, and after that any further gains are likely to be of no consequence. So competence levels off, but pay does not.

Pay increases given after someone has spent three or four years on an essentially unchanged job can, as a rule, be explained only as rewards for not having quit or been fired — not as compensation for greater productivity. They are longevity premiums, not merit increases, and it is their cumulative effect that ratchets pay levels ahead of the productivity rate — especially in companies with many senior employees.

Here's a question to ponder: Who in your company is accountable for the long-range effects (beyond this year) of this year's pay increases? In every company where I've asked the question, the answer turns out to be nobody. But we are all living this year with the effects of pay increase decisions made in previous years. In most cases, past decisions account for at least 90% of the total wage, salary and benefit burden your company will carry by the end of this year. And how heavy is that burden? It depends on your labor-cost ratio. If it is 20%, your company will have to work this year from January 1st until about March 3rd solely to meet the cost of commitments for which no one is any longer accountable.

Now then: is your labor-cost ratio in or out of control? Take a look at the promises you've made on benefits, at the ratio of net employment growth to average revenue growth, and at the ratio of average pay to average productivity. Then decide whether your successor is going to have to be merely capable, or extra-ordinarily lucky, to cope with the labor cost ratio you are bequeathing to him.

FROM : SAUL GELLERMAN
SUBJECT : PROMOTIONS: COMMITMENTS THAT KILL ORGANIZATIONS

In the magnitude of their long-term impact on the organization, decisions about whom to promote are a close contender with hiring decisions. Hiring puts absolute limits on the talent that will be available to an organization, but promotion sets the limits of its leadership. The quality of both decisions is critical. But the promotion decision is often made less logically — and certainly less systematically — than the hiring decision. The result, to put it simply, is managerial mediocrity.

Most organizations have no promotion list at all, much less thoughtfully-derived lists. In fact, most promotion decisions are made in a hurry — because a vacancy has occurred and it must be filled in a hurry — and are made on the basis of skimpy and largely irrelevant information about candidates on a haphazardly assembled list.

Granted, the moment when a managerial post will become vacant is not always foreseeable, but because every managerial job inevitably becomes vacant sooner or later — and more likely sooner, there is no good reason for not trying to foresee promotion decisions so they can be made systematically.

Typically, promotions go to candidates who have done their jobs well, who make the decision-makers feel secure, and who are conspicuous in some way.

This "system" — if we can call it that — does produce some capable managers. It also produces a lot of mediocre managers and overlooks a lot of potentially more capable people. In brief, it is inefficient.

Unless the two jobs are very similar — which is seldom the

case — doing one job well is no guarantee at all that the next higher job will also be done well. All too often, promoting the "best worker" leads to a double loss: you lose your best worker and acquire an inadequate manager.

In effect, using job performance as a promotion criterion treats managerial jobs as rewards to be given to the most deserving, rather than as responsibilities to be given to the most capable. It denigrates the management function and reduces it from the most critical component of organizational success — which it is — to something "anyone can do" — which it most assuredly is not.

The point is that doing a job and managing it are two very different tasks, requiring quite different skills. Some people are well-equipped for either role, but many more can manage a job much less capably than they can do it. Why? Because doing a job requires only skill at that job, but managing it requires the ability to influence the way other people do that job.

This accounts, in no small measure, for the fact that at the lower levels of management — the crucial level at which plans are converted into reality — technical competence abounds and leadership is all too often inept.

Most managers are quite aware of how much is at stake in a promotion decision, and they also recognize the weaknesses in the tools they are given for making that decision. For the most part, these "tools" consist of their own, and other people's, whims and impressions; hence both the possibilities and the consequences of an error are severe.

The result is that the lower levels of management tend to over-intervene in the work of their subordinates, and then to swing petulantly to the other extreme when they encounter inevitable resistance to what is seen — rightly or wrongly — as their tendency to push other people around. One can not help wonder how many unions have been organized, and how many existing unions have been driven into the arms of their militant wings of overzealous junior managers who feel that the first requirement of their jobs is to prove "who is boss" in their departments.

He who wishes to come to the attention of those who make promotion decisions, must first be distinguished in some way — be it relevant or not — from the mass of his colleagues.

Thus, one's chances of promotion increase if one works under a boss who is promotable, or if one is a protegé of a manager whose opinion other managers respect, or in a department or group from which managers have in the past been drawn in disproportionate numbers. Granted, none of this bears on one's ability to manage, but it bears very heavily on whether one is noticed.

None of these popular criteria — doing a very different job well, fitting a stereotype and being "noticeable" — shed much light on the question of whether someone can manage well. But in most companies they weigh more heavily in determining who will be promoted than do other factors. Thus in selecting its managers, the typical organization has a built-in bias toward bossy, technically capable people who can slip all-too easily into an adversary relationship with the people whom they are supposed to guide and motivate.

Companies that enjoy strong supervision at the first and second levels of management usually employ some combination of three methods:

1) They have analyzed the behavioral requirements of these jobs, so they know specifically what to look for. They are unlikely to be overly impressed by someone who is generally attractive but has no clear-cut qualifications for the job.

2) The "nomination" process through which candidates are recommended for the job is systematic and stringent. In fact, most candidates never get past this hurdle.

3) The best available candidates compete directly against each other, under conditions that simulate the supervisory job as closely as possible.

FROM   : SAUL GELLERMAN
SUBJECT : HIDING MANAGERIAL FAILURES

When it becomes clear that money has been invested unwisely, most companies elect to cut their losses, salvage what they can and redeploy their assets elsewhere. When it becomes clear that one of their managers is failing, they are likely to do nothing of the kind.

Of course, a lot depends on precisely what is meant by "failing."

Grand and glorious fiascos, in which orders are lost from previously satisfied customers, or production costs float out of sight, are usually dealt with severely. But subtler failings, which may persist unspectacularly forever, are far more likely to be overlooked. This is not because they are unrecognized or mistakenly considered trivial. Nor does the difference lie in cost to the company — because the cumulative cost of a lingering failure can easily exceed that of a sudden, splashy one.

The difference between tolerated and untolerated errors is visibility. Briefly, the manager who wounds his company in ways accountants can not detect is likely to go scot free, while the one whose damages head straight for this year's bottom line will be punished.

Moreover, the subtle sins that managers get away with are more likely to involve people, while the gross ones for which they are likely to suffer involve money. Ultimately, of course, people both cost and generate money, so the distinction involves no real logic. But the simple truth is that most managers would rather not punish other managers at all, and do so only when not to do so would be noticed.

With few exceptions, managers at the middle and lower levels (in other words, a majority of all managers) do not contribute to their companies directly, but do so through their influence on subordinates.

Consider the long-term effect on a department's efficiency of a manager who consistently demoralizes or demotivates a majority of his subordinates.

What kind of error rate, scrap rate, absentee rate, accident rate, turnover rate, re-work rate, customer complaint rate, equipment down-time rate, and failure-to-meet-schedule rate would you expect in such a department? If your guess is on the high side in each instance, you're probably right.

If you have managers whose subordinates work against them, or at least don't work willingly for them, it's probably no secret who they are. Their reputations are common knowledge among their peers. But they are forgiven, and the thought that possibly they might cause more trouble than they are worth never enters their colleagues' minds. Ask them why, and the initial answers will be charitable. Well, the fellow really isn't *that* bad, they'll say. Besides, he has a lot of good qualities: he's technically sound, thoroughly experienced, a loyal company man — and maybe he's got a particularly tough or inept group of subordinates.

Probe a little deeper, and you'll start ferreting out the real reasons for their forgiveness.

What you would hear, in other words, is a managerial version of the same litany used to justify unions, seniority and job security among the hourly workers whom these managers manage.

Thus the reasons managers are so tolerant of ineffectiveness in other managers are powerfully persuasive to them. What's more, many of them would protest quite sincerely that technical know-how — which is the main reason why most of them were made managers in the first place, and therefore most commonly their main strength — should weigh more heavily in evaluating one of their peers than something as slippery as getting along with people. But if technical ability deserves only secondary emphasis in selecting managers — as we have argued — it surely deserves only secondary emphasis in deciding whether to retain them.

And there's the rub. The main problem is neither technical ability nor any other criterion of managerial performance. The main problem is that the question of whether managers should be retained is raised so rarely that most companies are, in effect, permanently saddled with every promotion error they have made — and most of them have made plenty.

Make no mistake about it: this is no easy problem to cure, because in effect the doctor is also the patient. And this extreme difficulty in effecting a cure is perhaps the best argument that could be found for investing far more time, money and — above all — expertise in the process of managerial selection than it customarily gets.

But it isn't really intractable. Managers shrink from removing a colleague because they fear — wrongly, in most cases — that he would necessarily have to be fired; or that if offered a demotion he would regard that as a thinly-disguised invitation to resign.

But the simple truth is that most employees, including managers, are worth more to their present employers — simply because of their experience, and because their abilities are known — than they are to most other employers. Further, most managers are sensible enough to realize that, once they get over the inevitable shock of demotion. They are sensible enough to realize that if demotion is no honor, it is no disgrace, either. It is in fact the most humane way to correct a costly error and to redeploy what is surely one of any company's most valuable assets.

FROM : SAUL GELLERMAN
SUBJECT : HOW PERSONNEL
DEPARTMENTS TRY TO
PLAY IT SAFE

Raise an unorthodox suggestion at a personnel meeting or seminar, and the first reaction is almost predictable. Someone will ask, "Can you tell me which companies are using that?" As if other companies were better judges of what is right or wrong for the questioner's company than he is.

It isn't professional thoroughness but job security that motivates the need to know "Who else is using it." It's safer to be wrong on a bandwagon than to be wrong all alone.

All this is just another way of saying that many programs are selected because they are fashionable, or abandoned because they have become unfashionable; in both cases with little if any relationship to whether they do any good.

If another company is using a particular method, the only thing it proves is that the method has *current executive sponsorship* in that company.

In other words, somebody over there has been sold. But you'd better not assume that he's as hard to sell as you are, or that he's facing the same problems and has the same standards that you have. Above all, you'd better not assume that someone else's enthuasiasm means that a method "works."

In brief: the only sponsorship that isn't irrelevant is your own. Select *your* methods on the basis of results, and to hell with sponsorship.

The degree of fashion-consciousness among personnel departments can accurately be characterized as a sin, and that sin is incest. The extent to which forms and procedures are

278

lifted wholesale from some other company (which probably acquired them in the same way) is scandalous.

Perhaps the most common example of inter-company copying is performance appraisal. Personnel departments usually assume, as an article of faith, that every employee needs, has a right and is probably dying to know "where he stands" —whatever that means — and that the best way to let him know is to sit down with his supervisor with a filled-out form between them so they can discuss whatever the supervisor has written on the form.

But most supervisors don't like to do this, most employees can't remember whether it happened or not, and most appraisal programs need periodic applications of executive clout to cause them to be used at all.

The typical personnel department's diagnosis is that a better form is needed and that a better job of selling needs to be done on the supervisors. In other words, the prescription is for more of the same, only "better."

So they busy themselves with hunting for better forms or planning more elaborate role-playing sessions, seldom questioning whether the whole procedure is worthwhile. In most cases it is not. In fact, many of them are counter-productive, since they create an unnecessary adversary relationship in the worst possible place: between someone who is supposed to get some work done and his boss.

More than forms and phrases are borrowed. The belief that what the forms are designed to do is necessary, and the faith that they can actually do it, are borrowed as well. All this persists despite the everyday experience that performance appraisal seldom works, and that by honoring such programs in the breach most companies get along well enough without them.

Then why the faith, why the investment of staff time, why the mounds of paper and the periodic pious sermons on why appraisal interviews are good?

Mainly, I think, because of the idealistic hope that they will work — and the not-so-idealistic fear of being branded a heretic for saying that they don't.

New methods in personnel management are not "discovered." Rather, what is discovered is that they have begun to be used, or that they have acquired some articulate advocates. And then the rush is on. Books are written, courses are taught, contracts are signed. Managers by the dozens are put through programs which everyone hopes will make them more sensitive, less authoritarian, more employee-oriented. In most cases the managers themselves don't change, but their vocabularies do, brimming over with sophisticated jargon and — for a few months, anyway — enlivening their lunch-table conversations with the latest behavioral buzz-words.

Those executives who wonder what, if anything, the company has to show for all these exertions are given the "really" treatment. That is, they are reassured that if someone "really" understands it, "really" believes it, "really" commits himself to it, it's just got to work . . . etc. The "really" treatment is a reliable, tested escape-hatch: if the graduates don't improve, you blame the graduates and not the courses they were made to take. Then, predictably, another "breakthrough" will come along about the time the old one is starting to look a bit tattered, and it will probably be no worse than the one it replaces.

Personnel managers have to contend with human nature, which has taken millions of years to become what it is, and isn't likely to change quickly to suit anyone's convenience. Nevertheless, hope springs eternal. Personnel fads basically come from a desire to change the unchangeable — to escape from having to learn to live intelligently with people as they are.

Performance appraisal seeks to soothe people who may be unreasonable, or to edify those who prefer to live in a dream world. Human relations courses seek to soften people who have spent their lives learning to be hard, or vice-versa. Such changes are not quite impossible — just nearly impossible.

Hence the high failure rate and the search for newer, hopefully "better" panaceas. Rare indeed is the personnel director with the courage not to follow suit, even when logic and his entire professional experience tell him that what he is attempting is too grandiose to fit reality.

FROM : SAUL GELLERMAN
SUBJECT : KEEPING UNIONS OUT

Any candid union-oganizer will tell you that the key to success in his profession is target selection. After all, he has to live with a budget, just as you do; and like you, he is measured in terms of his cost effectiveness.

He can no more afford to squander his time and effort on employees who are unlikely to vote for representation than you can afford to pursue unprofitable markets. What is more to the point, he doesn't need to: there are plenty of ripe, juicy targets just waiting to be plucked.

Ranged against the organizers — but in a subtle sense, dependent on them for their livelihoods — are the lawyers and consultants who act as professional union-fighters. To successfully market their services, they too need susceptible targets: clients who are dumbfounded that the union got in the door at all, and terrified of what organization may bring. Fortunately for both union-organizers and union-fighters, there are enough somnolent personnel departments in nonunion companies to provide them with plenty of lucrative work.

No union-organizer who is paid for results is likely to put much reliance on so-called "troublemakers" or "agitators" — discontented employees who seek to convince their peers that a union is needed. Most employees know their own minds perfectly well, and are no more susceptible to blatant pro-union propaganda than they are to self-serving appeals by management.

The reason "troublemakers" are often found in companies that have been organized is not that they influenced the outcome, but that managements inept enough to lose elections

usually look for scapegoats. The organizer doesn't: he looks
for real grievances that can be exploited.

I'll state my own ideological preferences here, to the extent that I'm aware of them: I believe that working people
know what is best for them, and that they should have
whatever they want — unions if they want them and no unions
if they want none.

But I also believe that most employees who want unions
are likely to be dealing with 19th century managements — in
which case I'd wholeheartedly favor their protection by unions.
Further, I doubt that employees whose managements were en-
lightened (20th century managements, if you will) would see
much advantage in interposing a union between such a management and themselves.

What makes a company "ripe," from the union-organizer's point of view, is the number, extent, and above all the age
of the serious grievances he finds.

If he scouts a company in which grievances are few, mild,
rather localized, and of comparatively recent origin — indicating that earlier grievances weren't important enough to be
remembered — he will probably seek a more tempting target.
But if he finds the right conditions, he is likely to beat any combination of lawyers and consultants you can buy.

The most easily exploited grievances are: favoritism (or its
obverse, bias), arbitrariness in discharge or discipline, pay or
benefit disadvantages, and the absence of a protected channel
of appeal. The first two are related to the quality of supervision, while the third and fourth are matters of policy.

a) Favoritism

Charges of favoritism are usually traceable to nothing
more nefarious than supervisors trying to see that justice is
done. They want to reward the virtuous and punish the wicked:
that is, they want their hardworking subordinates to receive
what favors can be given, and consider it only fair that less-
desirable assignments go to the slackers.

The union promises even-handed treatment for all. Therefore, the practice of permitting supervisors to dispense small favors and small penalties creates an exposure that organizers can readily exploit. The best way to block this particular entry to your company is to insist that supervisors exercise their sense of justice solely with regard to large matters (for example, promotion); and that with regard to petty matters (for example, early departure) they treat everyone — without exceptions — with strict equality.

b) Discipline

What converts discipline from an uncomfortable fact of working life — which it is for any employed person — to a threat that requires protection at all costs, is uncertainty.

Most people feel safe (that is, able to look after their interests by themselves) when they are confident that they know the rules by which they are expected to play. But if the rule-enforcers are free to interpret them as they wish, or to invent new rules, the power balance shifts too far in the enforcer's direction. It was precisely to correct such imbalances that our basic labor laws were enacted in the first place.

The union offers written contract. Anyone who can read knows that those contracts include procedures for discharge and lay-off, so their appeal lies not in job security but in certainty. A contract doesn't guarantee, it just clears the air. The rules are spelled out, and an advocate is at hand to argue that the rules should be interpreted to the employee's advantage.

As in the case of dispensing favors, the union is simply offering protection against conditions which few people would willingly tolerate, and which any intelligently managed company has no need of. Again, the best way to block the union is to make it unnecessary, by providing what they offer without union dues. Any offenses for which punishment (including discharge) is considered necessary should be published, clearly and concisely, for all to see — along with a commitment that no one will be punished for any unlisted offense.

c) Pay Disadvantages

Most people want to be paid what their work is worth, and recognize, at least dimly, that this is related to what other people's work is worth. To be paid much less than none could presumably command elsewhere would be galling for anyone. The practical problem is that most people don't know the comparative value of their work: they only have their suspicions.

The less you know for certain about the market value of your work, the easier it is to believe that your pay is out of line. The union organizer need not be deterred by pay levels that are actually quite competitive, provided the workers have no firm basis for being convinced of that. All he has to do then is tantalize them with the prospect of "more."

There is a paradox here. Market forces usually move employers in the direction of competitive pay, with or without unions. Of course, unions influence the market price of labor (in both organized and unorganized companies), but do not counteract the market forces themselves. Consequently, most employees in most companies would find a marginal advantage at best if they were paid according to some other employer's rates, regardless of whether that other employer was organized or not. But if the actual pay advantage of signing a union card is only marginal, why are so many cards signed? Becuse the signers don't know that the advantage are marginal. Further, they don't know it because of a deliberate policy of their employer's personnel department. Pay comparisons, whether between workers in the same company or between companies, are usually taboo. This suits the union-organizer just fine, since it leaves him a wide open field. The preventives are simple and effective, but seldom used: if your pay is good, flaunt it. If it is not competitive, make it so, and then flaunt it.

d) Channels of Appeal

In a hierarchy virtually everyone is under someone else's thumb — even the chief executive is at least theoretically subject to some kind of collegial review. To earn one's livelihood in a hierarchy (as most of us do) is therefore to live in peril of someone else's whims. To be bearable, the system requires some method of keeping the fellow above you honest.

Unions offer to do this with a formalized grievance procedure. In effect, the union reserves the right to review your boss' decisions, and this very right is likely to restrain his rasher impulses. Even if your present boss is the soul of fairness and restraint, what guarantee do you have that he won't be in a foul mood next time he makes a decision about you? And what about his successor, and the successor after that? What if they turn out to be harsher than the fellow who makes decisions about you now?

Obviously, a grievance procedure that is spelled out in black-and-white has a powerful appeal. But as in the case of each of the other main exposures to being organized, this can be had without a union contract. Formal appeal systems, both to higher management or, in some cases, to groups of one's peers, work quite as well in nonunion companies as in organized firms.

The point of all four of these analyses is that it is much wiser to make unions unnecessary in the first place than to wait until the organizer has penetrated your company, and then rely on union-fighters to save you. After all, even the best union-fighters win a few and lose a few — and they don't guarantee which column you'll end up in. What's more, the aftermath of even a successful fight could involve as much bitterness and dissension as even the most predatory union would stir up. So fight if you must, but avoid it if you can — even at the cost of discomfiting your supervisors and your personnel department.

FROM : SAUL GELLERMAN
SUBJECT : LIVING WITH UNIONS IF YOU HAVE TO

The same managements which unwittingly invite the union-organizer and then fight him tooth-and-nail are, paradoxically, most likely to roll over and die should the organizer win. In brief, defeated managements tend to overreact and become subservient.

What happens next is that the union president becomes the *de facto* personnel manager. Disagreements on the shop floor are escalated to the executive suite, where they are settled more on the basis of *quid pro quos* than on whatever the merits of each case may have been. Supervisors who elect to confront the union are in effect engaging in a lottery, and quickly become convinced of the futility of standing up for what they regard as management's rights. At that point, management has been put to rout.

The contracts that are periodically negotiated are not nearly as important, in themselves, as the body of contract interpretations that gradually builds up between negotiations. The contract does not mean what it says; it means what it has in practice been interpreted to mean. When these interpretations are worked out between demoralized managers, on the one hand, and shop stewards who are probing to see how far they can stretch a point, the outcome is all-too predictable. The contract becomes, in practice, what the union wants it to become.

A unionized company does not have to centralize virtually all employee-relations decisions at the top level of its personnel or industrial relations hierarchy. It does so when it regards the union hierarchy, rather than the mass of individual employees, as the most appropriate focus of its attention. In such cases, the two power blocs square off and, in most cases, eventually learn the limits of their own and the other's power. Some kind of accommodation develops between them, and oddly enough this is sometimes referred to as a sound union-management relationship.

But this accommodation takes place at the expense of alienation between the parties the power blocs represent: the employees and their supervisors. Their relations, if they can be called that, become distant and stilted. In many cases they are virtual strangers to each other, despite nominally working together. But that relationship is still the hinge on which any hope of labor productivity must swing.

The unionized workers may be persuaded, but can not be commanded. If anything, therefore, a unionized company needs healthy relationships between supervisors and employees even more than a nonunion company does. Nothing less than productivity itself is at stake: the rate of equipment utilization, for example, may depend on whether a union member is inclined to help out a decent supervisor or let his disliked boss go to hell.

Therefore anything that builds simple respect and a mutual sense of shared obligation tilts the odds in favor of productivity. But neither is likely to develop in companies that centralize their personnel decisions, thereby discouraging supervisors from pursuing — much less cultivating — any kind of relationship with their subordinates.

Centralizing personnel decisions can be rationalized in many ways. What is at stake is too important to be risked of the impetuousness of some over-zealous underling. The contract is too full of nuances to permit anyone but an expert to interpret it. Keeping union relations firmly at the level of corporate vice presidents and union presidents (or better still, international vice-presidents) ensures that really big issues don't get beclouded by minor ones. And so on — but the real issue underlying all of these sophistries is that top management has a pretty low opinion of lower-level management.

This is one of those unfortunate situations in which it is hard to distinguish cause from effect. Yes, there are horrible examples in most companies of lower-level managers who commit truly stupendous blunders in their dealings with employees or unions. But most sins at this level are of omission, not commission — because most supervisors know darn well that they are both under-informed and under-supported.

For example, their subordinates are more likely to learn before they do of developments that affect them all — the union grapevine is both faster and more reliable. And if the supervisor is bold enough to take a stand in the face of some particularly flagrant violation, the odds are that he will be countermanded. Shop stewards quickly learn to be automatically adamant, regardless of the circumstances, on the reasonably safe assumption that the supervisor is probably unsure of his ground.

Thus in practice the two-way street implied by any freely bargained contract becomes a one-way street. Top management controls its relationships with the union, but the union controls the employees and the employees ultimately control productivity. And what do the lower levels of management control? That's a good question. But given what they so seldom get — thorough training, reliable communication, quick access to expert advice and encouragement by top management to manage actively — they can exert a positive influence on employees. And that can restore the two-way street.

What is a *really* "sound union-management relationship?" To measure it in terms of working time that is not lost to strikes is at best a minimum standard. The real test is the productivity levels that are achieved when workers are not on strike. That's what pays for everything: your salary, the employees' wages and benefits, the union's dues — everything.

FROM : SAUL GELLERMAN
SUBJECT : JOB ENTRY: WHEN AND WHOM TO HIRE

People flow continuously into, through and out of a company. Regulating that flow is the responsibility of the personnel department. If the job is done intelligently, the labor cost ratio will be relatively low, and the company can, unencumbered, go about its business of caring for the army of people who depend on it in one way or another. If the flow is not regulated intelligently, the ratio goes up and — sooner or later — somebody gets hurt.

It is the continual interaction between all of the many entries, passages and exits that determines, in the long run, how often the right person will be in the right place at the right time — and that, in turn, determines how often work will be done as intelligently as possible.

Entry: When to hire

The typical personnel department looks at too few candidates from not enough sources, thus maximizing its administrative convenience and minimizing the efficiency with which it uses available talent.

The result, given enough time, is an accumulation of people whose performance is somewhat better than marginal, who are regarded as having little if any potential for other kinds of work, and who for lack of variety become disinterested in everything but their paychecks and in whatever gossip they can share with fellow employees.

The basic problem is timing. Both personnel departments and individuals enter the labor market when it suits their purposes to do so. As a result, personnel departments encounter random supply and individuals encounter random demand. Typically, personnel departments conclude from this experience that it doesn't matter very much when you go shopping for talent, because the supply is more or less the same at all times. But it is only the same if you are looking for ordinary talent. If you are looking for people with out-of-the-ordinary capabilities, you have to be in the market when they are. Because their availability is unpredictable, this means quite simply that you must always be in the market.

Perpetual recruiting is the key to gradually raising the average internal talent level well above the external average. There is no other way to do it, short of building the kind of reputation that will make the most capable candidates seek you out — and that takes decades. The advantages of superior talent are huge: you can beat the pants off your competition in almost any sphere. There are three disadvantages, two of which deserve some comment:

The first is that perpetual recruiting may result in hiring in excess of current need, thus raising the labor cost ratio. Should you hire an extraordinary person, for example, when you are fully staffed and have no budget left for hiring? If you can satisfy yourself that his "special" qualities are both real and needed, then yes, you should hire him. Attrition will bring your headcount and payroll figures back into balance quickly enough.; and if you wait until your bookkeepers give a go-ahead signal, you'll have to content yourself with someone considerably less promising.

The second disadvantage is more apparent than real: a company that continually interviews applicants will obviously reject most of them. It will thus acquire a reputation for being very choosey, thereby discouraging many would-be applicants. This is true, and also desirable, since that kind of reputation will do much of your screening for you. The undeterred group of applicants will probably include more of the kinds of people you would like to hire anyway. As a rule, you will hire more motivation among people who are seeking a particular kind of job than you will among people who are just seeking any job.

The third disadvantage deserves only mention, not comment: Perpetual recruiting places an added burden on the personnel department.

Entry: Whom to hire

The first indicator we get of how hard people will work if they get a job is how hard they work to get it. All indicators are fallible, but as indicators go, this one isn't bad. Initiative and persistence in job seeking won't necessarily carry over into job-doing, but the odds that they will are fairly decent.

Therefore personnel departments should be receptive to uninvited job seekers who walk in or write in, and who keep trying to get past personnel to the department head for whom they want to work.

The same logic applies to internal candidates who persistently nominate themselves for higher-level jobs, with or without the endorsement of their superiors.

Assuming they meet whatever paper qualifications are required, self-nominees probably have about the same chances of success as the average management nominee, and deserve the same consideration. The obstacle here is that both personnel and line management are likely to consider such people a nuisance. To complicate the picture further, some self-nominees are misguided or foolish.

The most promising source of candidates is self-nomination, regardless of whether it originates inside or outside the organization. Those who seek a particular job or employer for a particular reason, and display some determination to get what they want, are already giving more reliable evidence of motivation to do the job well than any other source can give — including management nominators and outside psychologists. There may be superior candidates available from other sources, but the certainty with which they can be identified is less.

One more source must be considered: those whom the

company seeks out. This includes both campus recruiting and the use of management (or other) recruiters.

As for candidates turned up by recruiters: the best ones are likely to be initially disinterested, and to be genuinely (not playing) hard to get. They are usually well appreciated and well treated by their present employers. So you'll have to make them unhappy in their current situation. Be prepared to take their second "no" as final, not their first.

FROM : SAUL GELLERMAN
SUBJECT : A HARDY OLD FALLACY: PROMOTION FROM WITHIN

No personnel selection system can identify an outstanding candidate if he or she isn't in the candidate pool to begin with. Therefore, to maximize the effectiveness of your selection system, maximize the number of candidates. Again, this minimizes the administrative convenience of the system, but so be it. It also raises the old question of whether a company should promote from within or bring in outsiders. That short question needs a long answer.

Like company loyalty and the taboo on rehiring defectors, promotion from within is a fine old tradition that has largely outlived its usefulness. It belongs in corporate history books, not policy books. It's harmless enough, and in some ways even beneficial, when it doesn't deny the company access to the talent it needs to prosper; but it usually begins to have precisely that effect at about middle management level (or its technical equivalent).

Therefore when it comes to promotion the rule of thumb is to use internal sources when you can and external sources when you must. More precisely, you promote from within only when that doesn't mortgage the company's future. Employees deserve a monopoly on promotion opportunities to those many jobs which can not make or break a company — jobs in which, to be blunt about it, failure can be tolerated — but for all other jobs they should compete with the best the outside market has to offer.

Limited competition for promotion is actually a kind of "fringe benefit" for employees at lower organizational levels, and at those levels the company can well afford to grant it. But as more critical levels of responsibility are approached, it quickly becomes a dangerous practice.

Promotion from within is, after all, based on the fallacious assumption that in the undeparted residue of hiring that took place years or decades ago, you can always find someone who has grown to the dimensions of any job — no matter how demanding and important that job may be. Relying on that fallacy has moved entirely too much mediocrity from levels where it does not harm to levels where it does.

Promotion from within can be defended in a number of ways, some more sophisticated than others. The usual defense is that morale and motivation will suffer if promotional plums are handed to outsiders, who — having done their toiling elsewhere — are by definition undeserving. The triple specters of demoralization, unionization and turnover may be raised, and these are usually more than enough to frighten off the inquisitive non-specialist.

As a matter of fact, there is some truth in this defense but not much.

Most employees in hierarchies make their peace with the recognition that they probably won't rise as high as they might wish. They won't enjoy watching outsiders being brought in over their heads, but it won't ruin many dinners or spoil many nights' sleep, either. Unionization if it happens, is likely to have much deeper causes than jealousy. As for turnover, there probably won't be enough of it: people who feel stymied in their ambitions are often well-advised to pursue them elsewhere, but seldom do.

In brief, cutting of a previous monopoly on access to promotion undoubtedly hurts some people, but not nearly enough to outweigh the gains.

Another defense is that a moral principle is involved: the company should return the loyalty of those who have been loyal to it. Indeed it should, but how?

It's much too easy to overstate the value — even the moral value — of employee loyalty. In most cases it consists of not having quit or been fired, and almost never of having spurned attractive offers from other employers.

Surely it's excessive to offer protected access to key jobs as a reward for being uninteresting to other employers. Surely continued employment is an adequate reward. And the best way to guarantee that is to protect the company from disastrous mismanagement at all cost, including the cost of a few bruised egos.

More sophisticated defenses of promotion from within are that it enables an employer to skim the cream of the entry-level job market (by promising a glorious future as compensation for unattractive starting jobs), and to deter turnover by holding out the promise that patience will eventually be rewarded.

Both are true, but they have to be viewed in the context of offsetting points. A company that has a reputation for being inbred will have a tough time attracting sophisticated outsiders if it ever decides to change its policies: How many, after all, want to risk their careers in a company where their peers and subordinates have a vested interest in seeing them fail? As for deterred turnover, it's a mixed blessing at best — more about that later.

The most sophisticated defense of promotion from within is the least often heard, but the hardest to answer. This is: the most reliable forecasts of future job performance can be made about the people whose track records are best known, namely, one's own employees. That's true. There is always more certainty about what an insider can do than there is about an outsider's capabilities.

Here we must draw a rather precise distinction between what we think someone can do and our certainty that he can actually do it. The ideal situation, of course, is to be quite certain that someone is equal to a job. We can only have that certainty with an insider; but the higher the demands of the job we are considering, the less likely are we to find an insider about whom we feel that certain.

In practice, therefore, we often face a choice between the high probability of mediocre performance and a less certain possibility of superior performance. If the job is sufficiently important, the riskier course is usually wiser.

On balance, a fixed policy of promotion from within reduces a company's options in potentially critical decisions, and offers few substantial benefits. About the only context in which promotion from within makes sense is in a company that has built superior talent resources through years of sophisticated recruiting and development. If you're not there yet — and most companies are a long way from it — you're not ready for strict promotion from within. Use it selectively, and be candid about where your obligation to promote your employees stops.

In most companies, it doesn't stop until it reaches pretty close to the presidency itself — and that's much too high. As presidents know, better than anyone else, a capable president supported by a mediocre middle management has a tough row to hoe.

FROM   : SAUL GELLERMAN
SUBJECT : PASSAGE: REASSURING
THE "STAYERS"

If movers constantly present near-term problems for management, stayers inevitably present long-term problems. These are usually ignored until they are insoluble, and then either continue to be ignored (at great cost) or are solved brutally.

The problem with stayers is that they tend to become overpaid and/or underproductive. Both hazards can be managed, but seldom are, for all of the familiar reasons: it's inconvenient, untraditional, and requires inflicting pain now to avoid worse pain later.

Stayers want to believe (and therefore do) that the organization for which they work will endure and nurture them forever. To them, being employed is the equivalent of being adopted, and the organization — as distinct from the individuals who run it — is a dedicated and protective parent. It is, of course, nothing of the kind, although some personnel departments like to foster the illusion by implying, or at least not denying, that anyone who keeps his nose clean has a guaranteed job come hell or high water. Both inevitably arrive in the form of recessions, technological changes, mergers and acquisitions, competition or simply new managers with new ideas.

The simple truth is that the best security is not given by guarantees, but by supplying something that is in demand. People (and therefore organizations) break promises when they can't keep them or don't want to acknowledge them; but the laws of supply and demand have been faithfully delivering goods and paying incomes since they were first observed. And this means that an organization that is genuinely committed to

298

providing security for its employees had best keep their productivity and marketability high — and its own labor cost ratio low.

It is not in the stayer's long-range interests to stay too long in one occupational role. To do so runs the risk of making inevitable the very thing he is trying to prevent. The stayer's methods are to resist having to make adjustments and to preserve the *status quo*. His purpose is to avoid ever having to re-enter the labor market.

The problem, then, is to help stayer's cope, sooner or later, with what they don't want to cope with: change. In particular, the problem is to prepare them for changes that may not come until they are well into the second half of their careers, when change is cruelest and — diabolically — more likely.

There are two ways to do it: relocation and what for the want of a better term I will call "inoculation." Relocation solves fewer problems, but is simpler and more familiar, so it will be dealt with first.

Relocation

We usually think of relocating employees only when jobs themselves have been relocated; for example, when plants are shut down or opened. (Promotions and transfers also involve relocation, but these are far more likely to involve "movers" who welcome such changes.)

When opportunities to chase jobs or better opportunities in other locations are offered, even at company expense, to employees on the lower rungs of the organizational ladder, only a small minority are likely to accept. Ties to family and community, and simple inertia, are usually stronger than the temptation to make a new start elsewhere.

In effect, offers of relocation "select out" from a population that consists largely of stayers those few who have the instincts of movers. This is desirable — so desirable, in fact, that such offers should not be limited to those relatively few occasions when a company needs to balance a surplus of workers at one location with a shortage somewhere else. A certain number of transfers should be offered regularly to qualified volunteers. How many? As many as you can afford.

The advantages of voluntary relocation are that people with undeveloped potential can continue to grow, rather than stagnate; and that a constructive outlet is provided for energies and ambitions which, if thwarted, could easily be turned against the company that frustrates them.

Why is voluntary relocation not used more often? The main objections are cost, negative reactions by employees at the receiving locations, and fear that relocated employees may quit shortly after being relocated. Like most objections to seldom-used methods, each contains a kernel of truth, but are, on balance, insubstantial.

Relocation is costly, but like every cost this one must be balanced against the benefits and the alternative uses to which the money could be put. In each case there is a business decision to be made. Voluntary transfers should be a mutual option of management and the individual, not a fringe benefit doled out to anyone who qualifies. But people who are willing to pull up stakes and take their chances elsewhere are, by that very fact, giving fair evidence of motivation that would justify the expense. Screening out those who are unstable or unreliable should not be difficult.

Employees at receiving locations are likely to regard incoming transferees as interlopers. The reason is simple: most employees at the receiving location are likely to be stayers, and a mobile newcomer who has already received special treatment from management is, at best, not one of them and, at worst, a threat.

Therefore, someone who is timid or dependent on the fellowship of his or her workmates would be a poor choice for voluntary relocation: but by the same token, such a person is unlikely to volunteer. Thus the practical question is whether an initially chilly reception would seriously diminish the value of the transferee's work. It probably would not, especially if it is established that transfering, both in and out of the location, takes place fairly frequently.

When the transfer is into a larger labor market, there is some risk that the employee may elope after the company has picked up the moving bill. Moves to smaller labor markets (for example, to the comparatively rural areas where much industrial expansion has been concentrated lately) actually create the opposite situation: the transferred employee is far more dependent on the employer than he was. Some post-transfer elopements are probably inevitable, but they can be minimized by favoring longer-service employees (who would have a lot to lose by leaving) for transfers to larger labor markets.

Two more substantial arguments against voluntary relocation are less frequently heard. There are the possibilities that the individual may not adjust well to the transfer, or that it may cause serious disruption to members of the family.

The best way to assess the adjustment risk is by examining relevant records, but unfortunately these are scarce. Someone who has already moved around a bit (for example, in military service or schooling away from home) and has had no trouble can probably handle the stresses of relocation. Difficulty in previous moves is at least cause for concern. Without such a record, one has to rely on general impressions of adaptability. These are not very reliable; but fortunately, most people are fairly adaptable anyway.

Forecasting the family's adjustment is far more difficult, because clues are subtle and because it is questionable whether employers have a moral right to inquire into the kinds of issues (for example, the strength of the marital relationship) that are relevant. About all one can do is get the employee's assurance that he or she has thoroughly discussed the move with all adult members of the family, and that the adults have carefully considered the best interests of the children.

Inoculation

This term is borrowed from medicine, where it means deliberately starting a small infection to stimulate the production of antibodies which can then resist larger infections. The analogy for preparing stayers to cope with changes they would rather, but cannot, ignore is fairly accurate. You do it through deliberate, small, scheduled, relentless upsettings of the *status quo*, with or without an organizational need; and by openly calling attention to the impermanence of current arrangements. As with preventive "shots," the recipient will complain and occasionally howl; but that is better than indulging their instincts — because stayer's instincts are ultimately self-destructive.

The changes can be in personnel or in methods. Both are salutary, but changing methods is both a more effective "inoculation" and less obvious. Most jobs can be accomplished equally well in a number of different ways, and choosing between them is really more a matter of taste than of efficacy. Typically, it is the supervisor's taste or the industrial engineer's taste — occasionally it is even the individual employer's taste — that determines which methods become standard.

No method is addictive in itself; rather it is the length of time people have used it — how long they have had to convert it, through repetition, into an automatic, lulling habit — that makes a method dangerous. The danger is that people may eventually find themselves defenseless and impotent when the major change is thrust upon them. Their adaptive, coping, grappling skills may be flabby, so that a challenge they could have taken in stride when younger defeats them utterly when they are older. It is not age itself but the use to which people have put their years that makes the difference.

Many problems, let alone tragedies, are neatly finessed by periodically inviting those people whose jobs are linked to consider how they might be done differently — if not for the sake of efficiency, then for the sake of variety. Provided the suggested changes are not unsafe, illegal or excessively costly (what is excessive should be determined and stated in advance) such changes should be implemented — even when that means going back to ways that had previously been abandoned.

The usual objection to such changes for change's sake is that methods in use represent the distilled wisdom of many supervisors (or engineers), and that no good can come of tampering with what experience has shown to be the "one best way."

Nonsense.

In practice, the "best way" is always whichever method has the most support from whoever has to use it. No method is too sophisticated to be undermined by indifferent (or worse, hostile) implementation; and few methods are so hopeless that they can't be made to work, somehow, by implementers who are determined that they will work.

Will stayers join enthusiastically in periodic rituals designed to jostle them out of the old habits? Probably not enthusiastically, but they will join. Stayers (on average) are just as clever, observant and creative as movers — they are merely less motivated to apply these attributes. If management supplies the opportunities and scrupulously avoids belittling their contributions, the motivation to contribute should be sufficient. (Not spectacular, but sufficient.)

However, to avoid belittling won't be easy, because methods are the traditional franchise of the entrenched managers and professionals. They are unlikely to approve the delegation of even some of their professional functions to amateurs. It would be understandable, but disastrous, for them to over-react — that is, to see an employee-proposed methods change as far more sweeping than it is.

Responsibility for quality and productivity still rests with them, and therefore final decisions on methods also rest with them. They are merely asked to be as tolerant of such changes as they can bring themselves to be, because they serve a valuable purpose — two, in fact:

There will probably be at least a medium-term productivity gain (after an initial adjustment period when productivity may drop temporarily). More important is the inoculation effect — people who have gone through many little changes are much less likely to be disabled if, subsequently, they have to go through big ones.

FROM : SAUL GELLERMAN
SUBJECT : THE BOTTOM LINE: LIMITING THE LABOR-COST RATIO

The most important single service the personnel department can perform is to set limits on the growth of the labor-cost ratio.

In the absence of clear-cut standards against which to test plans affecting people, management will too often opt for expediency — in the mistaken belief that it is being "practical." The damnable thing about such expedient solutions is that their effects accumulate insidiously, until one day they are suddenly recognized for the unbudgetable, irrevocable and unmanageable horrors that they are.

Three main limits need to be set. In each case, a trade-off has to be worked out between immediate advantage and ultimate ruin, or in some cases between the acceptance of current turmoil and the avoidance of future disaster. These are not easy decisions to make, and for precisely that reason the best time to make them is well in advance — before the pressures for a quick, easy, expedient solution begin to mount. The limits that need to be set are on:

a) the number of full-time employees
b) pay increases that result solely from longevity, and
c) cost-of-living adjustments to pay.

a) Number of Employees: The biggest single factor in the labor-cost ratio is usually the sheer number of people employed, which is why it is very much in the company's interest to hold that number down. Most companies that attempt to do this at all use either the statistical approach (that is, betting on

attrition), or the brutal approach (lay-offs, forced early retirement or simply firing workers who have become redundant). In
either case, they attempt to correct a human surplus only after
one has been accumulated.

A more reasonable approach begins with the premise that
it is best not to let employment swell beyond a sustainable level
in the first place. This means recognizing that full-time
employees who have survived a few years of employment are,
for all practical purposes, tenured, and that barring their
departure or gross malfeasance, the company has assumed an
obligation to them that will only end when they die. (It may
even continue after that if its pension plan provides for a surviving spouse.)

"Tenure" derives from the simple fact that any company
that wishes to avoid endless restrictions on its productivity and
flexibility will recognize that it is not really free to treat
employees otherwise — with or without a union contract. A
union simply makes "employment shrinkage" more orderly
and more costly; in most cases it does not prevent it. On the
other hand, to alternate between inflated and deflated employment is an excellent way to acquire a union contract if you
don't already have one.

There are three ways to prevent the excessive growth of
full-time employment:

• *Don't let employment grow faster than revenues.* To be
more precise, don't permit the trendline for average increases
in headcount rise faster than the trendline for average revenue
growth, measured in constant dollars.

• *Get as much work as possible done by people on someone
else's payroll* — such as temporaries, part-timers and contrac-
tor's employees. Even if this should involve paying a premium,
it is only temporarily more costly than acquiring more full-
timers. What is far more important is that it permits business
contraction when it is necessary without having to renege on
your commitments to existing full-timers. More important, it

minimizes your exposure to the so-called "deadwood" problem — which in most cases consist of reasonably capable people who haven't had anything worthwhile to do for entirely too long.

• *Stimulate turnover.* You can do this by facing a sad fact of organizational life — which is no less a fact for being sad: anyone who has not moved vertically or sideways in five years isn't likely to, ever. It is much better in the long run, but more painful at first, to counsel such people while they are still marketable and mobile that they probably have a better future elsewhere than it is to let that dawn on them long after any opportunity they might have had is gone.

b) Longevity and Pay: When pay is economically sound — that is, when it exploits neither employee nor employer — it is tied to the market value of the work one is capable of doing. Thus it is limited by both the individual's ability and the job's demands. If we consider someone who is starting a new job, without prior experience, and assume that he has the requisite talents and receives adequate instruction, it follows that his pay should rise as his experience increases — and it usually does.

But it also follows that as his acquisition of knowledge and skill gradually flattens out — as it inevitably will, because all of us follow a learning curve, and eventually become about as proficient at any given task as we ever will be — that his pay should cease to rise further. (More precisely, his purchasing power should cease to rise, because this limitation does not rule out cost-of-living adjustments.)

But regardless of where people are on their private learning curve, in virtually every company, pay continues to rise inexorably, year after year, for everyone.

And there's the rub.

Beyond a certain point, pay increases given to people whose jobs have not changed are really longevity increases, no matter what they may be called — and continued longevity increases lead inevitably to overpayment. When large numbers of people are involved, they also lead to swollen labor-cost ratios.

So another limit that needs to be set is on the number of years of service in an essentially unchanged job for which pay increases (other than clearly-labeled inflation adjustments) will be given.

The figure will probably differ from job to job, but the important point is that this limit be set. And lest this seems too radical a proposal, note that, in effect, many companies are already doing precisely this through the simple, but dishonest, expedient of calling an inflation adjustment a "merit increase." This is the real reason the purchasing power of so many wage-earners has remained flat for the last several years. And it is no harmless euphemism to perpetuate expectations of unearned increases by miscalling them "merit increases.

To suggest an upper limit on increases that are given purely because time has elapsed usually arouses fears of turnover or unionization. With regard to turnover, the simple truth is that precisely because of their longevity of tenure (and consequent familiarity with the job and organization), most employees are worth more to their present employer than they would be to any other, and are already paid accordingly. This is why employees should be periodically encouraged to make the acid test of their worth on the job market — by soliciting job offers. Most of them will emerge from that exercise with renewed respect for what they already have.

With regard to unionization, management should not be reluctant to remind employees whose pay has plateaued that it would be no less plateaued, but at greater cost to them, were a union to come to their aid. Union contracts do not remove pay ceilings; instead they levy dues for negotiating them. And any union official who cares to be candid can testify that the competing claims of younger and older members has the effect of pulling demands for their pay closer together — in effect, limiting the pay advantage (but not the job-security advantage) of longevity.

Thus the company which protects the security of its senior employees by limiting its hiring, and which provides an adequate grievance process, has virtually nullified whatever advantages unionization might offer such employees.

Long-service employees are usually susceptible to feeling that they are taken for granted — and with good reason. For many of them, the sheer length of their employment is their principal accomplishment, and it is only human that they should want this to be recognized — and are hurt when it is not. So — beyond lapel pins and wall plaques — anniversary bonuses should be considered, for example, cash awards every five years or so. That's a more convincing way of expressing thanks, and a lot easier on the labor-cost ratio than a pay increase. Pay increases continue forever.

c) Cost-of-Living Adjustments: It would take a more qualified economist than I to say whether these attempts to keep employees "whole" in the midst of inflation are not inflationary themselves — I suspect that they are. A more immediate problem for management is finding the means to pay for them. The options are limited: "COLA" (which is not a beverage, but a payment) can only come from increased prices, increased productivity or decreased distributions to other accounts (including profits). Of these, the easiest and therefore most popular is simply to "pass the pain" of inflation to one's customers with a price increase.

Sometimes, even the most benevolent managements can not afford to provide a full adjustment to the cost of living for its employees. There comes a point beyond which the employees must begin to absorb a part of inflation themselves— and indeed, should inflation continue to worsen, a progressively greater part. Of course, anything less than a full cost of living increase amounts to a purchasing power decrease, and that is an ugly prospect for nearly everyone. Nevertheless, if economic conditions become too severe, employees might have to endure part of all of the pain of inflation.

Most working people are sensible enough to opt for what amounts to a pay cut if the alternative is loss of their job — provided, of course, they believe that the choice is really that stark. Therefore most companies could probably preserve both their employees and themselves without COLA, if they had to — if employees believed that their jobs were at stake. But that's a big "if." The problem, in brief, is how to prepare people for a crisis which everyone hopes will never come.

What must be done, is first: to devise a system of measurements that show whether the organization's survival would be threatened by continued granting of full COLA. This would no doubt include, but could not be limited to, a measurement of inflation itself. Second: to explain *in advance* — long before crisis points are reached — how the system works and how restrictions on COLA would, if necessary, be put into effect. Third: to report, periodically, on the measurements themselves — even when, as we all devoutly hope — they are nowhere near critical levels.

The point of the exercise is to ensure that if employees must be asked to sacrifice, it will come as an understood if unpleasant necessity, and not as a shock. Why? Because shock virtually ensures disbelief, which undermines cooperation — and cooperation is essential for surviving a major crisis.

To develop such measurements is beyond the sole competence of personnel executives, although they must be involved. Their most important role is first to make certain that the system is both intelligible and fair, and then to explain and defend it to their employees.

If COLA is financed by allowing the labor-cost ratio to rise, the profitability, if not the survival, of the company is endangered. The best solution by far is to finance the payment through productivity gains, in which case it isn't really COLA at all, but profit-sharing in the purest form. But productivity gains are a lot easier to talk about than to produce.

And if COLA can't be financed, it can't be given. If a flood rises high enough, everyone gets wet, and — to continue the analogy — it is better to be soaked aboard a raft that stays afloat than to sink it by trying to stay dry. That's why there can be no unlimited commitments to COLA, and why the consequences of each such adjustment need to be thought out in advance — far more carefully than they usually are.

Many personnel managers have agreed with this line of reasoning, but only to this point; then they say that they would not dare take such controversial action unless other employers went along with it simultaneously. Otherwise, they say, they foresee horrendous competitive disadvantages. But that would be true only if competitors could pay for COLA with productivity gains, or absorb higher labor-cost ratios, or were less blocked from passing along price increases than you. In other words, there is no competitive disadvantage unless one exists already.

When everyone is endangered, the competitive advantage lies with whoever has the best chance of survival — and putting limits on COLA is one way to boost those chances. ☐

SHIRT-SLEEVE APPROACH
TO
LONG-RANGE PLANNING

FOR THE SMALLER, GROWING CORPORATION

Robert E. Linneman

Dr. Robert E. Linneman is on the marketing faculty of the Temple University School of Business Administration. Experienced in marketing industrial products, he has helped in the marketing plans of over 45 companies. He has published articles in professional journals and in 1976 was a recipient of the Lindback award for distinguished teaching.

Benefits of Comprehensive
Corporate Planning

W hy consider formal comprehensive planning? There are two overwhelming reasons: Businesses that do generally (1) grow faster and (2) make more money. It's easy to see why. The end results of formal planning — explicit, written-out specific objectives, plans, control points, and back-up contingency plans — give you a clear understanding of your company and a firmer control over its future.

But by itself a formal plan is not enough. Consider an incident that occured several years ago. The director of marketing of a medium-sized bank, with the help of a consultant, developed a formal procedure for locating branch banks. The director of marketing presented the finished "model" to the bank's president, who was excited about the procedure: "This is the most creative piece of work I've seen since I've been with this bank. Implement it." The director of marketing then explained the procedure to other divisions (real estate, branch banking, and so forth). Everybody understood their roles. But one year later the model was junked, its very title a dirty word. Actually, the model was a good one. It failed because most of the bank's executives really didn't care whether or not it succeeded. In fact, because of existing rivalries, some were more interested in seeing it fail. When something went wrong, they wouldn't put forth extra effort to correct it. It wasn't *their* plan, after all.

This dismal case points to a significant truth: Only people who are involved in drafting plans are going to try their best to make the plans succeed. The key is managerial involvement. Nothing flatters people more than being taken seriously, and there is no better way to take managers seriously than to bring them into the planning process. The sense of a shared challenge and real responsibility helps generate a climate that encourages extra effort — as well as stimulating creativity and fostering a positive attitude toward change.

Moreover, the very process of involving management in formal planning improves communications, thereby pulling management together. The assembling of information from all vital areas enlarges managers' understanding of overall company operations. This increased knowledge makes it easier not only to spot problems but to see possible solutions. Beyond that, it makes it easier to see new opportunities — opportunities that might never occur to managers who remain isolated (comparatively) in their own domains.

Since planning and reviews will be scheduled at regular intervals, a formal approach also assures continuity. Of course, merely granting an adequate amount of time and effort to the process does not guarantee thoroughness, but it makes it possible. Because planning occurs on a regular basis, managers gradually become better planners.

Finally, planning *is* managing. Formal planning is one of the best ways to develop managerial skills. And having good managerial depth is one of the best ways to ensure the success of your firm.

Operational planning. Most firms, and certainly those of any size, have a written annual plan — an operational plan — which guides day-to-day company activities. An operational plan is a recipe for action. It specifies what gets done, who does it, and when. Since practically all firms require time — usually several years or more — to change the overall direction of their business, operational planning by itself is tactical in nature. It

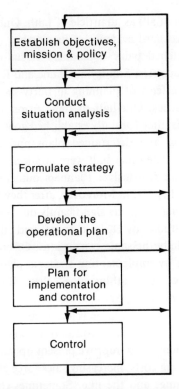

Figure 1. The Planning Process

is almost solely restricted to fine-tuning what the company is already doing.

Strategic planning. Strategic planning, on the other hand, involves looking into the future and deciding what the basic thrust of your business ought to be. It may result in a strategy that, over time, brings about fundamental changes in your business. The point of strategic planning is to decide a course today that will get the company where it wants to be tomorrow.

Benefits of strategic planning. No one disputes the benefits of formal operational planning. But for a long time managers had to accept the value of formal strategic planning (if they accepted it at all) as an article of faith. Only recently have studies provided hard evidence of its worth.

Using matched pairs — planners versus nonplanners — in the same industries, Stanley S. Thune and Robert J. House compared the effects of planning in thirty-six firms from six different industries. One-half of these firms were long-range planners; that is, they formally established goals for three years ahead or more, and determined plans and procedures for achieving them. The other half were non-long-range planners. The results were conclusive: Planners outachieved nonplanners, especially in growth. Moreover, after they had introduced strategic planning, planners significantly outstripped their own performance. Studies by H. Igor Ansoff and others have come up with essentially the same conclusions. Of course, this does not imply that by implementing strategic planning you'll be guaranteed success. Nothing does that. But, in general, strategic planning does pay.

Why is this so? One reason is that firms that do not engage in strategic planning tend to concentrate on what they're already doing. They try to improve present operations by lowering manufacturing costs, increasing sales force efficiency, beefing up advertising, and the like. Sometimes this works. But often the "try-harder" approach fails because external conditions have changed so that their present strategies — indeed, those that may have served them so well in the past — are no longer suitable. The results of such buggy-whip strategies are legend.

In contrast, strategic planning concentrates attention on what you should be doing now to prepare for, say, five years from now. This perspective encourages consideration of non-traditional approaches. And, it is more energizing in the sense that it forces you to think about where you want to be in contrast to where you will be.

You'll have to make many tough choices in long-range planning. For example, you must decide between: improving your competitive position or taking short-term profits; concentrating on existing markets or developing new ones; high-risk strategies or "riskless" activity; growth in one industry or diversification; growth by acquisition or internal growth; maximizing profits or considering social responsibilities. Of course, whether you engage in formal strategic planning or not, you still have to make these choices. In the final analysis, its not a question of whether you want to do strategic planning or not. You cannot escape the futurity of your actions. You either build a plant or you don't. You enter a new market area or you don't. You invest in R & D or you don't. And all of these decisions will have long-range implications. So the question is: Do you do strategic planning informally (intuitively) or formally? Formal strategic planning provides you with a framework for determining the best balance.

You may say, "Things are going fine. Why should I go through all the bother?" Let's approach that answer indirectly, with an example of the rapid impact of exponential growth. To begin, a pond has one lily pad growing on it. But every succeeding day the number of lily pads doubles. On the second day, then, there are two pads, on the third day four, and so on. Sixty days later, if growth continues, the pond will be entirely full. It's relatively easy to understand that only half of the pond is free of lily pads on the next-to-last day, the fifty-ninth. But it's usually harder to grasp that on the fifty-ninth day, just a week before the end, the pads cover less than 1 percent of the surface.

Unfortunately, complications that stem from faulty strategies often grow at close to an exponential rate. To make matters worse, strategic decisions are not self-regenerative like operating decisions. Operating decisions you are forced to make every so often, but, unless you have a formal review process, this is not so with strategies. At first, faults in strategy are hardly detectable, but toward the end they close in with remorseless swiftness. And it takes time to devise adjustments to your strategy, put them to work, and then turn things around. In fact, by the time it's obvious to everyone that your strategy is beginning to flounder, it may be too late to do anything about it.

So consider yourself fortunate (or skillful) if you're satisfied with your firm's current performance. And start strategic planning now. Close scrutiny of your company and its operating environment may uncover concealed threats. If so, you can make gradual changes now that can solve problems before they get out of hand. And the earlier you implement a change, the less disruptive it will be.

Perhaps the outcome of strategic planning is that you decide to continue to do what you've been doing in the past. In such a case, was your planning a waste of time? Not at all. As a result of formal strategic planning, you will have systematically examined where your present strategy will lead, and you will have considered the possibility of changing the thrust of your business. You are at least more aware of the risks and advantages in the course you have decided to follow.

Prerequisites for successful strategic planning. Experiences of hundreds of companies have shown that the following points, all of which are basic to successful strategic planning, need to be fully understood — and carried out.

• Include functional area managers in the planning process. Company managers, the people who run the firm on a day-to-day basis, generally understand their divisions better than anyone else. This practical knowledge is critical for the long-range planning process. It keeps planning down to earth. In addition, these are the people who will carry out the strategy, and its success depends on their cooperation. They are far more likely to be enthusiastic over a strategy they've had a hand in making.

• The involvement of the president (or chief executive officer) is essential. Mere support is not enough. After all, strategic planning, by definition, may change the thrust of the organization. Unless the president is involved — deeply — involved — in making such plans, he or she is not likely to approve them. Besides, deciding the future directions of the firm is the president's job. Anything less than full participation by the president will lead to disappointment for everybody.

• Make time for strategic planning. You can't wait until you have time available — job pressures are not likely to diminish. The time must be made. The time requirements are another reason why the president must actively lead the planning efforts. For if this responsibility is delegated to someone else, it soon becomes evident to everyone how the president rates its importance. Other top managers won't put their efforts into strategic planning either. They'll work on something which they think the president views as more important.

• Strategic planning must be integrated with operational planning. For the vast number of firms, the transition from short-range plans must be gradual; few firms can operate with one orientation today and an entirely different one tomorrow. In addition, some short-range commitments simply must be met. If they are not, you may lose your power to act (in plainer words, you may lose your job). On the other hand, you must think of the future. Consequently, it's usually best to develop operational and strategic plans concurrently. Short-range requirements may force you to modify your strategic plans, and vice versa. In any case, it's a hammering and fitting process.

• The strategy must be flexible. Strategy can be described as a company's reaction to the economic, social, and political environment, both as it is at present and as the company expects it to be in the future. There is very little the company can do to affect the environment; on the other hand, it does have control over its own response. The trick is to determine what the future will be like and devise a strategy that enables the company to operate successfully within it. Unfortunately, our forecasting skills leave much to be desired. It's necessary to develop strategy that has sufficient flexibility to succeed in a number of plausible future environments.

• Strategic plans must be continually reassessed. Don't expect to develop a strategic plan and then be done with planning. Thanks to the unpredictability of the environment, plans must be checked and updated. Most firms engaged in long-range planning examine their strategies once a year as part of the regular planning cycle — and on an ad hoc basis should critical elements of the environment turn out radically different from the forecasts. As a military strategist once remarked, "Planning is indispensable, but plans are useless." Robert G. Page, chief executive officer of Leesona Corporation, put it this way, "We're not slaves to our plan. It's a guide."

• Don't look for the universally ideal method of planning. No single method or planning applies to all companies; what works best for a given firm depends on several basic factors:

a.) Is management more comfortable, for example, with "by-the-numbers" procedures or a shirt-sleeve approach? A radical shift from one to the other usually must be made gradually. Then, management with experience in planning is more likely to use sophisticated techniques than management that is fairly new to the process.

b.) Size may also determine the method you choose. Large companies can usually afford the staff both to accumulate information and to help coordinate the planning effort. In smaller companies, these tasks must usually be carried out by the operating managers.

c.) The length of the planning horizon will vary with the firm's product. For example, a fashion goods manufacturer would find the fifty-year planning horizons of some petroleum firms totally unsuitable. In addition, planning would be highly decentralized in a conglomerate but centralized in a company with a homogeneous product line.

d.) Data, time, and staff availability obviously determine how sophisticated the planning will be. In some industries, data may be hard to come by. Then, sometimes staff may be limited in even the largest corporations.

e.) Finally, even for a given company, the ideal method of planning changes through time as management gains more experience in planning, as attitudes change, and so on.

This book presents a step-by-step procedure for planning. Although it is generally suitable for most firms just starting comprehensive planning, keep in mind you may have to make some changes to adapt to the "culture" of your firm.

Probably one of the greatest pitfalls for companies just starting strategic planning is trying to do everything "right" the first time through. As a consequence, they get bogged down on one or several steps. They never get through the planning cycle in time. Sometimes they give up in disgust.

Accept the fact that your first time through will produce only a rudimentary guide to action. Experience has shown that it usually takes about five years to develop "sophisticated" plans. But the benefits from even a rudimentary plan can be great. Remember that you can carry on planning at any level of sophistication you like. Just take care to follow all the steps described in the following chapters.

When should you start the planning process? Right now. Perhaps you think, "It's too late in the year. We're almost ready to make our next year's budgets." If so, why not run through the steps in a very general way taking only a few days? By doing this, you'll have a better feel for your strategic direction, thus improving the focus of your short-range plans. And you'll have gained practice; making the next planning cycle more productive. Then too, you'll have made the commitment, making it less likely that comprehensive planning will be put off until it's too late.

Organizing
for Planning

Organizing for planning in a centralized company.

The planning team. The planning team should consist of the firm's top management.

• Normally the team consists of top management — those officers who report directly to the president. If more than seven people are reporting to the president, perhaps there are too many people reporting to him, thereby cutting down his efficiency. Why not consider reorganizing *before* you set up the planning team?

• Is there someone who could make a valuable contribution but is not a member of top management? If you discover that your firm has a number of such people, two things are possible: Either the wrong people are in top management, or management needs to be restructured.

• If you dip below top management, can you afford to include everybody on the next management level? If not, who's going to feel hurt if he or she is left out? Do you really want to keep such people in the firm? And you should ask the same questions about someone with high rank whom you'd prefer to leave off the committee.

The president (assuming the president is the chief executive officer) should chair the planning committee; this will help underscore the importance of the planning team. If someone else serves as chairman, he or she should be unusually important to the firm, perhaps the heir apparent to the president.

The main advantage of the planning team is that it provides an orderly forum for members of top management to "have their day in the court" which boosts morale. People appreciate the chance to present their own ideas; at the very least it makes them more receptive to those of other people. Also, the interchange of ideas usually stimulates creativity, while the company-wide experience of the committee members keeps the plans realistic. Finally, people who participate in the decision-making process feel they have a greater stake in making the final plan work.

The final decisions are ultimately made by the president (again assuming the president is the chief executive officer). He or she must be careful, however, to encourage creative dissent during the meetings. The value of the discussions diminishes drastically if people feel it is pointless (or unwise) to present ideas the president may disapprove of. Similarly, it is up to the chairman to make sure that a clique or an overly aggressive individual doesn't push everybody else to the sidelines.

The major drawback to the planning team is readily apparent: Committee meetings seem to be non-productive. And it's dismaying to see a collection of the firm's most highly paid officers tied up in committee meetings when so much needs to be done out in the plant. Yet despite this shortcoming, committee meetings are usually the quickest way to a satisfactory result.

To avoid tying up executives when it's really not necessary, sometimes companies use subcommittees made up of planning team members, whose functions might be to evaluate acquisitions, new plants, and so forth. These ad hoc task forces usually include only those members needed to gather information or make analysis.

How much do planning team members need to know? This is a question that has been raised at many seminars — by presidents of closely held businesses. In such firms figures of the business are not known to the outside, or even some of the key employees who might be on the planning team. The presidents are usually concerned about releasing such figures for several very good reasons: If key employees know how profitable the business is, they may start up competing businesses of their own. If too many people really know the business, it's more likely that competitors will find out important information. If hourly employees find out the profitability of the firm (and the more people who know the profitability of the firm, the more likely it is that they will find out), they're more likely to demand higher wages.

The answer that comes out of these discussions is that there are no rights or wrongs about what should be revealed to key employees. It's a personal choice. The decision boils down to weighing the benefits of involving others versus the loss of secrecy and the costs of doing all planning by yourself. There's a general agreement that if you want others to be on the planning team, these people have to know the firm's objectives, financial strengths and weaknesses, and past successes and failures. Otherwise, they won't be competent to make any meaningful systematic contributions.

Use of planning coordinator. Many companies have found that designating someone to *coordinate* the planning process reduces the work of the chairman and the other members of the team. The person's duties usually include recommending the planning format, scheduling meetings, keeping minutes, helping to gather data and assembling and distributing the plans. Usually the planning coordinator is a nonvoting, ex officio member of the planning team.

It is generally accepted that the planning coordinator's role is not to develop plans but to facilitate the process. Do not underestimate the requirements for the job, however. As one of the leading authorities on planning, George Steiner, points out, a good planning coordinator should have a thorough understanding of the firm and its operations. He (or she) should have a close working relationship with the president and the respect of its operating managers. He must be sensitive to the kind of information necessary (and acceptable) for managerial decision making, but never give the impression that he is making the decisions for managers. Overall, he should serve as a catalyst in the planning process.

Steiner also emphasizes that operating managers should view the planning coordinator as someone available to help them, not as a watchdog who will turn them in as soon as something goes wrong. The coordinator, then, must not be responsible for seeing that the plans are carried out. The coordinator who must report to the president that the performance of one of the operating managers isn't up to snuff loses the trust not only of that manager but of the others as well. After all, anyone might be next. Who can remain open and free with a potential executioner?

Most smaller companies cannot afford a full-time coordinator. Many elect to settle for less than the ideal by using a part-time one. These persons usually lack many of the qualities listed above, or because of the nature of their job, perform fewer of the tasks that might be carried out by full-time planning coordinators.

In companies with no planning coordinator, the president usually assumes the responsibility for planning formats, scheduling the meetings, and putting together the plans. One president of a company with $2,000,000 in sales, emphasized that he wanted to be the "scribe" in order to underscore the importance that he attached to the planning process. Actually, you'll find that if you stick to the procedure recommended in this book, you'll have less writing than you probably expect.

The use of consultants. By now it should be clear: Consultants should not do the planning. Consultants should be used only to suggest planning procedures, to provide information (such as competitive data), or to evaluate the feasibility of particular plans. In certain instances you might wish them to *suggest* strategies. But remember, consultants should serve only in an advisory or facilitating capacity. Managers must do the planning.

Organizing for planning in a decentralized company. The corporate planning team will include, quite obviously, top management of the corporation. In some instances, division managers are the top management, but the larger the company, the less likely it will be that division managers will sit on its corporate planning team.

The division planning teams closely resemble those of the centrally organized company. These planning teams set up planning timetables (within corporate limits), determine divisional strategies and action plans, discuss objectives, strategies, and forecasts with corporate management, and authorize the preparing of detailed plans for functional areas after corporate management approves their (divisional) plans.

Step 1: Establishing Objectives, Mission and Policies

Before you can do any kind of planning, you must decide what you want your company to be like. This means establishing your objectives, your mission, and your policies. It's usually best to determine your objectives first. But, all three are interrelated, a fact the planning team should keep in mind.

Establishing objectives. After you've decided who is going to be on the planning team, the next step is to set objectives. Remember that here goals and objectives are used interchangeably.

Make sure that your objectives don't emerge like some corporate goals — "to maximize profits," for example, or "to produce profits in order to return to shareholders adequate dividends and to have ample funds for long-term investments." These "objectives" are unlikely to cause any argument; they are vague enough to mean all things to all people. Vague objectives can create confusion among those engaged in strategic planning even when only a few people are involved and they are in continual communication.

At the very outset of strategic planning make sure there is a common understanding among management about what the company wishes to accomplish both within and by the end of the planning horizon. Here's how to construct meaningful corporate objectives — objectives that provide direction for the planning process.

Interim objectives and objectives for the planning horizon. First determine your "planning horizon" — how far in the future you wish to plan. No single time span is proper to all because needs vary from company to company. The length of the planning horizon usually varies with "turnaround time" — firms with heavy, fixed commitments usually plan further into the future than companies without such investments. However, many firms have discovered that five years is about right. It's far enough ahead so that they can make strategic changes. On the other hand, a five-year span is not so far away that it seems "blue sky."

Occasionally some people object to a planning horizon as lengthy as five years. Usually they will cite the fashion goods industry: "How can you plan ahead for five years? Because of the rapid change within the industry, about six months is about as far as you can plan." As far as product planning goes, this is true. But such a narrow view of planning misses the essence of strategic planning. The benefit from strategic planning is taking the long-range view of the business and asking such basic questions as "Are there trends occurring in this industry that may make our business less (or more) viable in the future? Are there any actions that we should be taking today to protect against (or capitalize on) these trends?" Such actions might range from upgrading personnel, modernizing production facilities, investing more in research and development, or changing channels of distribution, to taking steps to change the major thrust of the business.

When you've decided upon your objectives for the end of your planning horizon, determine your objectives for the first year. If you're experienced in long-range planning, you may wish to set objectives for the second and third years as well. But if youre're just starting, settle for the first and fifth year. Keep the process as simple as possible.

Corporate level objectives. The first objectives within the firm should be set at the corporate level. After these goals have been established, develop plans to achieve them. These plans become the goals for the next level of management, and so on.

Too frequently top management fails to determine the company's objectives. The reason given usually goes something like this: "In our firm we can't do things this way. Actually, each division has to set its goals first. Then we take the sum of these goals — the composite — and this gives us the goals of the firm. This is the only way goals can be set realistically." What this really means is that lower-level managers decide the destiny of the company. There's a hand on the tiller all right, but it's three decks down, in the engine room. A judgment is unavoidable; when the top management allows others to decide the system's objectives, the wrong people are in top management.

In differentiating between goals and the means for accomplishing goals, it is also important that one recognize which echelon of management is under consideration: A goal at one level of management might be a "means" (plan) at another. For instance, the intent "to increase manufacturing capacity by 50 percent in five years" would be a goal for the manufacturing department, but it is not a goal at the corporate level. At the corporate level it would only be part of the master plan. The corporate goal should be expressed in terms of what it really wants to obtain: for example, $1,000,000 in net profit after taxes in five years.

Making objectives specific. It is always easier to agree on broad objectives than on specific ones. But a broad objective, by definition, leaves much open to interpretation. By contrast, a specific objective promotes unity of purpose: Everyone knows what must be accomplished. Knowing where you want to arrive also enables you to evaluate the various ways of getting there. Moreover, you're in a position to measure your progress en route and, if necessary, to make adjustments.

"Measure" is a key word, because a specific objective is concrete and measurable, whether in dollars, percentages, or proportions. For this reason, "maximizing profits" is not a specific objective, for how can you tell when the company has maximized profits? At best such a goal indicates a broad aim. Suppose, however, a company determines that over a five-year period it plans to increase its profits to $400,000 after taxes and its annual sales to $4,000,000. These are specific objectives because they describe exactly what the firm wants to achieve; progress toward objectives of this kind can be measured every step of the way. And when the firm gets there, it knows it.

Sometimes it's difficult to hammer objectives into specificity. The following process is typical. A planning team states its broad objective of "maximizing profits." The members must then forge an agreement about what maximization of profits actually involves. Reconciliation can be a monumental task. The members' concept of an acceptable level of profits may vary widely. No doubt disputes of this nature explain why many companies have vague goals. Avoidance of establishing specific goals saves thought and argument, but in shirking the task, the firm, unfortunately, forfeits the benefits of management by objectives.

Of course there are many cases in which quantitative terms cannot fully describe what one wishes to accomplish. In these instances a compromise is necessary, and you may have to express what you want to achieve in the most concrete qualitative terms that the situation permits.

Establishing objectives of every key area. Setting objectives would be far simpler if a company had only one major objective it wished to accomplish. But most firms have several. Consequently, the objectives for each key area must be concretely defined. Objectives for key areas help avoid ones that are overly broad.

A word of caution: Be sure that you establish objectives only for key areas. Lengthy lists that include trifling goals are impractical. They can also obscure, through sheer numbers, the ones which really count. The common key areas are profitability, growth, dividends, stability, and — where information is available — relative ranking.

Relative ranking. When data is available and publicized, there is a fifth area that is commonly used: relative ranking. Most top executives of a company are interested in maintaining, or achieving, a certain relative rank among firms with whom they are normally compared. This is for an obvious reason: If the firm is at the bottom or its rank is slipping, stockholders are not going to be satisfied with the present management. Therefore, many firms use relative ranking as a target.

Exciting yet believable objectives. Mediocrity is no more interesting in a corporation than in an individual, and the company that sets up uninspiring objectives invites a potentially fatal case of passivity in its employees. Highly creative and agressive people gradually wilt if the atmosphere around them is dulled. The mediocre quickly become even more so. On the other hand, absurdly high objectives are just as bad. It does little good to establish objectives at high level if no one really believes that the company can achieve them. In such a case only half-hearted efforts will go into developing plans and putting them into action.

Where then, should a firm set its goals? Perhaps this has been best summarized by the former chairman of A. T. & T., Frederick R. Kappel: "Part of the talent or genius of the goal setter is the ability to distinguish between the possible and the impossible — but to be willing to get very close to the latter." Note, however, that an attainable goal that nobody believes in is little better than one that really is impossible. Part of the "genius" of top management is to convince everybody that they *can* rise to the challenge.

Ranking objectives in order of importance. There are two major problems in deciding what the firm's objectives should be: The first is that there's never enough time or resources to work toward all of the things you'd like to accomplish. The second is deciding on the proper level of desired accomplishment.

To handle the first problem, use a procedure recommended by Kepner and Tregoe. Place objectives in one of two groups: *must* objectives and *want* objectives. Must objectives are absolutely essential. Want objectives are important, but not absolutely essential. Must objectives are to be attained at all costs. There is no hierarchy among these objectives. They all have to be reached. And here — on must objectives — is where you'll spend your resources.

Now for deciding the proper levels. For each must objective, determine the minimum acceptable amount necessary to create the necessary vitality and excitement in your company (stockholders, executives, workers, and even "external" members, such as suppliers and customers). These levels, then, become minimum acceptable levels of performance.

Anything besides the must objectives and minimum levels of performance, then, are really want objectives. If there is a surplus left over after allocating resources to achieve the must objectives, it can be used for achieving want objectives. Kepner and Tregoe's book provides further information how want objectives might be ranked and utilized. But for most companies, isolating the must objectives and minimum levels of acceptable performance provides adequate direction. So for all practical purposes you can forget about the objectives you placed on the want objective list.

Objectives subject to revision. Objectives that you set today may become obsolete within a short period of time. While working through the planning process, for instance, you might find that there is no way you can reach the predetermined objectives. Or, after the plan has been implemented, environmental conditions might change. When you replan you might find your previously set objectives impossible to attain. If this happens, change your objectives.

Before you set objectives, however, make sure that the planning team is also familiar with mission and policies. As pointed out previously, these three — objectives, mission, and policies — complement each other and may partly overlap.

Stating the mission. After you have decided what it is that you want to achieve (objectives), the next step is to specify the mission. The mission stakes out broad areas of business in which the firm can, or perhaps cannot, operate. In other words, the mission decides the playing field.

It's best to arrive at a common understanding of the general mission of the company early in the planning process. Although everyone may have a general idea of what this is, chances are that putting it in writing will help people to think it through more carefully. A carefully expressed mission helps narrow the search for suitable strategies by indicating what broad areas (industries, geographic areas) of business are acceptable. There's no point wasting time on ideas that the company is not prepared to accept.

After you've conducted the situation analysis and the examination of the environment, you may decide to revise the mission. Or you may wish to do so later because an unexpected opportunity has arisen. In any case, there's no harm done. The mission is not graven in stone. It expresses the philosophy of an evolving institution. Its function is perpetually contemporary: to let management know at any given time which areas of business are acceptable and which are not.

The mission should point in the direction of acceptable strategies and to an industry or subindustry affected by identifiable external forces and where, hopefully, statistics will be available. Too broad a mission is not much help. You probably lose more than you gain by saying, "We're not in the bicycle business, but in the transportation business." What does transportation business mean? Air, surface, water, underwater, space? What mode of travel? Jet aircraft, glider, supercargo, sailboat, spaceship? To what class of customer? Industry, government, individual?

On the other hand, the mission should be stated broadly

enough to allow for creative growth. It would be better to state the mission as being in "environmental cooling systems for industry" rather than in the "air conditioning business." When possible, the mission should describe both who the customers are and what services the firm performs for them.

Stating policies. Now that you've decided what it is that the company should accomplish (objectives) and what types of general activities the company should or should not engage in (mission), the next step is to determine corporate policies. These are rules of behavior that govern top management action, both within the company and in the company's dealings with other businesses and the general public. Whereas the mission stakes out the playing field, policies specify the rules of the game.

Policies delineate courses of action that will be acceptable to the company and, like the acknowledgment of the mission, help to focus the search. For example, the owner-president of a company with 35 employees claimed that it was a policy of her company to provide jobs — and growth opportunities — for employees of the company. Another company (about 300 employees) had as a policy that the firm would not seek expansion through innovation. Rather the firm would grow by utilizing its marketing skills and by capitalizing on its well-known name. Some companies have policies concerning ownership: retention of family control or even sole ownership. Then too, some companies, in order to avoid overdependence on one or two customers, target the maximum percentage of total sales to any one customer. These examples point out how important it is that members of the planning team fully understand the firm's "rules of conduct"; it saves quite a bit of thrashing around.

Getting the job done. You should be able to set objectives, mission, and policies in several meetings. A guiding rule is not to strive for perfection. One president remarked that his planning team had been trying to decide upon proper corporate objectives for three months. They had been meeting one afternoon every other week, but in spite of all this time spent, they still hadn't arrived at any conclusions. No one had ever told him it could be done in a few hours. In retrospect, he realized that they could have set tentative objectives — and mission and policies, too — in two meetings. Revisions could have been made, if necessary, as they progressed through the planning cycle.

Step 2: Conducting the Situation Analysis

Corporate plans are based on assumptions about company strengths and weaknesses. It follows, then, that the accuracy of your assumptions, in part, determines the effectiveness of your strategies. A thorough appraisal of your company will point out strengths which can be capitalized on for internal expansion, diversification, or both. Conversely, it should indicate internal weaknesses, which unless corrected, signify that certain strategies should be avoided.

Surprisingly, many firms do not have a solid grasp of what makes them successful. An executive vice-president of one of the largest marketing research companies in the United States once commented on this puzzling fact. Many of his company's clients, he said, lacked well-organized data bases. In fact, many did not even have a list of their key customers. It's easy to understand how such companies might overlook both market opportunities and ways to improve their operating efficiency.

The situation analysis offers another benefit. All companies have an abundance of beliefs about the firm's strengths and weaknesses. Unfortunately, too many of these beliefs are myths. They may have been fact at one time, but times and conditions change and to further complicate communications, often — even among top management — there's no common agreement on myths. The situation analysis provides the plan-

Table 1. Explanation of P. & L. and Balance Sheets and Common Ratios

Consolidated Income Statement ($000)

Sales	12,100
Cost of goods sold (including selling costs)	8,460
Depreciation	900
Interest	740
Pretax income	2,000
Income tax	800
Net income	1,200

Consolidated Balance Sheet ($000)

Assets		Liabilities	
Current assets		Current liabilities	
Cash	200	Accounts payable	500
Marketable securities	100	Bank note	1,900
Accounts receivable	1,300	Long-term debt	5,500
Inventories	1,500		
Total current assets	3,100	Total liabilities	7,900
Long-term assets		Shareholders' equity	
Land	800	Common stock	100
Plant and equipment	9,000	Retained earnings	4,900
	9,800		5,000
Total assets			
Current & long-term	12,900	Total liabilities & equity	12,900

Common Ratios

Liquidity ratios
Current ratio:
Current assets ($3,100) compared with current liabilities ($2,400) = 1.29 to 1
Quick ratio or acid test:
Deducting inventories from current assets and comparing the remainder ($1,600) to current liabilities ($2,400) = .66 to 1

Profitability ratios

Return on assets:
Net income ($1,200) compared with total assets ($12,900) = 9%
Return on invested capital:
Net income ($1,200) compared with shareholder's equity ($5,000) and long-term debt ($5,500) = 11.4%
Return on shareholder's equity:
Net income ($1,200) compared with shareholder's equity ($5,000) = 24%

Leverage ratios
Debt/equity
Long-term debt ($5,500) compared with owners equity ($5,000) = 1.1 to 1
Current liabilities to equity:
Current liabilities ($2,400) to owners equity ($5,000) = .48 to 1
Times interest earned:
Earnings before interest and taxes ($2,740) compared with interest ($740) = 3.7 to 1

ning team with a common factual understanding as to what the firm's strengths and weaknesses are.

You may feel that a formal situation analysis would be a waste of time in your case because your planning team already has an accurate understanding of your company. Perhaps it does. But it is hard for anyone who is deeply involved in what he or she is doing to be completely objective about it. If management has committed itself to a course of action, even subconsciously, it becomes easy to downplay or even ignore evidence of potential weaknesses in that course. At the same time, it is easy to perceive strengths that do not exist. A formal study helps to minimize these possibilities.

So conduct a formal evaluation of your company's resources and capabilities before you form strategic plans. Include every major functional area within the organization. For instance, in a centralized firm (or a division within a diversified corporation), there should be an audit of major areas such as manufacturing, R & D, finance, marketing, and manpower. These individual analyses would then be consolidated into a summary statement of the firm's present strengths and weaknesses.

The members of the planning team should take an active role in the analysis. This will help them to better understand the firm's points.

Conducting the analysis. The following recommends the "ideal" way of conducting the situation analysis: Getting bogged down in the situation analysis is an all too common problem. There are some rules of thumb that can make the difference between success and chaos.

Keeping the task manageable. On the first go-around, don't try to gather all the facts you'd like to have. It's impractical — if not impossible — to make a complete diagnosis of your firm. Accept the fact that you'll have to make "best estimates" about many things. If you try to gather everything, you'll never finish the planning cycle. And you'll have the same experience as the firm that started formal planning with a zest but never got any further than the situation analysis — because the president had insisted on gathering all the facts.

Setting up timetables. Decide at the outset when the situation analysis must be completed. Besides a completion date deadline, set up timetables for each task. If you allow people a nebulous period of time to complete a job, you invite procrastination. Moreover, only timetables enable coordination of the various stages of the overall effort. Decide on what needs to be done and set dates for every step as well as for the completion of the functional area analyses and their consolidation. In addition, functional area managers should set up timetables for completing tasks within their individual areas of analysis.

Keeping the situation analysis relevant. There are all sorts of information that are "interesting" or "nice to know," and there may be a place for it but not in the situation analysis. Limit your study to information that suggests action. For instance, manufacturing will be looking for ways to improve productivity. Marketing will be looking for insights into possible opportunities for product line expansion and/or pruning, new products, geographic extension, and the like. If the situation analysis fails to provide insights of this sort, it's a waste of time.

Deciding what should be analyzed. No single format will fit the needs of all corporations, and for a basic reason. The evaluation must include the firm's significant areas, and those that are "significant" will vary from company to company. Even so, there is much common ground.

Regardless of the company, or the industry it's operating in, there must be an analysis of absolute strengths and competitive posture. Looking first at absolute strengths, this analysis highlights what "tools" the company has to work with. For example, what kind of production facilities does the company have? How much working capital? What is its customer base? What kind of skills do its employees possess? The purpose of this analysis is to assure that each member of the planning team will better understand the strengths and weaknesses of the other functional areas. And, of course, such an examination forces functional area heads to make systematic analysis of the points of leverage (and vulnerabilities) of their own departments — no small benefit!

For some of these factors you may wish to (and should) gather data to establish historical trends. Many companies go back five years. Use charts and graphs if they will make the relevance of the data more obvious.

The analysis of competitive posture is usually more difficult. It's more subjective. But it needs to be done. For example, many ratios — such as debt/equity — are only meaningful when compared with other firms in the same industry. Another situation: Total sales may be less meaningful than market share (sales may be climbing but the company's market share may be dropping precipitiously, foreboding all kinds of trouble). The planning team is the logical group to perform this analysis, because the conclusions they reach will have a major impact on strategy selection.

You won't be able to examine everything the way you'd like to, so concentrate on gathering the information that will be of real help to you in laying out strategy. There are no hard and fast rules as to how detailed or time-consuming your examination should be, but two common-sense rules offer a measure of assistance.

First, take a hard look at those items that could really make a difference. For example, major products should receive much closer examination than those which are "incidental." As for minor items — these are important, yes. But the greatest potential for increased sales and profits probably lies in the major items. You may have to lump many minor items together and make a cursory examination of them — especially the first time through the planning process.

The second general rule: Consider how thoroughly you

know the various elements, and spend more time evaluating those you don't know so well.

Nothing makes these choices easy, but it may help if you keep the following questions in mind: How much will it cost in terms of time and/or money to get this information? And how much might it cost in profits if I don't?

Devising forms. Have all functional area managers prepare forms appropriate for their individual areas. Do so before you start collecting data. First of all, forms will force you to think about what you're going to do before you start to do it. Specifically, forms will make you decide both what it is you're going to analyze and how deeply you will be going into it. Forms will also make it easier to delegate some of the routine chores of gathering information, since they will enable subordinates to better understand what data you want them to get.

Forms serve another important function. Since functional area managers conduct their own analyses, they may find it difficult to be objective. They may be afraid to "tell it like it is" because a straight-forward report will reveal past errors (either theirs or their superior's). Even if they try to be frank, they may subconsciously distort the presentation to make their past efforts look better than they were. You can help avoid self-serving situation analysis reports by presenting, discussing, and revising forms at a planning team meeting before any information is gathered. Not only will this create a unity of thought about what information is needed, but it will also produce data that are more objective.

Analyzing available secondary information first. Analyze available secondary information first. Not only can you save time, but you learn right away about areas in which your information is poor. Also, the more you know at the outset, the more efficiently you'll go about collecting information and the right information. But the above is pretty "academic" for your first time through the situation analysis. If you only have two months to complete it, you're not going to be able to do

Sample Forms for
Various Functional Areas

MANUFACTURING EXPENSE ANALYSIS
(current dollars)

	19__	19__	19__	19__	End of Last Year
Sales Volume (in dollars)					
Direct labor costs					
Dollar cost					
Cost/sales ratio					
Engineering costs					
Dollar cost					
Cost/sales ratio					
Indirect labor costs					
Dollar cost					
Cost/sales ratio					
Operating expenses					
Dollar cost					
Cost/sales ratio					
Depreciation					
Dollar cost					
Cost/sales ratio					

Concluding Comment:

Figure 2. Manufacturing

DISTRIBUTION AND INVENTORY CONTROL
(current dollars)

	19__	19__	19__	19__	End of Last Year
Sales Volume (in dollars)					
Inventory Raw Materials Inventory/Sales Ratio					
Work in Process Dollar Volume Inventory/Sales Ratio					
Finished Goods Dollar Volume Inventory/Sales Ratio					
Distribution					
Inbound Dollar Costs Distribution Costs/Sales Ratio					
Outbound Dollar Costs Distribution Costs/Sales Ratio					

Concluding Comment:

Figure 3. Manufacturing

KEY CUSTOMER ANALYSIS (Customers who account for more than 10% of the total sales volume)

Customer	End of 19__	End of 19__	End of 19__	End of 19__	End of Last Year
Customer 1					
Sales (current $)					
Profitability					
Relationship (Excellent-good-poor)					
(Estimated share of customer's purchases					
&bull;					
&bull;					
&bull;					
Customer n					
Sales (current $)					
Profitability					
Relationship (Excellent-good-poor)					
Estimated share of customer's purchases					

Concluding Comment:

Figure 4. Marketing

LIQUIDITY AND STABILITY

Measures of Liquidity and Stability	End of 19__	End of 19__	End of 19__	End of 19__	End of Last Year
Cash flow					
Current dollars					
Constant dollars					
Working capital					
Current dollars					
Constant dollars					
Debt-Equity Ratio					
Acid Test					
Current Ratio					
Interest Coverage					

Concluding Comment:

Figure 5. Finance

much primary research. About all that you'll be able to gather is information from company records, trade associations, syndicated industry studies, and the like. And you'll have to depend on "best estimates." Always keep in mind you can't do everything the way you'd like to the first time through. However, you can take steps now so that the next time you'll have more of the kinds of data you'd like to have.

Summarizing findings. Each functional area should summarize its key problems and opportunities *on one page* to show the following:

A. Absolute strengths and weaknesses.
   1. List the absolute *major* strengths of the functional areas.
   2. List the absolute *major* weaknesses of the functional area.
B. Present competitive posture.
   1. List the *major* points of leverage of the functional area.
   2. List the *major* points of vulnerability of the functional area.

Absolute strengths and weaknesses (Category A) are those that are independent of competition. For example, the firm may have a sizeable cash surplus. List the amount. On the other hand, the firm's managers may be close to retirement. List this as well.

Category B contains the points of strength and weakness that reflect the company's current competitive position. The company might enjoy a superior distribution system, for instance, while its manufacturing division may be hard pressed by innovations in production methods developed by competitors.

Normally only a few issues developed in the situation analysis are "key." These should be summarized on one page. The rest of the analysis serves as backup material.

Have each planning team member present his or her situation analysis to the group. (Copies should be delivered to the planning team several days before the meeting to make sure that everyone has a chance to analyze them ahead of time.) Thrash out any differences, and then consolidate all the important corporate issues *on one page.* This, then, is the consolidated situation analysis of the firm.

Getting the job done. It may be that at this time, you feel the above procedure is just too complicated for your planning situation; particularly the steps involved with the form design and form approval. Then simplify. For example, in one company each functional area manager prepared a list of strengths of his or her own area, the overall strengths and weaknesses of functional area interface, and, in addition, statistical data to support these conclusions. The president just filled out a list of points of leverage and vulnerability of the firm. These lists were circulated to members of the planning team ten days prior to a meeting where there was an evaluation of lists and data, consolidation, and, where necessary, assignments for future study.

There are many other variations. While deciding the process best for your company, keep in mind, the more the procedure is simplified, the more you run the risk of losing objectivity as well as perpetuating "myths." However, on the other hand you have to consider practicalities. A simplified procedure may be the only way to get strategic planning started and to get through the planning cycle.

It's important to recognize that how the situation analysis is handled will set the tone for the remaining steps of the planning process. This is the first time it's going to take independent work on the part of the planning team members. It's up to the president to make sure that the job is done thoroughly by everyone. If one, several, or all of the members do haphazard jobs, the president must send them back and have them redo their work until it's right. This will let the planning team know that there's a real importance attached to the planning function.

Step 3: Strategy Formulation — Anticipating Future Environment

You've determined your objectives, mission, and policies. You've also examined the strengths and weaknesses of your firm. The first part of strategy development is to forecast the future environment your firm will operate in. The need to do so is obvious. Few strategies work equally well regardless of prevailing business conditions. For example, a strategy including high debt/equity ratio will work better during times of inflation and easy money than during recession and tight money.

Unfortunately, the future has become increasingly hard to pin down. Too many key factors are simply too unpredictable. To mention a few root causes: There are more inventions leading to more rapid product obsolescence. There's more government intervention (which is usually not predictable). And then there's the rate of inflation. For example, in a recent seminar a group of corporate planners were asked what they thought the rate of inflation would be in five years. The range: between 2 and 27 percent. Imagine, back in 1963, asking a similar group to predict what the rate of inflation would be in 1968. Probably the range would have been somewhere between 1 and 3 percent.

Often the planning process involves using a single "most probable" forecast as the basis of thinking. Estimates are made of uncontrollable make-or-break variables — such as competition, industry growth, and inflation — and then a strategy is developed to achieve the company's objectives. But what happens when, because of faulty forecasting, the assumed values of one or more key variables are wrong? What seemed to be a solid strategy might prove surprisingly treacherous under these different, unplanned-for conditions. Even tactical contingency plans may fail to compensate for the faulty strategy.

As a consequence, many companies of all sizes now measure their strategies against several possible future environments, relevant to their businesses, as a formal part of their planning procedures. This chapter explains how you can use multiple futures to give you a better idea of plausible environments in which your company may be operating. Although it doesn't cover forecasting techniques, it does point out how you can integrate your forecasts, arrived at by conventional methods, in developing multiple futures.

The overriding benefit of constructing multiple futures is already clear: It enables you, even forces you to see how a strategy might fare in the event of an unexpected (but possible) future. There are other benefits. Awareness that the future may wear "different faces" will alert you more fully to the need for a flexible strategy, and for contigency plans as well. Further, the act of committing alternative futures to paper helps clarify your assumptions and variables, and hence the logic of your arguments. Even the process of writing down assumptions and variables has benefits.

Formally writing out multiple futures in corporate planning also helps improve communication. There are less likely to be misunderstanding among members of the planning team. And it's a process that most executives enjoy.

Of course there are potential disadvantages as well. Too much worry about possible dangers, for instance, can lead to timidity and risk avoidance. Certainly, the safest path is seldom the most rewarding, and you're being paid to evaluate and accept risk, after all, not simply to avoid it. Since you've already set your objectives, however, you're less likely to fall into this "no hits, no runs, no errors" trap.

Another criticism might be that examining multiple futures takes too much time. It can, of course, if you let it, but it doesn't need to involve much more work than traditional forecasting. In addition, you can — and at first you probably should — design multiple futures on a shirt-sleeve basis. Finally, it could happen that all the futures you plan for turn out wrong. Even so, a technique like this will leave your company better prepared to deal with the unexpected.

Following is a step-by-step procedure for incorporating the concept of multiple futures into strategy planning. Although designed with smaller companies in mind, larger companies that want to keep planning simplified will find it equally useful.

Let's assume that you have established your objectives, mission, and policies, and have conducted the situation analysis as well. You're now ready to start the following process: First, determine the factors relevant to your business that you are sure will occur within your planning time frame — these are your assumptions. Second, list the key uncontrollable variables that could have make-or-break consequences for your company. Third, assign a range of reasonable values to each key variable. Finally, develop at least two but no more than three plausible futures that your firm could find itself operating in. One of these futures should be the most probable case, and the other(s) should represent the most plausible (worst case and/or best case) futures. When these are completed, the planning team develops a strategy for the most-probable-case future, and measures it — adjusting it for responsiveness, when possible — against the other future(s) the company might face. A more detailed step-by-step approach follows.

Stating assumptions relevant to your business. Assumptions are factors you can forecast with almost complete certainty. Calculated natural resources (in some cases) or the number of sixty-five-year-olds five years from now (in all cases) are examples. Or it may be that members of your planning team are *sure* that some things will happen. If that be the case, consider them assumptions. There is no sense changing these values and designing multiple futures around changes. No one will consider the alternatives realistic.

Other projections, such as the rate of economic growth, are unpredictable and should be classified as variables. Variables differ from assumptions in that assumptions must be thought to be accurate and conclusive; a high probability of occurrence is not enough. A test: If some members of your planning team doubt its value, consider it a variable.

Listing key variables. After you have defined your assumptions, you need to identify the variables that will be important to your business in the future. Try to use key variables that are commonly predicted and monitored, such as GNP and the rate of inflation. Easily identifiable vital signs facilitate forecasting and simplify control.

You can keep the planning task on a shirt-sleeve basis by limiting key variables to no more than four or five by using the following guidelines:

• Omit variables having a low probability of occurrence and a low potential impact. On the other hand, include those with low probabilities but high impact.

• Consider the timeliness of the variable. Because the future is so unpredictable, it is more important to include an event that is likely to happen or have an impact in the next few years than one that may not happen or be insignificant until near the end of the planning horizon.

• Omit disastrous events. Events that would cause total disaster — such as a major nuclear war — should not be considered seriously.

• Aggregate when possible. For example, the factors in economic growth include expenditures on consumer, investment, and government goods. If only the economic growth rate is relevant, use it as the representative variable for your analysis.

• Separate dependent from independent variables. Check for interdepedence. Is the value of one variable based upon the value of another? If so, then remove the dependent variable. Keep a separate list of dependent variables for use in helping to describe the multiple futures.

Assigning reasonable values to each key variable. Pick a reasonable range within which each variable may vary, and divide the range into two or three sets of values — a "most probable case" and the extremes. What is "reasonable," of course, can only be determined by common sense. However, reject values so extreme that they seem absurd.

To forecast the values of these key variables, you can follow the same forecasting procedures you've been using in the past. The only difference is that you're now trying to predict the extremes as well as the most-probable-case forecast. To maintain objectivity, you may want to seek the opinions of exports, trade association officials and staff. Or, if relationships permit, customers and suppliers.

Describing plausible futures in which your company may operate. The end result is the description of possible futures in which you may be operating. Do this by selecting a value for each key variable; estimating the resulting interactions between key variables, dependent variables, and assumptions; and writing a brief description of the future under this set of conditions.

You'll find the following suggestions helpful.

• First take your most-probable case values of each variable and put together the most-probable-case future. This you normally do intuitively. Only now, you are putting down this picture of the future in written statements. The written statements are necessary for two major reasons: You can better link together (describe) the effects of variables (for example, increased competition and increased inflation); and you'll improve communication among members of your planning team.

• Write from the viewpoint of someone standing in the

future (at the end of your time frame) describing "present" conditions. Your description should point out potential problems and opportunities facing firms in your industry. Keep in mind that you are describing a setting in which your firm may be operating. As a consequence, for now keep your firm — out of the portrayed future. Once you've put together these alternative settings, then you can go about seeing what courses of action your firm should take.

• Limit yourself to one or two paragraphs. Use concrete terms and classifications, and don't worry about the elegance of your sentence construction. Simple clarity is much more important. You'll probably be surprised at how easy it is to put together a story line after you've merely listed assumptions and variables. In fact, in some cases listing them may be all that is necessary.

• Besides the most probable case, describe at least one, but not more than two, alternative futures. You may wish to use only one other alternative future. Most companies that develop only two futures develop the second one for the downside. If you develop two alternative futures, the third should be for optimistic conditions. Regardless of whether you develop two or three, make sure that the alternative futures (other than the most probable case) have a moderately high probability of occurrence, or else no one will pay serious attention to them.

• Make sure that the multiple futures are significantly distinct from each other. In fact, it has been recommended that you develop "deadly enemies" futures ("deadly enemy" futures refer to those in extreme contrast to the most probable case. In this sense the best case future can be a "deadly enemy"). After all, you're trying to find out what will happen if you follow one strategy and a much different environment should occur.

• Keep the length of each multiple future roughly even. People tend to give more credulence to a longer description.

Step 3 (continuation) : Strategy Formulation — Guidelines for Strategic Action

Strategies enable you to move from where you are today (as revealed by the situation analysis) to where you wish to be (as indicated by your objectives). They are the general courses of action you follow within the parameters set by mission and policies, in order to achieve certain levels of profitability, growth, or whatever your objectives might be.

In this chapter a number of types of strategies and guidelines for their use are given. The guidelines are general rules of thumb that apply to smaller, growing companies. Because of your company's special circumstances, some might not hold true for you. If you don't follow one or more of these guidelines, however, make sure you have a good reason for violating the general rule.

Identifying basic strengths and building upon them. Identify what your company does well. This may be harder to do than it seems. Often firms operate under fixed attitudes inherited from the past and assume that what they are most accustomed to doing is what they're best at. Use your situation analysis to counter these natural biases. It will help you identify where the firm already has or could develop an advantage over its competition.

Such an analysis requires objectivity. You may find it helpful to rate your company's strengths as if you were an outsider — an outsider who is interested in acquiring a company

356

in your industry. Always ask: What are our core strengths? Overall, basic strengths divide into those of the market and those of technical skills.

Just because customers value your name for one product does not necessarily mean they will hold your other products in high regard. It's the customer who determines the market, not the seller.

The second area of core strengths is in technical skills. For technology to be a source of strength, however, it must be a proven skill rather than knowledge of theory. The technology must also be sufficiently distinct for your company to make its product a leader with your target market. It's best to stay out of areas where customers do not — or cannot be "taught" to — appreciate your excellence. Xerox found this out during its unsuccessful foray into the computer industry.

Besides asking, "What are our basic strengths?" you must also ask, "What makes us subject to precarious exposure?" There are three major sources. The first can be described as "rigor mortis," which sets in when existent power centers protect their positions by fighting every major change that is proposed. The usual ground for resistance is that change involves difficulties too great to overcome. Innovation, however, is essential. The wars of tomorrow will not be fought on the battlefields of yesterday. The massive guns of Manila, for instance, could have blown the Japanese Imperial Navy out of the water in 1941. Enemies had always attacked Manila from the sea. But the Japanese approached from inland, a direction in which the guns could not fire.

It's hard to shake methods that have been successful. But always ask yourself whether these methods will be successful in the environments of tomorrow.

The second source of "precarious exposure" stems from failing to see a future that has (in effect) already happened. Many things cannot be predicted with certainty, such as wars, the rate of inflation, competition, and so forth.

Take a close look at the environment that is relevant to your business. If you can gather any information, demographic or otherwise, that partially "creates" the future, don't ignore its implications.

The third source of "precarious exposure" simply involves being the wrong size. The Boston Consulting Group has pointed out that economies of scale govern the costs of production and/or marketing in many industries. In such industries costs usually decline 20 percent to 30 percent with every doubling of volume.

When there are economies of scale in production and/or marketing, and when there is little brand preference, firms that cannot gain enough market share to be cost competitive should get out of that business. It is always better to be a major producer for a small market segment than a small producer (relative to others) in a large market segment. In other words, try to be the dominant producer.

Using the opportunity chart. The opportunity chart presents four sectors you should examine in developing your strategy, numbered in the order they should be investigated.

Let's take a look at each of these sectors. The opportunities suggested by "present products/present markets" would involve selling essentially the same products (requiring the same manufacturing technology) to the same markets (using the same marketing skills). For example, a manufacturer of automobile mufflers for domestic cars (selling to the after-market) might increase its product line to include mufflers for foreign cars.

Opportunities in the "new products/present markets" sector would involve using present channels of distribution to reach present customers, but making more than model changes or line extensions in the product. Often, though not always, this requires new manufacturing technology. For example, the muffler manufacturer might begin producing silicone lubricants for sale to after-market distributors.

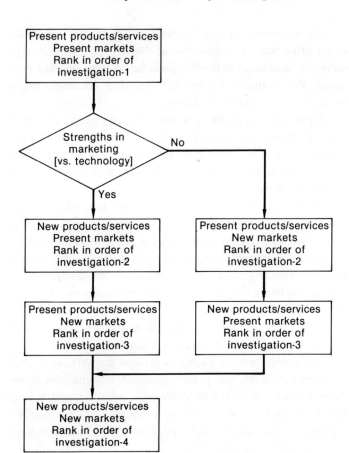

Figure 6: The Opportunity Chart

Opportunities in the "present products/new markets" sector often require using different channels of distribution to serve new markets for products similar to those already produced. For example, the muffler manufacturer might begin selling to automobile manufacturers.

Opportunities in the "new products/new markets" sector involve expansion requiring both new manufacturing technology and different marketing skills. For example, the muffler manufacturer acquires a firm that manufactures recreation tents.

In examining your possibilities, start first with present products/present markets. If you can't satisfy growth and sales here, move on. If your core strengths are in technology, then see if you can increase sales and profitability by selling present products and/or services to new markets. Conversely, if your core strengths are in marketing, make new products/services to your present markets your second order of investigation. The last sector that you should examine is in new products/services to new markets, because here it's a new ball game.

Naturally, present products/present markets, new products/new markets, and present products/new markets sometimes overlap. It's hard to distinguish which should belong where. And sometimes a company is equally strong in marketing and technology. In that case it doesn't matter which of these sectors it examines first.

Company after company has found that the areas that offer most profitability and growth are those that they know best. Now this doesn't mean that you won't wind up finding your greatest opportunity in new products/new markets. But you should only undertake this investigation after you have examined the other three sectors.

Question of scale. An important question to ask is, "Will the proposed change be worth the trouble?" A small program may prove successful — but will such a success make a significant difference to your firm? Too many small programs are likely to overextend managerial expertise.

No one has expounded on this problem better than Peter Drucker: *I have been reading for years the acceptance speeches of Nobel prize winners. Again and again one hears them say, "What started me on the work that led to this achievement was a chance remark by a teacher who said, 'Why don't you try something where the results really make a difference?'"*

If it won't make a major difference, you can't afford the time and effort.

Minimizing limitations (and capitalizing on advantages) of scalability and size. Consider scalability. Every cook knows that some recipes cannot be doubled. The same is true in business. The success of many small firms, for instance, stems from the customized service they afford their clients. When these firms grow beyond a certain size it is unlikely that they can give clients the service that made the firms successful in the first place. Or it may be that some skills are "unique" to certain individuals and are not duplicable. A small, extremely successful truck rental firm was considering expansion; their proposed strategy was essentially one of continuation. Their core strengths were in the two partners who were extremely shrewd in buying used equipment at bargain prices and who possessed ingenious mechanical skills enabling them to fix up and modify the equipment so it would be serviceable. These two partners were actually overextended, however, and it was highly unlikely that they could hire, motivate, and supervise people who possessed the same qualities that they did. This does not mean that this firm should not try to expand, but to do so by extending their present method of operation would appear to be folly.

Look for the crumbs. There are always segments of the market that larger companies do not find attractive. Seek these out.

Don't try to be a mass marketer. Instead, cater to the needs of a specific segment of the market. If possible, position yourself uniquely. At all costs avoid head-on clashes in promotion and distribution with large companies. They simply have more resources than you do. They can buy better distribution facilities, they can afford better "brains" to develop promotion programs, and they can hire more — and better — salesmen.

Coming to grips with the "precarious exposure" of size. There are three ways to deal with the problem of being the wrong size. First, change what you do. A small chemical company, for example, unable to compete with larger established firms, might switch to consultative selling.

Second, acquire what you need. Consider acquisition or merger. A company that needs an expanded distribution system for its product, for instance, might look at a company that already has such a system.

Finally, if you cannot change what you do or gain what you need through merger and acquisition, consider selling it, either all or in part.

• **Don't invite competition when you can avoid doing so.** It boosts one's ego to give success stories at trade conventions and the like, but such publicity may awaken sleeping giants.

• **Withdraw when the large companies become your direct competitors.** Perhaps you've staked out a market segment that large competitors neglected until now. It may have grown to the point where they find it attractive. Regardless of why they attack, retreat unless you have a competitive advantage in the field.

• **React quickly.** One advantage of the small company is its ability to respond swiftly to opportunities in the market. Keep your organization flexible, your management prepared to capitalize on market developments as they occur. Similarly, be ready to shed in a hurry any products or services that are no longer profitable.

Pruning your product line. Many companies, both large and small, suffer from having too many unprofitable products.

The 80-20 principle is usually in effect: 80 percent of the profits come from 20 percent of products. If this is true in your firm, consider shrinking the line. Studies show that high growth — high profit companies are usually those where the president cuts losses. And quickly.

Getting rid of the losers can be difficult. There is always the hope that some day the product will become a winner. Or there is sentiment attached to the product. Or pride. For example, the president may have recommended its addition, and it is difficult (and maybe dangerous) to confront him (or her) with the advantages of dropping it. And he may find it painful to admit he was wrong, not only to his subordinates and the board of directors, but also to himself. For this reason, often new management is able to turn a sluggish company around because they aren't burdened with emotional ties and promptly shed unprofitable products (and customers and personnel).

Of course, in some cases loss leaders must be retained to round out the product line. But often the need for them is imaginary, based more on emotional than economic grounds.

Step 3 (continued) : Strategy Formulation — Putting it All Together

The search for effective strategies, like all steps in planning, can be frustrating and unrewarding unless you approach it in a disciplined fashion. Here are steps that will help reduce the frustration level. And they'll increase your odds for finding a suitable strategy.

Setting time limits for strategy development. Failure to work by a schedule will provide only another dismal proof of Parkinson's First Law: "Work expands to fill the time allowed for it." Not only will the job drag on endlessly, but new and viable strategies are less likely to develop from it. By default, you may well be left with the strategy already in operation.

Also specify what resources are available for expansion (new facilities, increased promotion activity, stepped up R & D expenditures, and the like) and/or diversification. (Could you afford to acquire a firm? If so, what's your top limit?) These facts are readily available from finance's situational analysis.

Reviewing previous steps. In order that the planning team keep them firmly in mind, review the corporate objectives, mission, and policies; the situation analysis; and the analysis of environment. In brief, objectives determine what the firm intends to accomplish; mission and policies help keep the search within reasonable bounds; the situation analysis provides agreement about company strengths and weaknesses; the analysis of the environment depicts plausible future environments.

Gap analysis. A common sense rule of search states: "Know as much as possible about what it is you are looking for." To make sure that you do, perform gap analysis; that is, decide what kind of shortcomings you'd have if you continue your present strategy. Since you know the specific objectives of the firm as well as its risk posture, and you have already constructed the most-probable-case future, you can figure out where the gaps are likely to be.

A question that often comes up is, "While putting together our plans, what kind of dollars should we be working with? Current or inflated dollars?" Of course, in deciding on your strategic plan you'll take into consideration possible impacts of inflation. But as far as making tentative projections, keep things simple by working with current dollars. But generally it's easier at this stage to use current dollars.

Naturally you'll want to design your strategy for the most-probable-case future. But you'll also want to consider how effective this strategy would be in the worst-case future since you may wish to modify the strategy so that you'll have an escape hatch. At any rate, you should give the worst-case future consideration during strategy development.

It may be that you don't have any gaps. At this point the planning team may decide that the objectives are high enough and it's perfectly desirable to continue following the same strategy. If so, skip, "creative hypothesizing." Or the planning team may decide that, although there aren't any gaps, the objectives should be set higher to have more "stretch."

But, more likely, gaps will be a way of life.

A final check. Before proceeding, make a final check of your tentative strategy. Review the strategy contigency guidelines. Have you really stuck close to them? It is remarkably easy to inch away, in very small steps, so that we hardly realize how far off base we are. Then, there are some general questions you should ask.

First, is the strategy consistent with the style and philo-

Key Areas	Five Year Objectives	"Most Probable" Case Forecasts	"Most Probable" Case Gaps
Earnings			
Sales			
•			
•			
•			
Return on investment			

Figure 7

sophy of management? In his book *The Corporate Man,* Antony Jay reports an incident that in various guises we have heard over and over again. A new headmaster of an English boarding school was determined to initiate major changes. Unfortunately (for him), his proposed reforms encountered entrenched resistance from his staff, and he accomplished only a little of what he wanted to do. The situation in a business can be just as touchy — corporate strategy must be in reasonable harmony with the attitudes and philosophy of management.

Second, is there an ample supply of critical resources? According to Murphy's Law, "If things can go wrong, they will go wrong." Not only is that "law" cleverly put, it touches on an unpleasant truth. A gambler once approached this point in a different way. "Don't prepare just for average bad luck," he said, "but for outrageously bad luck." If such luck comes your way, will you have an adequate supply of critical resources? Money? Manpower? Physical facilities? Raw materials? Energy?

Testing the adaptability of the proposed strategy. Although you've taken into consideration the worst-case future while designing your strategy, pause for a moment and check the flexibility of your strategic plan in your worst-case future.

Can the strategy adapt itself to these conditions? Or does its effectiveness depend on the values of the key variables in the most-probable-case future?

This check may encourage you to modify the strategy in order to increase its adaptability. Or you may wish to discard the tentative strategy entirely and redesign a completely new one. Or you may decide the risk is worth taking and that no change is necessary. Or you may decide to develop contigency plans.

Developing contingency plans. There is one constant: The future is unpredictable. And Murphy's Law points out which way things are likely to go. (O'Leary's Corollary: "Murphy was an optimist.")

Contingency plans are normally developed after you've decided on your strategy, but you should consider contigency planning as an integral part of strategy development. In fact, an examination of possible contigencies may lead you to change your strategy in order to generate a more flexible stance.

If you're developing contigency plans for the first time, and if your planning team is not sophisticated in planning, be sure to keep the process simple. As one executive (of a very large company) cautioned, "Contingencies tend to be downside and people do not like to anticipate negative situations. If people do not like to plan in general, contigency planning becomes an even more difficult task." So accept that the contingency plans will be much less than ideal, but keep in mind that even a very crude plan can have great benefits.

Determining key contingency events. Although there are many possible contingent events, begin with contingency plans for no more than one or two. To help isolate the most important, closely examine the worst-case future you developed. The key variables in this future spell out the events to be considered. However, it may be that your planning team decided that there were no specific contingencies that were deemed as real issues. In that case, don't bother with contingency planning. Your planning team will only view contingency planning as an unnecessary chore.

Specifying trigger points. A trigger point indicates when a contingency event has developed sufficient impact that the contingency plan should be implemented. For example, your strategy may be dependent upon a maximum of 7 percent inflation. You may decide that your plan is "triggered" when inflation reaches 8 percent or higher for six months.

Select a trigger point for each key contingent event. It simplifies monitoring if you use commonly reported events, such as GNP, rate of inflation, retail sales, money supply, and company sales.

Developing contingency actions. In developing contingency actions, follow these guidelines:

• Keep the plans simple, particularly when developing contingency plans for the first time. Avoiding complex plans will make preparation easier. Limit contigency actions to one page.

• Consider positive as well as negative reactions. To illustrate: In the event of a contingent downturn, a negative reaction would be to discharge personnel. A positive reaction would be to expand to unaffected markets. Positive actions usually help morale. Furthermore, they're more likely to improve your profits and competitive position.

• Estimate the funding necessary for implementing the contingency action. Make sure funding requirements are realistic and available; recognize that what is "realistic and available" usually varies with psychological perspectives. While business is on the upswing, management is usually optimistic, and funds are approved in this perspective. When profits are threatened, however, management may change its stance and reject what it had previously viewed as reasonable.

Before moving on, recheck your strategy. The contingency plans you've developed may reveal unexpected vulnerabilities in your strategy. You may wish to revise the strategy in order to reduce your exposure to hazards.

Making financial projections. Through the process of developing the corporate plan, you already have an idea that your proposed strategy and first-year plans are on target with objectives. Now make a rough calculation. The figures you use for this need have only ballpark accuracy — that is, just enough detail to prove that your proposed plans are realistic.

Here's what to do: First, based on your strategy and most-probable-case future, forecast sales for your five and one-year plans. Then, forecast expenses needed to support projected sales, that is, consider production, inventory, marketing, finance and personnel costs. Forecast capital requirements for plant and equipment, inventories and receivables. Then prepare pro forma balance sheets, P. & L. and cash flow statements. Finally, compare the financial forecasts with objectives. If you're off, one or two actions are in order: Search for more effective strategies or, as a last resort, modify goals downward.

Putting the strategy in writing. To make sure that the strategy you have hammered out is difficult to misinterpret — to forget — formalize it by writing it down. Do so concisely. But make sure that it is explicit enough to provide guidelines for detailed operational plans. It should include three major parts:

Part 1. **Basic strategies** — types of products and/or services to be offered and target markets and the means by which these markets will be reached.

Part 2. **Contingency plans** — contingency plans for the worst-case future (and when appropriate, for the best-case future).

Part 3. **Timing and financial projections** — a timetable indicating major events such as the introduction of a new product or the entry into a new market area; major capital required for new production and distribution facilities, inventories, and receivables, and the times these funds will be needed; and projected sales, expenses, and profits for Years 1 and 5.

Step 4 : Developing the Operational Plan

Operational planning means deciding what is to be accomplished, who does what, when it should get done, at what cost, and, in addition, setting up control points and methods of monitoring. It involves developing plans for the corporate level, functional areas, and lower echelons of management. This chapter describes developing the operational plan at the corporate and functional levels.

Perhaps you're reasonably satisfied with your present system of operational planning, and you see how you can blend in the strategic plan. If so, don't make any major changes. Do what you've been doing. It's always a mistake to introduce procedures that aren't really necessary.

If you're not satisfied, the following procedures will help you set up operational planning that will better suit your needs. Of course, the procedure recommended here may be too simple or too advanced for your firm. Then make adaptations.

The operational plan. At the corporate and functional levels, operational planning involves three steps: putting together the detailed operational plan; preparing pro forma profit and loss and balance sheets; and making final adjustments.

Putting together the detailed operational plan. As far as the operational plan themselves are concerned, naturally, you'll want to keep them as short as possible. But you'll have to itemize major expenses, incomes, and timetables — enough, at least, to show the mesh between functional areas and to be able to construct pro forma P. & L. and balance sheets.

In order to accomplish this, functional areas will have to prepare plans for their areas. To make sure that all of the important areas are covered, have them follow the same format. Standardization will enable members of the planning team to analyze various functional area plans much more quickly. They'll know where to look for certain items.

Here's a recommended format:

THE (MANUFACTURING) PLAN
19xx

Objectives — what the functional area is supposed to accomplish during the year.

Situation analysis — summary statement of the functional area's strength and weaknesses.

Environmental forecasts — external environment, as relevant to the functional area.

Summary description of the (manufacturing) plan — outline of the functional area's general thrust for the year and statement of relationship of the functional area's annual plan to the general strategy of the firm.

Detailed plan of action.

Contingency plans — key threats and proposed actions to counter them.

Required resources.

As a general rule for smaller companies, the plans for each functional area should not exceed ten to eleven pages. More specifically, objectives should take up one-half to one page; the situation analysis, one page; environmental assumptions, one-half to one page; the summary description of the plan, one page; the detailed plan of action, five pages; required resources, one page; and contingency plans, one page.

As you can see, you have already done part of the work in the previous planning steps — objectives, situation analysis, and environmental assumptions. The functional areas can extract appropriate parts; their major effort will be in developing the plan of action. There's a lot that could be included in this section, so don't get bogged down in detail. But certainly you'll want marketing, for example, to estimate sales volumes from each of the product lines and major customer, as well as the cost of obtaining those sales. To ensure realism, have marketing make a comparison between what they expect in sales from the coming year and what they actually achieved in the year past. The marketing plans should also describe environmental conditions, including the probable activities of major competitors.

Again, there is no point, for instance, in having production struggle to work out the details of factory loading and sequencing, although they will have to do this eventually. What you want now is a general idea of how production intends to produce — at a certain cost — that volume of products that marketing expects to sell. For this, you need cost estimates of energy, raw materials, labor, and equipment. (An overly detailed plan will become useless if the planning team should have to make revisions in the corporate plan.) So you can check for realism have production, also, compare its expectations for the coming year with its achievements during the previous year.

While forecasting the most-probable-case environment for next year, you probably came up with some projection for next year's inflation rate. If you didn't, do so now. (It may be that for your business you'll need to project not only the annual rate of inflation, but also the quarterly rate, or perhaps even the monthly rate.)

Use this inflation rate to adjust your first year's objectives. Quite obviously, if there is an appreciable change in inflation rate, and you don't adjust your growth and earnings accordingly, you'll be getting a distorted picture of your results.

Next, have functional areas use the same inflation rate in developing their plans. Remember that this will take considerable translation on their parts.

There must be close cooperation between the various functional areas while they prepare their plans. For example, manufacturing cannot make production schedules until it has sales estimates. Similarly, marketing may have to change its plan in order to achieve manufacturing cost efficiencies. Manufacturing must likewise consult with personnel about labor costs; and so on. This interchange, besides being necessary, can have additional benefits. While working out detailed plans, unexpected opportunities as well as problems are exposed. Close coordination among the functional area managers makes it easier to take advantage of the former and better deal with the latter. Besides, it helps functional area managers to understand better the problems of other areas and to think more of the firm as a system. Be sure to let them know they've got to work together. And that it's their responsibility to do so, and to make it work.

Of equal importance, at this time there should be a general agreement, within each of the functional areas, as to department heads' plans and budgets for the coming year. For example, the director of marketing should consult and work very closely with the sales and advertising managers. In fact, the director of marketing should have them develop tentative plans for their departments. This is necessary so that later on, when department heads submit formal plans and budgets, these will be in line with the overall functional plan. But there's no need to have department heads prepare formal plans and budgets now. All you want is a general agreement. There's usually some last-moment negotiations involving "final" functional area plans and budgets, and these will almost certainly require changes in department heads' plans and budgets. Department heads should be conscious, however, of the importance of their estimates — and that later on they'll be expected to live up to their commitments.

While examining each plan, make sure it is geared toward

achieving the basic strategy. For example, does the proposed action follow the strategic direction indicated by the market opportunity/company strengths matrix? If the product falls into the earn/protect category, for example, is promotion highly selective? Are pricing policies likely to stabilize prices for maximum earnings?

Closely examine the reasonability — the logic — of each plan. Do production schedules seem realistic? What about materials availability? Warehousing for raw materials and finished goods? Do sales forecasts seem reasonable given projected economic conditions and the past history of key customer's purchases? Be particularly on the lookout for "hockey stick" projections: plans that show a quantum leap to being "there" tomorrow without specifying how to get there.

Besides checking each plan, of course you'll have to analyze carefully the fit of the functional areas' plans. For example, do the production and inventory schedules meet the demands of sales? Is there adequate cash available (through cash on hand, lines of credit, factoring of accounts receivable, and/or cash flow) to finance increased production and sales costs and accounts receivables?

What happens if a functional area plan should not conform to the firm's strategy, fail the test of logic, and/or give a poor fit? Straighten it out now. If it's something the functional area manager can do, have him do it. But if he can't do it, and the problem area is critical to the success of the corporate plan, it will require the work of a sub-committee or the whole planning team. Hopefully it won't require radical changes in the corporate plan. But face the fact that it may.

Preparing pro forma profit and loss and balance sheets. Once the functional area plans are in order, prepare pro forma P. & L. and balance sheets to see how close you are to your one-year objectives.

Finalizing the operational plan and making final adjustments. If you're lucky, you're right on target. If you're very,

very lucky, you may have surpluses of profits and cash flow. In such a case, why not make "insurance" investments to strengthen your future position for the second, third, fourth, and fifth years? Such investments might include improving production facilities, increasing expenditures in R & D, opening of new territories, and/or manpower development. And your job's done.

But probably there's going to be a gap between what you'd like to achieve and what the P. & L. and balance sheets show. If you've been working carefully through the planning steps, the shortfalls will likely be minor. You'll probably·be able to make necessary adjustments by cutting costs, or increasing income, through a change in one or more of the functional area plans. Probably the gap will be in one of three areas: sales, earnings, or return on investment.

After you've taken a hard look at capital investments, check other ways to reduce cash requirements. Can marketing open up new territories by using manufacturers' representatives instead of a direct sales force? Can you reduce inventory? How about cash management — is your checking account's balance too large? What about your credit policy — could terms be tightened? Are you maximizing potential cash flow from accounts payable?

But in bringing your short-range plans in line with objectives, don't make cuts recklessly. Make sure that you're not sacrificing long-term opportunities, thereby putting your strategic plan in jeopardy. □